D0997186

HOME RUN

HOME RUN

Great RAF Escapes
of the
SECOND WORLD WAR

---

by
Richard Townshend Bickers

LEO COOPER
LONDON

First published in Great Britain in 1992 by
LEO COOPER
190 Shaftesbury Avenue, London WC2H 8JL
an imprint of
Pen & Sword Books Ltd,
47 Church Street, Barnsley, South Yorkshire S70 2AS

A CIP catalogue record for this book is available
from the British Library.

ISBN: 0 85052 301 X

Typeset by Yorkshire Web, Barnsley, S. Yorks.
in Plantin 10 point

Printed by
Redwood Press
Melksham, Wiltshire

CONTENTS

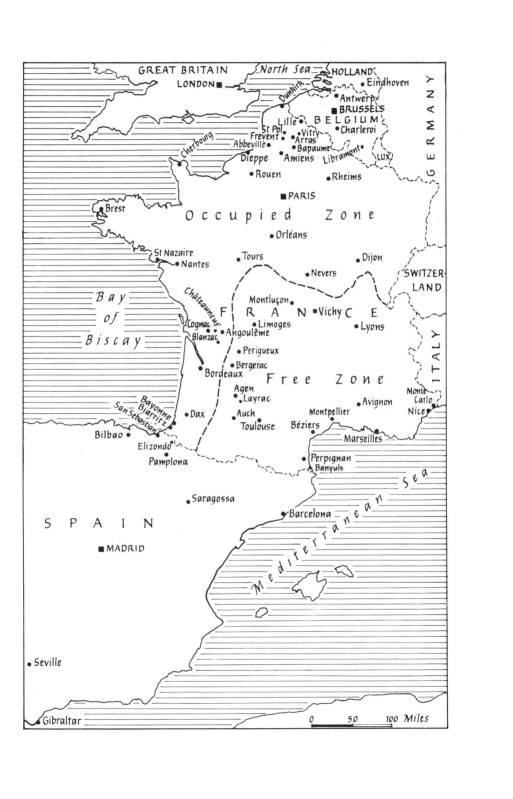

GREAT BRITAIN   North Sea   HOLLAND
LONDON ■   • Eindhoven
Dunkirk   • Antwerp
Lille   ■ BRUSSELS
St Pol   • Charleroi   BELGIUM
Frevent   • Vitry
Cherbourg   Abbeville   • Arras
Dieppe   • Bapaume   Libramont
Amiens   LUX
• Rouen   • Rheims
■ PARIS
Brest   O c c u p i e d   Z o n e
• Orléans
St Nazaire   • Tours   • Dijon
• Nantes   SWITZER-
• Nevers   LAND
B a y   Châteauneuf   Montluçon   • Vichy C   E
o f   F   R   A   N
Cognac   • Limoges   • Lyons
B i s c a y   Blanzac   • Angoulême
• Perigueux
• Bergerac   F r e e   Z o n e
Bordeaux
Agen   Monte
Bayonne   • Layrac   • Avignon   Carlo
Biarritz   • Auch   Montpellier   • Nice
San Sebastian   • Dax   Toulouse   Béziers
Bilbao •   Marseilles
Elizondo   • Perpignan
Pamplona   Banyuls
• Saragossa   Barcelona
S P A I N
■ MADRID
M e d i t e r r a n e a n   S e a
• Seville
Gibraltar   0   50   100 Miles

GERMANY   ITALY

FOREWORD

YOU ARE A FIGHTER PILOT or member of a bomber crew, shot down over German-occupied France, Belgium, Holland, Italy or Jugoslavia. Whether it is by day or night and whether you baled out or crash-landed, your first emotion is not fear, but anger.

You are faced with what the R.A.F. calls a 'bind', a tedious chore; to make your way home without being caught. You know that this will entail much discomfort as well as danger. You will have many miles to tramp. You will sleep rough and be hungry and thirsty; in autumn and winter, wet and cold. If you are on a day operation, your plans for that evening, or, if on a night sortie, for the following day, will have 'gone for a Burton'. The girl with whom you had a date will be tearful and worried. The evening out in the local town with the crew or fellow pilots will have to wait, maybe for months. Your parents, and your wife if you have one, will be distraught with anxiety when you are reported missing.

You are not idle while these melancholy thoughts flash through your mind. If your aircraft was on fire when it hit the ground, enemy troops guided by the blaze will be hurrying to take you prisoner. Ammunition, and perhaps bombs, will be exploding and heard for miles around. If the aeroplane is not burning, it is your duty to set it alight and that will bring Jerry in large numbers as fast as his jackboots and vehicles can move. If you have parachuted by day, hundreds of hostile eyes will have seen you. The brain in many a square head will have calculated where you will come down and triumphant Krauts bristling with weapons might soon be swarming around you.

Such fear as you presently feel is caused by the thought of months or years as a prisoner of war. Of the enemy himself, you have no trepidation. To the British fighting Services the German is a figure of fun, despite the atrocities of the SS and Gestapo. You respect his fighting qualities but deride his ludicrous goose-step march, his ponderous sense of humour, his tendency to shout and bully, his robot-like lack of imagination and obedience to any authority.

If you evade immediate capture, your first contact with the native population will be a nervous business. There is the problem of communicating in a strange language. The natives are suspicious, knowing that Germans disguised as Allied aircrew frequently try to trap them into giving help, for which the penalty is death. If you accost someone on the road or a farm worker in the fields, you might be brusquely turned away or happen upon a traitor who will pretend to succour you, but hand you over to the enemy. If you knock on somebody's door, you run the same risks and one even worse; perhaps German troops are billeted in the house.

But there are others, who are alert day and night to welcome and help you. One or more of them could also have seen your aircraft on fire, heard you crash or watched your parachute descending, and will soon be at your side to aid and abet you.

Immediately on the defeat of Belgium and Holland in May, 1940, the withdrawal of the British Expeditionary Force from France in June, and France's capitulation a few days later, active resistance to the Germans by the native populations began. At first, those Belgians, Dutch and French who were brave enough to defy the occupying power could do little for British officers and men who had been left behind when their comrades departed. Shelter, food, civilian clothes and money were all they had to offer, at the risk of brutal reprisals by the enemy for doing so. Soon, some were able to supply those who had evaded, or escaped from, capture with false identity and travel documents.

It was in France that most of the Allied airmen, soldiers and sailors left adrift after the evacuation from Dunkirk and other ports were in hiding. This was also the country that shared a frontier with neutral Spain, whence a successful evader or escaper could eventually return to Britain via Gibraltar. By the end of 1940 the French Resistance movement already had some semblance of organization: in the north, where most Allied fighting men had found themselves abandoned, and in the south, where there was an established system for moving them across the Spanish frontier or having them picked up from a French Mediterranean beach.

It was in the vast area between, which had to be crossed in order to reach safety, that the greatest danger of discovery lay. For Allied fugitives, this meant becoming prisoners of war. For their French helpers, it meant execution. When France capitulated, Germany divided it into two main areas; the Occupied Zone and the Free Zone. In the *Zone Occupée*, the Pas de Calais comprised a third area, the *Zone Interdite* (Forbidden). The *Zone Libre*, the so-called Free Zone, constituted the part of France ruled by a puppet Government, based in Vichy, that was under Nazi surveillance and infested by the Gestapo, the Nazi Secret Police, in plain clothes. In 1942 a paramilitary police force, *La Milice* — literally The Militia — was formed in the Free Zone and reached a strength of 30,000. These men, in black uniform, were volunteers and therefore traitors, detested by their compatriots not only for going over to the enemy but also because their cruelty equalled that of the Gestapo and SS.

The main escape lines across France originated at various places in a 180-degree arc north of Paris. They converged on the capital, then followed four main routes southwards.

The towns on these routes and the Zones into which France was divided are shown on the accompanying map.

Resistance groups were also active in all the other German-occupied European countries and gave essential help to Allied aircrew evaders.

CHAPTER ONE

THE FIRST ESCAPE LINE

ON THE COLLAPSE of France and the evacuation of the British Expeditionary Force, several hundred British servicemen who had been left behind were not taken prisoner. The speed of the retreat to Dunkirk and other places on the Channel coast had left some of them cut off from their units, some in hospital; some had deserted. Those who reached the south of France were able to enjoy a certain liberty of movement, and at once a few people of outstanding character and resourcefulness began to devise means of harbouring British soldiers and airmen and helping them on their way to England.

The first sanctuary and source of general help was the Seamen's Mission in Marseilles, which existed to provide simple amenities for British and Americans of the merchant marine. From May, 1940, it was run by Dr Donald Caskie, a clergyman of the Church of Scotland who had previously been minister of a church in Paris and was now being provided with funds by the American Consulate. The Mission sheltered a great number of Britons awaiting the opportunity to leave France secretly.

One of the first British officers to take a lead in the escape operations was Captain Ian Garrow, a brawny member of the 51st Highland Division. He had fought his way to the coast after the French Army had given in and the enemy then surrounded the Highlanders. Garrow was one of the handful who managed to evade capture and reach Marseilles. With other officers and men he was interned there in Fort St Jean; but they were allowed out every evening after five o'clock. Instead of setting about contriving his own departure from France, he considered it his duty first to see to the liberation of his juniors in rank of the Highland Division. He had the financial resources to rent a hotel room from which to conduct his clandestine work.

A most generous supporter of the escape line was Louis Nouveau, a Marseilles businessman. On his first meeting with Garrow, at the flat of a French couple who had befriended several Britons, Nouveau realized that this large Scotsman was involved in secret work. Their friendship quickened and Garrow asked him for financial help. Nouveau gave him a handsome sum, his own money plus some from friends. Subsequently he supplied nearly half a million francs for Garrow. In normal times this would have been remitted to a British firm with which Louis Nouveau had dealings; Garrow arranged for the War Office to pay the firm.

In the north there was Henri Duprez, owner of textile factories in Roubaix. From the earliest days of the German occupation he had been harbouring, clothing and providing money for British airmen and soldiers who were trying to escape from France. He had been put in touch with an Englishman, known as Captain Cole, who helped them and was financing him liberally.

An eighteen-year-old Frenchman, Roland Lepers, who was relying on Cole to get him to England to join the Free French Army, had been working with him, mainly as an interpreter in northern France. Early in 1940 this youth had led a party of British evaders to Marseilles, where he met Garrow, to whom he extolled Cole's work. When he returned to Lille he bore a message from Garrow inviting Cole to a meeting. 'Captain' Cole was only too pleased to travel to Marseilles and become part of an escape line that was officially sponsored by the Secret Intelligence Service. This not only enhanced his status but also put more money into his sticky grasp. Soon he and Ian Garrow were working together and Cole was conducting a substantial number of British escapers and evaders from the north at frequent intervals. He was also gathering, for the British, much information on troop movements and military installations.

Initially Cole had raised funds for housing and feeding fugitives and paying rail fares by obtaining contributions from numerous people in and around Lille. Now Garrow was supplying him with generous sums of money that were sent to him by Donald Darling, a member of British Intelligence, stationed at the Embassy in Lisbon. Cole, whose dishonesty exceeded his undoubted boldness, was pocketing some of it.

A few months earlier, Germany had forced the Vichy Government to move all British ranks who were interned in Marseilles to more secure quarters in a former barracks, St Hippolyte-du-Fort, near Nîmes. Warned of this, Garrow had stayed behind with the Rodocanachis.

Dr Rodocanachi, then sixty-five years old, was another vital member of the secret network. Of Greek parentage, but born in England, he had qualified in medicine in France. In 1914 he had volunteered for the Royal Army Medical Corps, was turned down on some technicality to do with his nationality, joined the equivalent French Service and won several decorations. His wife, Fanny, was a partner in his clandestine work in the Second World War; eight years his junior, she was also a product of mixed cultures, born in France and brought up in Britain.

They were a couple who possessed both dignity and that elusive quality, style. Taffy Higginson, whose story is told here, recalls that on his first evening in their home Mrs Rodoconachi changed into a formal dress and asked him to take her in to dinner on his arm. It was a frugal meal, but old-fashioned decorum was observed.

Before the war the American Consul in Marseilles had appointed the doctor to examine foreigners seeking refuge in the USA. After the fall of France, he became the official physician to the Mission for Seamen and was soon inviting British officers to his home. Among these was Ian Garrow, of whose undercover rôle a common acquaintance had told him, and to whom he instantly offered the use of his flat for meetings with his collaborators and as a lodging for British officers on the run.

One of the toughest, most gifted and versatile members of the escape organization was Dr Jean-Marie Guérisse, who began the war as a thirty-year-old medical captain in the Belgian Army. On the conquest of Belgium he escaped to England. Wishing to serve in a combat capacity, he adopted the *nom de guerre* 'Patrick Albert O'Leary' and volunteered to serve in Special Operations Executive, which ran all manner of clandestine operations.

He made friends with another independent character, an English-speaking Frenchman named Pérès, captain of the *Rhin*, an armed 1,500-ton Q ship, who had sailed his vessel to England when his own country succumbed and changed his name to Langlais. The Admiralty took the vessel over, re-named her HMS *Fidelity* and commissioned her master. When he found that the gold lace on his cuffs was wavy, whereas on other captains' it was straight, he asked why and was told that this was to distinguish regular officers from peacetime part-timers and wartime holders of temporary commissions, who were admitted only to the RN Volunteer Reserve, familiarly 'the Wavy Navy'. He retorted that neither he nor his ship would fight or even leave port unless she did so with Captain Langlais RN on the bridge. After weeks of argument, the Admiralty compromised by allowing him to wear RN rank insignia. Meanwhile he had acquired a mistress in the Women's Royal Naval Service. He insisted that she must be allowed to accompany him aboard. More time was lost before the bemused Sea Lords gave way again and the lady was installed as Second Officer.

Patrick O'Leary had confided to nobody but Langlais that he was a doctor. He sailed in HMS *Fidelity* as First Lieutenant, with the rank of lieutenant-commander and wearing RN gold braid, having quoted the favour done to his captain as a precedent.

The ship was operating in the Mediterranean. In the small hours of 25 April, 1941, O'Leary took part in landing two men by rowing boat on a French beach near the Spanish frontier. Returning to the ship, the boat capsized in a sudden high wind. O'Leary, the sole survivor, swam ashore and was arrested by coast guards. He masqueraded this time as a French officer trying to get away to England, so was sent to Toulon for court martial. During the trial he 'confessed' to being a French Canadian. No mention of him could be found in French naval records, so he was automatically incarcerated in St Hippolyte-du-Fort.

Garrow was informed about O'Leary's imprisonment, suspected that he was a German spy who had been planted among British prisoners, and went to see for himself. He quickly established O'Leary's authenticity and integrity. On the information O'Leary gave him, Garrow made inquiries through Darling, adding that O'Leary had volunteered to stay and help him. London confirmed O'Leary's identity. His escape from prison had to be arranged and was duly accomplished.

CHAPTER TWO

FLIGHT LIEUTENANT GUY HARRIS

ONE OF THE MOST familiar Shakespearean quotations is, 'Some men are born great, some achieve greatness, and some have greatness thrust upon them'. To paraphrase it, one might reflect that most aircrew who evaded capture did so by their own efforts and the help of friendly people in an enemy-occupied country who were brave enough to defy the Germans. And there were some, made helpless by injury, who had evasion thrust upon them.

Guy Harris was an unlikely prospect for dependency on others. An excellent pilot, quiet, modest and sociable, ebullient when there was a party on in the mess, he was typical of the efficient, dedicated officers who made the Royal Air Force their career. He had the self-reliance and confidence of someone who knows precisely what he is about and can take care of himself in any circumstances. At St Paul's School, which had dominated public school boxing since the 1870s, he won his first team boxing colours. He coxed the London Rowing Club crew that won the Thames Cup at Henley in 1935. In 1938 he coxed the club's crew that competed in Portugal against eights from the host country, Holland, Belgium, France and Germany, the last-named picked by Hitler to row in the next Olympics. The British boat won the two main events.

At the age of sixteen he was driving his own Morgan three-wheeler and learning to fly at Brooklands Flying Club; he made his first solo at the earliest permissible opportunity, on his seventeenth birthday, 17 October, 1934. On 15 November of that year he qualified for his Private Pilot's (A) Licence. He entered the R.A.F. on a Short Service Commission on 27 January, 1936, was awarded his wings on 7 October and joined No. 32 Squadron at Biggin Hill eighteen days later. On 19 August, 1938, he passed his Commercial Pilot's (B) Licence, and his Second Class Navigator's Licence on 21 February, 1939.

When the Blitzkrieg's massive assault by dive bombers and tanks thundered into Belgium and Holland, Flight Lieutenant (later Wing Commander) Guy Harris, who had flown Gauntlets and Hurricanes in 32

Squadron for more than three years, was commanding A Flight of No 253 (Hyderabad State) Hurricane Squadron at Kenley, where it had moved the previous day. He had been posted to the squadron, at Manston, on 12 November, 1939. He recalls: 'On May the tenth, 1940, I was awakened by my batman with the news that it was a lovely day and Hitler had invaded the Low Countries.'

The squadron had been formed in November, 1939, with some twenty pilots straight from flying training schools, where, as embryo bomber pilots, they had flown twin-engine Oxfords. They were now to fly single-engine fighters and had to graduate on obsolescent single-engine Fairey Battle bombers first.

The squadron became operational on 5 April, 1940, at Northolt and spent the next two months on standby or readiness and on occasional scrambles in pursuit of Bogeys (unidentified aircraft) or Bandits (hostiles) of whom they never caught a glimpse.

Guy recalled: 'April 22 was a memorable day, as Squadron Leader Elliott, Pilot Officer Douglas Bisgood and I escorted Mr Winston Churchill's Lockheed Hudson from Hendon to Le Bourget. We were entertained to a champagne lunch in the French mess, where I tasted my first Gauloise.' This agreeable introduction to flying over France was followed by another visit in dour contrast. 'On 16 May Flight Lieutenant Humphrey Russell, who was in charge of the Biggin Hill Operations Room, and I ferried two new Hurricanes to Glisy, near Amiens, where we left them with many others as replacements for those squadrons already in France.' The speed of the German advance was made threateningly obvious by 'the sight of numbers of civilian cars, all with mattresses tied on the roof, tearing along the road past the aerodrome'. There was no Lucullan entertainment this time; 'We spent the night in a hangar and next day returned to England in a Handley Page Harrow transport.

'I was ordered to take my flight to Vitry-en-Artois, near Châlons-sur-Marne, on the 18th with six Hurricanes of 111 Squadron, who were also at Northolt, led by their CO, Squadron Leader Thompson. We took off at 5.15 am and nine of us landed at Vitry. One section had turned right instead of left at Calais, but turned up later. The aerodrome was occupied, I think, by 87 Squadron (Hurricanes) plus a few Gladiators. My first impression of the pilots stationed there was of their dull black shoes — some were white round the edges — which contrasted sharply with our shining ones polished by our batmen.

'We sat around in the sun and were presently told we would be escorting Blenheims on a bombing raid. This did not materialize. A dogfight developed over the aerodrome and someone said, "Don't wait for orders; scramble". As I was strapping myself in I noticed someone coming down by parachute.

I learned later it was Fred Rosier — later Air Chief Marshal Sir F.E.Rosier GCB CBE DSO — who was badly burned.' (See Taffy Higginson's story.)

By the time Guy was airborne and had gained height, all trace of the dogfight had vanished. Seeing some Hurricanes, he caught up with them and, unexpectedly, found from their markings that they belonged to 32 Squadron from Biggin Hill, which he had left six months ago. 'So once again I was flying alongside my old friends. No doubt they wondered who I was, but I could get no response when I called up on the R/T.' The H.F. radio sets then in use had only one channel and 32 and 253 Squadrons apparently were not on the same frequency.

'We were flying at about 10,000 ft when a Henschel 126 army co-operation type passed beneath us. Immediately a couple of Hurricanes dived in pursuit of it, so I joined in with them. It at once went down to ground level with two of us chasing it around trees and haystacks. To my surprise I was the only one left firing at it. The rear gunner had by now disappeared [a gentle euphemism for "been pulped to jelly by .303 bullets"] and eventually it nose-dived into a field and burst into flames.

'My feelings on seeing this were mixed; exhilaration at having shot down an enemy aircraft, but rather guilty because I had been firing at him with eight guns and he had been firing at me with one or possibly two. I learned years later that Sergeant North, flying the other Hurricane, had been shot down by the rear gunner but had forced-landed unhurt. If I had known, I could have tried landing beside him and somehow packing him into my Hurricane to save him a long trek home.

'While searching for Vitry again I wryly reflected that in my first encounter with the enemy I had to carry out the very manoeuvres that could have been responsible for my presence in France with 253, i.e. low flying. This practice was severely frowned upon in the pre-war R.A.F., but in October, 1939, when I was Squadron Adjutant on 32, it was decreed that all pilots should carry out low flying in the vicinity of Biggin Hill; but not below 250 ft. I got carried away and perhaps interpreted this too literally; flying up the valley that runs along the edge of the airfield, certainly 250 above sea level, which was the floor of the valley, but still some 100 ft below the level of the station buildings. Unfortunately, at the moment that I passed below the level of the Officers' Mess, the Station Commander, Wing Commander Grice, was just sitting down to his tea. He did not stay to enjoy it, but rushed to the telephone to find out who was flying the Hurricane that had just passed below him. Strangely enough, my posting to 253 Squadron, with promotion to flight lieutenant, followed shortly after this.

'But back to Vitry. This appeared below me, rather to my surprise, since we were not controlled from the ground as in England; in fact I do not remember once speaking to anyone on the ground by R/T when over France.

Consequently we had to find our way around a strange countryside. After refuelling and rearming and a bun for lunch, we were sent off on an offensive patrol in the afternoon. We soon ran into a number of Me110s and in the ensuing dogfight I followed one round and round, firing at him with no visible effect − full deflection shooting was not my strong point − while he in his turn was despatching what appeared to be strings of red tennis balls towards me from his rear gunner. His shooting was as bad as mine, but I got the impression that he was using a cannon. Then suddenly the air was clear of aircraft, so I landed at Vitry, as did the rest of the composite squadron.

'While we sat around our refuelled aircraft, awaiting the word that would send us back to England again, we saw a Hurricane dive vertically into the ground in a pall of black smoke. "Poor old Soden," someone said. We had been talking to him earlier on, but did not know how he had been shot down...' (Flight Lieutenant Ian Soden was commanding B Flight of 56 Squadron, to which Taffy Higginson belonged, on detachment with Rosier's flight of No 229, forming a composite squadron.)

'Then we noticed a line of Dornier 215s in the far distance, passing from our left to right at low level. "Ha", we said, "whom are they going off to bomb?" We found out pretty quickly when we looked to our right and saw they had changed direction and were now heading straight for us at a height of 30 ft. There was a mad rush away from our machines and we dived into a shallow ditch at the edge of the field. From there we fired our revolvers at the Dorniers as they swept down our line of Hurricanes, releasing showers of small bombs; some exploded on impact, while others lay around on the ground. Six Hurricanes had direct hits and burst into flames, mine included, in which I had left a rather nice toilet kit in a leather case.

'This rather upset our plans for the return to England. Squadron Leader Thompson decided that he, Flight Sergeant Brown from his squadron and I should take the three undamaged aircraft back, leaving the rest of the pilots to make their way home as best they could. They all eventually arrived, while we had an easy flight back. I was feeling a bit emotional on the way home, as it had been the most eventful day in my life so far.'

Guy says that it surpassed even the day, some two years before, when he had 'flown a Gloster Gauntlet into the target aircraft, another Gauntlet, while practising a No 1 Attack'. He omits to mention that the accident was not his fault, but an error of judgment by his flight commander, who, making a dummy attack immediately before him, did not leave him enough room to break away. 'On that occasion I had found myself hurtling backwards through the air until I realized that I had to pull the ripcord. Having done this, I was very relieved to see another parachute away down below me, which meant that Flight Sergeant Hooper, the pilot of the target aircraft, was safe.'

Britain was now in its most critical period of the war to date. Antwerp had fallen and German Panzer units had taken St Quentin and Cambrai. Air Marshal Sir Hugh Dowding, Commander-in-Chief of Fighter Command, was under constant pressure from Churchill to send more fighters, which he needed for the defence of Britain, to help stem the enemy's swift advance across France.

'When I got back to Kenley on 18 May, my flight was minus five pilots and aircraft, so it was with a little surprise the following morning, when I was talking to my girlfriend, Janet, on the telephone, that I heard my name called on the Tannoy and was told that A Flight was again to join up with 111 Squadron and carry out an offensive patrol over France, taking off from Hawkinge after lunch.

'Squadron Leader Thompson duly led his combined squadron across the Channel into France, where we ran into wave after wave of Heinkel 111s that stretched as far as the eye could see. I edged my section in between two V formations of Heinkels, echeloning them to starboard in the laid-down No 3 Fighter Command Attack, so that they each had their own bomber to attack. Mine was on the outside left. I opened fire and saw white smoke coming from his starboard engine.

'However, at this moment someone delivered me a sharp blow in the back with a red-hot hammer, which shook me a bit. So I broke away to port and dived away to size up the situation. I found that my right leg did not work and that there was blood oozing through my jacket, by my right thigh.'

With characteristic lack of drama, Guy adds, reasonably enough, 'I concluded that I had been shot.'

He goes on: 'The aircraft seemed to be flying normally, although I could see some holes in the starboard wing, which should not have been there. I turned north-west, where I hoped to find the Channel, and tried to work out whether I had enough petrol − and blood − to get back to England. But, as I had little idea where I was, this was going to be difficult. I then remembered that Janet's mother had given me a small flask of Courvoisier brandy which was in my tunic pocket. This I managed to extract and felt much better after drinking it.

'After flying for another half-hour I came to the coast and, seeing an airfield below me, decided to land, and made a remarkably good landing in spite of having no flaps and a punctured tyre. Not being able to taxi because of the tyre, I had to switch off the engine and sit there feeling rather foolish, as I could not get out of the cockpit. However, help soon arrived in the shape of Squadron Leader John Kirk, who, with his corporal, got me out and into his car.

'He drove me to No 1 General Hospital in the casino on the seafront at Dieppe, the town where I had landed. There he rounded up some doctors and got them to operate on me. Everyone was very busy evacuating and our arrival must have been a nuisance.'

When Squadron Leader J.E.Kirk returned to England he wrote to the Officer Commanding 253 Squadron on 27 May, 1940, describing the event. The date on which it occurred was, in fact, the first day on which the possibility that the British Expeditionary Force would have to be evacuated was discussed by telephone between London and the commanders in the field. Kirk wrote:

'On Sunday, 19 May I was on Dieppe aerodrome with a small party of men trying to refuel aircraft as they arrived. At about 1530 hrs a Hurricane made a landing − a perfect one too − and swung round in the middle of the aerodrome and stopped. I hurried across to it, thinking the pilot might be wounded, and was greeted with the remark, "Sorry to litter up your aerodrome like this, sir, I didn't know I had got one through the tyre".

'The pilot, F/LT Harris of your squadron (I believe his Christian name was Guy), had a bullet through his leg. The bullet had gone in above the knee and had come out at the back of the thigh. I lifted him out of the cockpit and, as I knew it would take me some time to get an ambulance, put him in the back of my car and took him down to No 1 General Hospital Dieppe.

'The hospital was completely deserted of doctors. My corporal and I lifted Harris out of the car onto a stretcher and carried him into the hospital entrance. I then spent twenty minutes finding a doctor, only succeeding when I had found the Officer Commanding Dieppe Sub-Base Area and told him in front of his entire staff what the situation was and what I thought of it.

'I went back to the hospital to see Harris and found that he was being attended to. What I wish to bring to your notice was the grand courage of the man. Although his wound must have been giving him hell he never made a sound and whilst he was in the car talked away about his fight and his squadron as though that was all that mattered.

'I promised him that I would go to see him the next day and take him his maps through which the bullet had passed, but unfortunately I had to move my unit during the night and the maps were left in the Watch Office at Dieppe aerodrome. As luck will have it, however, when mopping up the blood in my car we found the steel core of a German armour-piercing bullet which must have fallen out of his clothes and I also have his "Mae West". If you can tell me where he is I am sure he would like to have them.

'I sent you a teleprinter message from Dieppe telling you what had happened to Harris. I hope you received it in good time.'

Guy recalls: 'When I came round after the operation I was presented with a little box containing bits of metal casing from a bullet. The actual armour-piercing bullet with a needle tip was found by Squadron Leader

Kirk when he was mopping up the blood in his car. He would have brought it to me the next day, but he had to move his unit that night, so he sent it to 253, who passed it on to me eventually.

'This bullet had entered my back just to the right of my spine and travelled through the top of my right thigh, where it had emerged and lodged in my clothing.'

It was not long before he was put on a stretcher to be taken out to an ambulance. 'I then realized that I had not got my watch and wallet and someone fetched these for me. I should have asked for my tunic also, as this contained a very nice cigarette case, a twenty-first birthday present; and it was my best uniform tunic.

'I was put into an ambulance with three Army privates and was rather surprised by their language — four-letter words were not quite so common as they are today — and their low morale. I must have given them a talking to, as they did quieten down; or it might have been because we were showered with cigarettes, sweets, soap, razor blades, etc; they must have been getting rid of the NAAFI stores in Dieppe.

'After some hours in the ambulance, we were told that our hopes of a quick return to England had gone, since two hospital ships, which were to have taken us, had been bombed and sunk in Dieppe harbour. This,' says Guy, with a further absence of dithyrambics, 'came as a surprise, as we had heard no noise of aircraft or bombing.'

Guderian's 19th Panzer Korps was barely 50 miles away, having raced nearly 350 miles in nine days. Four other Armoured Corps were sweeping across France to the north of the 19th. Calais, Boulogne, Dieppe and Dunkirk were under threat.

'We were driven off to another hospital somewhere outside Dieppe. I was carried into a ward and in the bed opposite mine sat Pilot Officer Brian Young, who had been Assistant Adjutant on 32 Squadron at the outbreak of war. His Hurricane had burst into flames and the top of his body and face was one mass of burnt flesh, which was why he was sitting up in bed. He was amazingly cheerful. His first words to me were to ask how Janet was. To add to his troubles he had been shot at, and wounded, by the French while he was descending by parachute. He survived all this and ended his career as Commandant of the R.A.F. Regiment.'

Soon after his arrival, evacuation of this second hospital began. 'In the middle of the night I realized I was the only one left in the ward.' For a fit, strong and healthy young man, to be unable to walk, dependent on others for his removal before the imminent arrival of the enemy, there must have been an eerie, totally dispirited sensation of doom. To one who had spent over four years immediately preceding the war training, and preparing himself mentally, to fight Nazi Germany, the feeling of frustration at the prospect of being eliminated from the battle line so early was perhaps the worst of his predicament. 'There then entered a little procession led by the Matron, carrying a bottle of whisky, followed by two doctors.' Their phlegmatic reaction to misfortune matched his. 'They said, "We are awfully sorry, but the Germans are very close and we cannot get you away, but we are going to stay with you and we will get taken prisoner together." They then sat down, opened the whisky and we drank to this rather gloomy prospect.'

How long would it be before he saw his parents, his sister and Janet again? The indignity of being captured while he lay immobilized... the boredom of a prison camp... the probability of many years' deprivation of flying, which had been the focus of his life since boyhood. At the age of twenty-two, it would be a dismal end to all his hopes and aspirations.

Suddenly there was the sound of a motor vehicle arriving. Was it the precursor of the tread of jackboots and the phrase, which soon passed into cliché and music-hall jest, but authentically was a favourite utterance of the Germans, 'For you the war is over'?

'Within a short time, however, another doctor arrived with the news that an ambulance had turned up outside, and so they carried me out to this and we set off into the night, to arrive finally at a railway station where an ambulance train was waiting. I was loaded into a covered truck with "Hommes 40 Chevaux 8" painted on it, which had been fitted with tiers of racks to take stretchers and provided with windows. In this we puffed slowly across France.'

The Germans entered Abbeville on the evening of Guy's departure from Dieppe.

It seemed like days before the train stopped at Le Mans. 'There I remember lying on my stretcher on the platform while a little conference went on above me to determine whether I was fit to carry on in another ambulance to another hospital. It was decided that I was, so I was driven 100 miles to Rennes; and very glad I was to be put in a proper bed and cleaned up.'

By the time he left there, a week later, Boulogne and Calais were on the brink of being overrun and the British Expeditionary Force was being evacuated from Dunkirk. It would not be long before 15th Panzer Korps turned south-west, towards Rennes and the ports nearest to it.

An ambulance took him to St Nazaire, where he was put aboard HM Hospital Ship *Somersetshire*. 'Absolute luxury. I was asked if I would prefer Guinness or beer before dinner. Never has Guinness tasted so good. We docked at Liverpool in early June and transferred to another Army hospital in Ormskirk.' He spent some weeks there. Then 'I was recaptured by the R.A.F. and transferred from Ormskirk to the R.A.F. Hospital at Halton.

Finally I was sent to that most marvellous of all R.A.F. hospitals, the Palace Hotel in Torquay.'

He and Janet were married in September and he was finally discharged from hospital in November, 1940, with his flying medical category restored.

'I am eternally grateful to the Army Medical Services and the QAIMNS for caring for me and transporting me from Dieppe to Ormskirk without my feet once touching the ground.

'Three moments stand out during this period. The first was the episode of the Matron, doctors and whisky. The second was when our train was somewhere on the way to Le Mans, pulled up, in pouring rain, alongside another train. Through our windows we could see we were opposite an open truck in which were our doctors and nurses from that same hospital; a joyous reunion for us all. Finally, just before we were moved from Rennes to St Nazaire, I jokingly remarked to my nurse that although I had been in France for about two weeks, I had not had any champagne. That girl slipped out of the hospital and brought a bottle which she presented to me as I was being carried out to the ambulance.'

Guy Harris had not rubbed shoulders with the enemy, as other evaders and escapers were to in the streets of many French towns and villages during the coming five years. He had been entirely in the hands of his own compatriots, men and women, on his way from acute danger to safety. But his was a genuine evasion and one of the war's earliest; along, of course, with thousands of other wounded British Servicemen who were snatched almost from under the tank tracks of the speeding enemy and whisked home.

Soon after returning to his squadron in November he was posted to a Hurricane operational training unit and detached to the Central Flying School to do an instructors' course. A year later, promoted to squadron leader, he found himself at an O.T.U. in Aden as Chief Ground Instructor. A course at the Middle East Staff College, Haifa, was followed by Staff appointments, culminating in May, 1944, with a wing commander's post as Senior Air Staff Officer at H.Q. Levant in Jerusalem.

Back to Britain in March, 1945, and thence to Germany, where he was Liaison Officer at Gatow. Here, he 'acquired one of the more interesting trophies of war, namely Hitler's lavatory seat from the Berlin Bunker'.

A.D.Godley wrote of the motor bus:
'What is this that roareth thus?
Can it be a motor bus?
Yes the smell and hideous hum
Indicate Motorem Bum...'

One wonders what he would have written about the article on which Hitler's bum had reposed.

Of all people whom one would have expected to continue flying professionally, Wing Commander Guy Harris was prominent. When he left the R.A.F. in December, 1945, he joined the British Overseas Airways Corporation, was seconded to Iraqi Airways and made the inaugural flight from Baghdad to Basra. In 1946 he resigned, relegated aviation to the background as a hobby and made a successful career in property development.

CHAPTER THREE

SERGEANT P. T. WAREING DCM

ON 25 AUGUST, 1940, the Battle of Britain was officially half-way through its eighth week. The weather was fair in the early morning, then became cloudy.

No 616 (South Yorkshire) Squadron, of the prewar Auxiliary Air Force, equipped with Spitfires, was stationed a few miles beyond the southern outskirts of London at Kenley. Before the war all Auxiliary pilots were officers. On the declaration of war their numbers were increased by the arrival of several R.A.F. Volunteer Reserve sergeants. These were weekend and spare-time amateur flyers, like the commissioned young gentlemen of the A.A.F. Unlike the latter, whose tunics were lined with red silk to distinguish them from the professionals of the Royal Air Force, who wore regulation black linings, NCOs' tunics had no linings at all.

Naturally, there was a degree of rivalry, sometimes of aloofness, between the three forces. The level of skill was high in all of them, though the regulars had the greatest number of flying hours. In enthusiasm there was no disparity; the R.A.F. earned their living in the air and the others gave up their free time to aviating. The VRs, however, all belonged to a pool, whereas the Auxiliaries, being organized in squadrons, had the same team spirit as the professionals and it was not always easy for NCOs who wore a 'VR' patch on each shoulder to feel that they were unreservedly welcomed by officers sporting a brass 'A' on their lapels.

When it came to the crunch, they were all equally committed and honours were evenly divided. The top-scoring pilot in the Battle of Britain, Sergeant Jim 'Ginger' Lacey, was a VR, serving with an A.A.F. squadron, 501.

Sergeant Philip Wareing had joined the R.A.F.V.R. early in 1939. He was posted to 616 Squadron while they were still at their peacetime base, Leconfield, Yorkshire. They had moved to Kenley on 19 August. On the 22nd Philip Wareing scored his first victory in action.

During the morning of 25th several spoof raids over the Channel appeared on the radar. It was not until 1730 hrs that 50-plus enemy aircraft were plotted near St Malo and were joined by another 50 over Cherbourg. Behind it, another formation 100-strong was heading for Weymouth. These two waves bombed several places along the south coast.

At about 1830 a third raid numbering 100 bombers and escorting fighters attacked Dover and the Thames Estuary. Philip had already flown two operational sorties that day when his flight was sent up to intercept the new mass of raiders. The Hurricanes and Spitfires met the enemy in mid-Channel and Philip opened fire on a Messerschmitt 109. His bullets hit it so effectively that it turned tail. He chased it, but before he could finish it off he found himself over the French coast. Flak batteries gave his aircraft such a hammering that he had to bale out, came down near Calais Marck aerodrome and was instantly surrounded by German troops.

He was taken to Brussels by car and flown from there to Germany, where he was put in Dulag Luft (aircrew transit camp) near Frankfurt. While there, he was subjected to one of the Germans' less intelligent ploys; an obvious impostor, who tried to persuade him to give information, allegedly for the Red Cross, about his squadron and the airfields on which he had been stationed. Being less stupid than his interrogator, he refused and was shunted off to Stalag Luft 1 at Barth.

Like every conscientious prisoner of war, his thoughts were much occupied with trying to find a way to escape. Two officers did manage to do so, which prompted the enemy to move all the prisoners, on 18 April,1942, to a new and supposedly escape-proof prison camp, Stalag Luft 3, at Sagan on the North German Plain.

Five months later, several officers who had been making a nuisance of themselves to their gaolers were moved to Oflag 21B at Shubin, in Poland. Philip volunteered to accompany them as an orderly.

It was not long before he learned from fellow prisoners that many Polish civilians were pro-British enough to take the risk of helping anyone who tried to escape. Determined to get away, he prepared for it by equipping himself so that he could take immediate advantage of any chance that came. To simulate civilian clothes, he had loosened the stitching around the pockets of his tunic, his pilot's wings and sergeant's chevrons, so that he could easily rip them off. He had changed his blue trousers for a faded pair of Army khaki and wore Army boots. He had fashioned a cap from an old pair of R.A.F. trousers. In his pockets he carried shaving gear, a comb and a mirror. He also had a home-made compass and three maps made in the camp.

The orderlies were taken regularly to the railway station to fetch rations, coal and Red Cross parcels, but they were under heavy guard, one escort to every two airmen. The R.A.F. NCOs had the good sense not to give their guards any trouble and in due course the escort was reduced to four for every party of ten orderlies.

Late on 16 December, 1942, during Philip's third trip to the station under the new arrangement, one of his fellows dropped a load of bread that he was carrying. In the ensuing fuss, while the escorts' attention was on the spilled loaves, Philip slipped between the lorry that had brought them here and a goods truck. He crawled under the truck, across the rails, then bolted across two more sets of rails and two platforms. The lorry driver, a German soldier, started his engine at the moment when Philip began his dash for freedom. Its noise so effectively drowned warning shouts that nobody fired a shot at him.

Darkness was gathering as he hurried from the station to hide in the woods and marshes beyond Blumenthal village. For food he had his day's ration of hard biscuits and a lump of Red Cross cheese, some Horlicks tablets, a block of sugar and a piece of chewing gum.

He spent that night in a wood, on a bed of small fallen branches. When daylight came he did not move until after 0930 hrs, when he set out to walk to Blomberg. There, seeing a bicycle which nobody was keeping an eye on, he stole it and rode off along the road to Danzig. It was a decrepit machine and he kept dismounting and pushing it as a relief from its hard saddle and the effort of pedalling uphill. Night fell, but there was ample moonlight and he took the risk of crossing a bridge across the Vistula, despite the police and sentries who guarded it.

At 0800 hrs on 18 December he arrived at Graudenz and made his way to the docks, where he looked around for a ship flying the Swedish flag. There was none, and to linger would excite suspicion, so he went to the railway station, intending to take a train to Danzig. None was shown on the departures board. Again, to wait without making any enquiry might make him conspicuous but wandering about the streets might equally invite curiosity. He resolved his dilemma when he saw a German prop a shiny new bicycle on a stand and walk away. Leaving his old one in its place, he mounted the replacement and was gone. Back to the Vistula bridge and, seizing his opportunity while the guards were having an argument, he recrossed it.

Out in the countryside once more, he saw a milk churn beside a farm gate and paused to drink before settling down to snatch some sleep in a haystack. At 0400 hrs he woke and pressed on until he saw a British soldier working on the road with a party of Germans. He had a quick talk with him, following which he turned back to seek help from an allegedly friendly Pole, but was unable to find him.

He spent the night in an empty, unfurnished house, where he barely missed being discovered by a caretaker whose flashlight beam just failed to light on him. He continued his ride the next day and reached Danzig, where he slipped into the docks without being stopped by police or troops. A Swedish ship was loading coal. He strode up the gangplank as though he were a member of the crew, unchallenged, and straight into the hold. Cranes were dumping more coal around him, until the hold was three-quarters full and some Russians, under German guard, came aboard to trim the cargo. One of the Russians saw him. Philip quietly got it across to him that he was an English pilot. This was relayed to the others, who turned a blind eye to him.

Early the following morning, 21 December, a two-hour routine search of the ship began before she was allowed to sail at 0900 hrs. Philip stayed below for two days, was seen as soon as he went up on deck, and was brought water and bread by members of the crew during the rest of the voyage. One of them eventually informed the captain that there was a stowaway and on arrival at Gothenberg Philip was handed over to the police, who notified the British Consul. He was · given decent clothes and stayed at Police Headquarters, but was allowed out during the day, until someone from the Embassy came to take him to Stockholm on 28 December.

After a comfortable week there he was flown to Scotland on 5 January, 1943; perhaps the most anxious hours of his whole journey, he said, because enemy fighters patrolled the route, on the lookout for aircraft transporting ballbearings and clandestine passengers.

Sergeant Philip Wareing was the only pilot shot down over France during the Battle of Britain who succeeded in escaping from a prison camp and making his way home. For this display of initiative, resourcefulness and courage he was awarded the Distinguished Conduct Medal. He was soon commissioned and after a few months spent giving talks on escape and evasion he continued his service as a flying instructor. He died in May, 1987.

CHAPTER FOUR

FLIGHT LIEUTENANT
F. W. 'TAFFY' HIGGINSON DFM

AIRCREW OF THE peacetime Royal Air Force had no illusions about their prospects of survival in the event of war. Any at North Weald, Essex, who had been optimistic about their chances were abruptly made aware of reality during the first week of hostilities. Wing Commander F. W. 'Taffy' Higginson, OBE, DFC, DFM, who had joined No. 56 Squadron as a sergeant pilot in April, 1937, recalls that the Secretary of State for Air, Sir Kingsley Wood, visiting the station, informed the assembled fighter pilots that the war plan was founded on the assumption that their average life would be three weeks: 'So you had all better make your wills!'

Wood had previously been Postmaster General. The affinity of a postman's or sorter's philosophy with a fighter pilot's is not immediately obvious. Whether he was being tactlessly jocular or scrupulously honest, their response was typical in its ribald attitude and probably astonished him.

Petrol was rationed and the allowance was meagre. One pilot spoke for the rest: 'In that case, may we be allowed to use Service petrol in our cars?'

The ironical question was as dismissive as a two-finger gesture.

'Not in my bloody aeroplane, you don't.'

The stricture expressed more than innate decisiveness and determination. There was also the assurance and authority engendered by eleven years of Service discipline and training, fortified by the confidence acquired through achievement. Together these qualities had formed a character well equipped to triumph over adversity.

Three centuries earlier, Francis Bacon had written: 'The virtue of adversity is fortitude... the heroical virtue'. Flight Sergeant Pilot Taffy Higginson was in considerable adversity at this moment, about to be stranded on the wrong side of the English Channel with the enemy hard on his heels. The manner in which he dealt with the threat foreshadowed his attitude and actions in the face of even greater calamities that awaited him in the near future and would test his capacity for 'heroical virtue' to the full.

On 10 May, 1940, the eight months of stagnation since Britain and France took up arms against Germany, the 'Phony War' or 'Sitzkrieg', had blazed into sudden death and destruction; the Blitzkrieg, Hitler's simultaneous air and land assault on Belgium, Holland and France.

The Luftwaffe's Order of Battle comprised 1,210 fighters and 1,680 bombers. Facing them, the French Air Force had 750 fighters of six types, all inferior to the British and German, of which only 584 were serviceable. The hard knuckle in the defence of France was provided by eight Royal Air Force fighter squadrons stationed there; six flying Hurricanes, two flying Gladiators but converting to Hurricanes. One more Hurricane squadron was added at once. More fighters, all Hurricanes, were sent from England, some daily from dawn to dusk, others to stay for a few days. It was the R.A.F., better organized, trained and equipped than *l'Armée de l'Air* and with higher morale, that provided the most effective opposition to the invaders.

On 16 May, B Flight – six aircraft – of 56 Squadron, led by Flight Lieutenant I. S. Soden, joined a Flight from 229 Squadron commanded by Flight Lieutenant F. E. Rosier (later Air Chief Marshal Sir Frederick, GCB CBE DSO), to form a composite squadron at Vitry-en-Artois.

Among the 56 Squadron Flight was Taffy Higginson, who by now had 750 flying hours in his logbook. On the first patrol, the following day, he was detached to attack an aircraft that he identified as a Fieseler Storch. This was small, slow, highly manoeuvrable and could take off and land in the length of a cricket pitch. For a Hurricane, with its much bigger turning circle and a minimum speed that exceeded the Storch's maximum, to engage one was like a hawk trying to out-manoeuvre a humming bird. 'I chased it around trees and other obstacles, but failed to destroy it.' He was not the only Allied fighter pilot to have this experience during the next few years.

On B Flight's second patrol Taffy Higginson shot down a Do215 twin-engine bomber. On the third, the flight met seven unescorted He111s: 'We had all the time in the world to get behind them and we shot down five of them'; one fell to Taffy. His last sortie of the day yielded no action.

The first two tasks on 18 May were patrols that brought no contact with the enemy. The third 'was supposed to be an offensive patrol near the battle front, but we were jumped by a large number of Me109s and there was absolute chaos. I fired on one aircraft without success and when I got back to base I was told we had lost Ian Soden.'

On the 19th, after two unproductive patrols, the five remaining B Flight pilots were ordered to rendezvous with bombers flying out from England to attack targets on the battle front. While taking off, they were attacked by Me110s, 'and in the ensuing shambles Flying Officer Tommy Rose and

Flying Officer Barry Sutton were shot down. Barry survived, badly burned, but Tommy was killed.' The three survivors took off once again on a local patrol and ran into twelve Me110s that were about to strafe the airfield. They shot down four of these, one bagged by Taffy: but, meanwhile, the Dornier 215s that were accompanying the Messerschmitts destroyed nine R.A.F. aircraft parked on the airfield.

When they landed they were shocked to find how few officers and men were left, how many aircraft had been destroyed or badly damaged, and the chaos that reigned. 'Everyone seemed to be running all over the place with nobody in control.'

Flight Sergeant Spreadborough, in charge of B Flight's ground crew, asked, 'What should I do, Taffy?'

'Commandeer a vehicle and get all the ground crew out of here as quickly as you can.'

Flying Officer Ereminski, a white Russian, and Flight Sergeant Higginson, the only pilots left of the six who had flown out from England three days before, took off for Norrent Fontes, a more westerly airfield.

Neither of them had a map. 'After we had been flying for half an hour or so, I told Ereminski I would land at a field and find out where we were.'

This he did and eventually they found their way to their destination. Hardly had they touched down again when the Group Captain in command ordered Flight Sergeant Higginson to return by road to Vitry and destroy any Hurricanes and petrol that remained.

His aeroplane was still intact and he was there to fight, so, 'Why me, sir?' he asked.

'Do as you're told.'

Back to Vitry, then, in the Group Captain's car with its driver; slowly, against a tide of refugees on foot and in a variety of vehicles, and retreating soldiers. The Germans were so close by the time they arrived that small arms fire was within hearing. Taffy shot holes in the petrol cans, struck a match and tossed it into the vapour, then recoiled smartly from the conflagration before it ignited him too. But it took more than one bullet to spring a leak in the two remaining Hurricanes. As soon as they were ablaze he jumped into the car and the driver accelerated away. The enemy was closing on the airfield perimeter.

By the time they were back at Norrent Fontes, Taffy's own Hurricane was the last remaining. The driver jammed the brakes on beside it at the same instant as a strange pilot was climbing into the cockpit.

'I grabbed him by the collar,' Taffy recalls, 'and dragged him off the wing.' "Where d'you think you're going?" I asked him.'

"To England", he said.' It was then that the poacher was disabused of this intention by the rightful owner's uncompromising retort: 'Not in my bloody aeroplane, you don't.'

The return flight to North Weald took one hour and thirty minutes, making a total of seven hours and forty minutes for the day.

B Flight's survivors returned from France as the pressure on Fighter Command began to increase. While the land battle moved southwards towards the Weygand Line, where the Allies were trying to hold the enemy advance, the air fighting continued unabated. Early each morning the squadron took off for Manston, the airfield nearest to the Channel coast, from where they flew four or five patrols every day over the beaches of Dunkirk and Calais. The main tasks were to give long-range air cover over the battle area until the evacuation of the British Expeditionary Force was accomplished and to escort bombers attacking the invasion barges that were assembling in the Channel ports. On one of these operations Taffy shot down a Me109. On another, sadly, he saw his brother-in-law, Sergeant Elliott, go down in flames over Dunkirk. The British forces had begun to fall back on Dunkirk on 26 May. The last were taken off on 4 June. Until 19 June others were embarked at Le Havre, Cherbourg, St. Malo, St. Nazaire and Nantes. Throughout it all, No. 56 and all the other Fighter Command squadrons stationed in southern England were giving the Army and Navy protection from enemy air attacks.

Then came the Battle of Britain, during which Taffy was awarded the Distinguished Flying Medal in July, and added six and a half confirmed victories to his total.

For 56 Squadron, this epic period of conflict against odds of never less than three to one was a grimly unrelenting time of weariness and daily expectation of death or injury. Fifty-six was a squadron with a cavalier reputation for dash and gaiety as well as outstanding performance in battle. In 1917 it had been the first squadron in the Royal Flying Corps to which only the best pilots were posted. Its first Commanding Officer, Major R. G. Blomfield, brought to it a distinctive style; one of his enterprisingly flamboyant innovations was to scour the Corps for first class musicians, conscripted from fashionable London hotels and restaurants, and form an orchestra to play for his officers nightly at dinner.

His pilots were as strongly individualistic as he. At London Colney, where the squadron was formed, they adopted the habit of landing by setting their wheels down on the ridge of the hangar's sloping roof and rolling down it on to the ground.

This whole ethos remained unchanged twenty-three years later. 'We drove frequently to London and went round the night clubs,' Taffy says. 'If we were a bit tired, it was probably more from late nights than from fighting all day!' Among the cars that made these sorties, his Opel, 'Esmerelda', was probably the most overloaded. They fought with the same zest, too; having scored thirty-five victories over France, they shot down eighty-eight more of the enemy in the Battle of Britain.

On 18 September, at the height of the battle, Flight Sergeant F. W. Higginson DFM was commissioned. He says, 'I was also dubbed "Taffy", like all Welshmen in the R.A.F.; as all Scotsmen are "Jock" and Irishmen "Paddy", a custom that makes it easier than having to remember everyone's Christian name.'

To become an officer was within the reach of every R.A.F. apprentice who entered No 1 School of Technical Training, Halton.

Pilot Officer Higginson was ambitious in the way of all natural leaders and those who take pride in excelling at whatever they undertake. He had now won his spurs in air fighting. The way there had been a long one. It began on the day in January, 1929, when, one month before his sixteenth birthday, he first put on R.A.F. uniform, in those days, a high-necked tunic, breeches and puttees.

'We felt very privileged to be there and were proud of our uniform.' Entry to Halton was a considerable achievement attained by passing a stiff examination and character assessment.

No. 1 School of Technical Training (Boys) was founded in 1920 by Marshal of the R.A.F. Lord Trenchard 'the father of the R.A.F.'. Its pupils have always been known as 'Trenchard's brats'. It should be remembered that the true progenitor of the R.A.F. was Lieutenant-General Sir David Henderson, who was the first commander of the Royal Flying Corps, from which the R.A.F. evolved, and deserves due recognition as the grandfather of today's Service.

Young Taffy Higginson's upbringing had prepared him well for the rigours and vagaries of communal life away from home, among strange companions, under strict discipline. 'We were a close family. My father was a proud member of the Swansea Constabulary, a keen disciplinarian and a devout Christian, who believed that Sunday should be spent in the house of God.' In all weathers, he walked six miles a day in term-time between home and his grammar school near Swansea, which produced many Welsh international rugger players and was where he first played the game at which he was to enjoy considerable success over some twenty-five years.

The Halton system was designed to mould an intelligent youth into a tough, practical and self-reliant man skilled in his profession. For three years Taffy Higginson's life consisted of drill and physical training, of long days spent on engineering and academic studies, with reveille at 6.30 am and cease work at 5.30 pm; of one half holiday a week for recreation on the playing fields and in the swimming bath; of church parade every Sunday; of winning distinction at rugby football, boxing and golf.

Pay was three shillings (15p) a week, of which one shilling was retained to pay one's fare home on holiday at the end of term. Taffy Higginson learned the habits of hard work and thrift. Not least, he absorbed the unique infusion of comradeship and Service tradition, and developed the resilience necessary for stoicism under military discipline and spartan living. Any breach of rules incurred at least seven days' confinement to quarters, with sundry other restrictions on the defaulter's freedom and an hour on the parade ground in the evening. Punishment could not deter some 240 energetic, growing youths with healthy appetites from occasional mischief, such as making use of an underground heating duct to crawl the long distance from your barrack block to the cookhouse. Timing was critical, to ensure that no cookhouse staff were present when you surfaced.

Taffy's was one of the first courses to be trained as metal riggers and given a further year on engines, so that they could do all the maintenance on an aircraft. 'We were also highly suitable to be air gunners,' he says, 'because if you had to fly in the aeroplane as well as maintain it, you made damn sure it was serviced as well as possible.'

Posted to No 7 Squadron, at Worthy Down, near Winchester, which flew the Vickers Virginia four-engined bomber, he duly occupied the rear gun turret of the aircraft he maintained. His reputation on the rugger field and in the boxing ring continued to grow. He was an effective hooker who turned his lack of height to advantage by swinging on his two props, which the laws then allowed; and as a lightweight boxer he reached the semi-finals of the Hampshire Championships.

For a very few candidates from the ranks, there was access to a pilot's cockpit. Only those with the highest assessments for conduct, character, intelligence, prowess at sports, ability at their ground trades and flying, if they had volunteered as air gunners, were considered. In August, 1935, Taffy began pilot training. He gained his wings on 30 June, 1936, and joined No 19 Squadron. In October he was transferred to No 56. At the outbreak of war he had logged 625 pilot hours.

On 1 September, 1940, his squadron, which had suffered heavy losses during the Battle of Britain, was posted to Boscombe Down to re-equip and train new pilots. This station was the Aircraft and Armament Experimental Establishment, so the arrival of an operational squadron was warmly welcomed by the station commander, Group Captain Ramsbottom-Isherwood (who later took the first Hurricane squadron to Russia).

In the Royal Air Force, as in the Royal Flying Corps a quarter-century earlier, it was experience rather than rank that dictated who would lead a formation. Pilot Officer Higginson, who was already leading B Flight in the air, was nominated flight commander designate. On his busiest day to date he had flown six sorties. The most he had flown in one week was 39, and 59 in a fortnight. The move from south-east England to Wiltshire did not mean that the squadron was on rest, but the pace did diminish; by the end of October he had flown only twelve more operational sorties, but shot down two more Messerschmitt 110s and a Dornier 17. Between 10 July and 31 October, the official duration of the Battle of Britain, he had survived twenty-four combat engagements.

At Boscombe Down there was more time for training, morale-building and relaxation than during the previous five months. He decided that the squadron needed a mascot, and found a suitable one in a pet shop – a small monkey with an engaging personality, which the Squadron christened 'Me 109'.

'We thought the world of Me 109. He really was a great chap.' Me 109's antics in his cage were a constant source of amusement. When the station commander held a cocktail party in honour of No 56, everyone felt that its mascot would enhance the occasion, so his cage was brought into the Officers' Mess ante-room. The monkey was by now accustomed to being the cynosure of attention, but the crowd of strangers and the novel presence of attractive, scented lady guests in these normally masculine surroundings, excited him to excel in his efforts to entertain. Encircled by admirers, stimulated by even more than the usual adulation, inflamed by feminine exclamations of enchantment, he suddenly resorted to the act of self-gratification for which his kind are notorious and which had once earned Onan such dire Biblical condemnation. One might almost say that Me 109 was swanking. There was much giggling and blushing among the female onlookers, embarrassed confusion on the part of their hosts. He was rushed from sight and never again introduced to a mixed gathering.

December saw the squadron's return to North Weald. In January, 1941, Pilot Officer F. W. Higginson DFM was promoted to Acting Flight Lieutenant and appointed B Flight's commander.

Work now consisted largely of escorting bombers attacking targets in northern France, a type of operation code-named 'Circus'. The whole of Fighter Command welcomed this assumption of offensive operations after so long on the defensive, but these soon proved costly in the loss of both bombers and fighters.

'February, March and April were extremely busy and we flew on almost every day.' The emphasis was on convoy patrols, sweeps over the French coast – intended to provoke the enemy fighters to come up and do battle – some night patrols and some high altitude tests with the new Hurricane IIs. This routine continued throughout the spring and early summer, until, for Flight Lieutenant Higginson, 17 June, 1941.

On that day the Squadron was detailed as close escort to a formation of Blenheims that were to bomb targets near Lille. The Hurricanes flew at bomber height, in the middle of the formation and on both flanks. Spitfires provided high cover. The attack completed, the Circus was on its way home when, 'There was suddenly an enormous bang and a cannon shell went through the bottom of the aeroplane, taking away my control stick.' The close escort had been relying on the Spitfires high above them to give warning if enemy fighters approached. The mission having been completed successfully and the way home apparently clear, Taffy was feeling comfortably secure. The attack came as a total surprise. 'The Hurricane went into a vertical dive. I undid my straps, slid back the hood and was more or less sucked out of the aircraft.' He pulled the rip cord, the parachute opened and, 'After the tremendous noise, all was peace and quiet and the countryside below looked absolutely delightful and attractive in the summer sunshine. How little did I know what was to follow.'

'He that hath wife and children hath given hostages to fortune,' Francis Bacon warned, 'for they are impediments to great enterprise, either of virtue or mischief.'

At twenty-eight years of age, Taffy Higginson's hostages to fortune were his wife Shan and two sons, Paul aged three years and Peter, one. He was about to prove that wife and children were the greatest possible incentive to sustain his determination to evade capture, through the darkest times that lay ahead.

There was also his religious faith to support him. 'I am a committed Christian,' he emphasizes, 'and from this I derived great nourishment.' His belief in God gave him strength now, as it had always done.

On 19 June, Group Captain Vincent, Commanding R.A.F. North Weald, wrote to Shan:-

'Please accept my sincere sympathy for the loss of your gallant husband. I trust most sincerely that he is a prisoner and honestly feel that there is a very good chance that this may be so. "Taffy" was such a grand chap here, so gallant and gay, that it seems impossible that he could be anything but a prisoner and making an awful nuisance of himself with the Huns! He was one of seven pilots that we lost from North Weald that day, and they went down because they were doing their job so outstandingly well that the bombers, who were their personal responsibility, reached the target and our country again in safety. We have the following telegrams from the A.O.C. of No 11 (Fighter) Group and No 2 (Bomber) Group which are self-explanatory.

' "The fact that the bombers reached their objective and arrived home in the face of heavy opposition reflects the greatest credit on the escort wing.

I deeply regret that this magnificent performance involved the loss of several most valuable pilots."

' "The close escort today by 56, 242 and 306 Squadrons was much appreciated by bomber crews of 2 Group. Please convey our thanks to Squadron Commanders and pilots taking part for the admirable way in which this was carried out."

'Taffy's loss was a great one to us at North Weald, as he was so universally popular, so please ask me if there is anything I can do to help you, and accept the sympathy of all his many friends at North Weald.

Yours sincerely...'

Taffy comments, fifty years later, 'Something must have gone wrong for so many to have been shot down. It was said that the high cover were in the wrong place.'

He landed on the edge of a wood. He had lost his left flying boot, which he presumed had been a casualty of the explosion in the aircraft. After burying his parachute and tunic, he waited until it was dark, then set out along the road to the first friendly-looking house, where he knocked on the door and asked if they could provide him with a boot. He had to rely on what he remembered of the French he had learned at school, gestures and the hope that whomever he spoke to would understand a few words of English. 'They were very kind indeed. They gave me a pair of boots and took my remaining one as a souvenir.'

He resumed his trudge, intending to walk all night but not knowing where the road would lead him. As dawn was breaking he looked for somewhere to hide during daylight. He made for a farm, where he found a woman at work in the yard, whom he asked if he could sleep in the barn. She agreed, but he had hardly made himself comfortable when in came her husband, 'who told me in no uncertain terms to get up and go: *fiche le camp*. Of course I had no alternative.'

A further hour's walking brought him to a village. There was a café on the corner where another road joined the one he was on. 'I thought, "To hell with it, let me get something to drink".' So he went in and bought himself a beer, then tramped on feeling reasonably confident 'because the place was not crawling with German soldiers'. He had covered a mile or so when a van overtook him and pulled up alongside.

He asked the driver for a lift.

'Where are you going?' the driver asked.

'St Omer.'

'But you are not a Frenchman, are you?'

'*Non, je suis aviateur anglais.*' One wonders what pang of nationalistic guilt this staunch Welshman suffered. But, of course, to the French all Britons, whether Welsh, Scots, English or Northern Irish, are 'English'. *Britannique* is one of the most rarely used words in the French vocabulary. 'Can you help me?' Taffy added.

'Yes, certainly.'

Taffy boarded the van, the driver turned and took him back to the village, Fauquembergues, where he stayed for a few days with a member of the Resistance.

'From there I was taken to Lille, where I was introduced to an Englishman, Paul Cole, known locally as "Monsieur Paul", with whom I stayed for a week or so.'

This tall, thin, ginger-haired man of thirty-five, with a clipped moustache, was wearing plus fours. He claimed to be an Army captain, cut off from his unit when it retreated to Dunkirk. He was such a caricature Englishman that the first sight of him must have alarmed most of the evaders to whom he was entrusted. Moreover, as the latest dependant on his protection at once heard, he spoke French with a grotesquely anglicized accent. Could this obvious non-Frenchman be expected to deceive the Germans about his nationality and lead anyone safely past the Gestapo and SS, let alone fool the ordinary enemy soldiery?

In fact, for a foreigner to delude the majority of Germans that he was French was not difficult. Few Germans, particularly the rank and file, knew the language. Those who had acquired a small knowledge of it could not differentiate between regional accents and foreign ones. Moreover, Cole had taken the ingenious precaution of having his false identity card endorsed to state that he had a speech impediment. Whenever accosted by the German military he adopted a stumbling, incoherent delivery.

To any compatriot, despite Cole's attempt to mimic a 'genteel' accent, it was obvious that he was a Cockney. His features did nothing to recommend his integrity either; pale and ferret-faced, with close-set, shifty eyes, a long, inquisitive nose, a thin-lipped pursey mouth whose bogus smile was as devious as a huckster's, as dehumanised as a hangman's. This mean, pinchbeck fellow yet imbued in his protégés a feeling of trust, gratitude and admiration.

His ill-favoured appearance did not deter women from succumbing to the sexual magnetism that he evidently possessed. No sooner did he find himself 'separated' from his Army unit than he began living with the wife of a café owner absent on military service. At the same time he was enjoying the favours of several other women and became well known for his lechery wherever he went.

Taffy Higginson habitually takes a benign and Christian view of his fellow humans, but he has his full measure of shrewdness. It is a considerable tribute to Cole's talent for confidence trickery that, during their close association, Taffy never suspected his guide and mentor's duplicitous nature.

Cole's source of false documents was François Duprez, a municipal official in La Madelaine. Although in his early thirties, he was exempt from conscription because he had lost a leg in an accident three years before the war. From the time that France surrendered he had worked against the Germans – first by hiding British troops in his house – and was one of the earliest members of the Resistance organization.

After Taffy had shaved off his moustache, Cole photographed him for the identity card that Duprez duly supplied. This certified that the holder had been discharged from the Army as mentally deficient, another spoof to explain his difficulty in understanding what was said to him and in replying.

Next came a visit to l'Abbé Pierre Carpentier, vicar of the parish of St Gilles in Abbeville, another member of the Underground. In appearance and character the priest was the antithesis of Cole; sturdily built and good-looking, he conveyed an instant impression of dependability. Taffy describes him as 'a marvellous chap'. A former French Army chaplain, he now contributed to the safe passage of evaders by forging permits that enabled them to leave Abbeville for the south. He also supplied false identity cards. Stationers sold blank cards and all café-tobacconists sold the tax stamps for them. The difficult part was to make a copy of the rubber stamp with which the Town Hall imprinted identity cards and to forge the signature of the relevant official; which this parish priest had learned to do. Taffy's immediate destination was Marseilles, via Paris, under Cole's guidance; thence, on to the Spanish frontier and ultimately Gibraltar.

Taffy was in the Forbidden Zone, whose southern boundary was the River Somme, on which Abbeville stands. The Occupied Zone was accessible by a bridge, patrolled by German troops, who demanded both an identity card and a transit pass; but the latter did not bear a photograph, so was re-usable by clandestine travellers. Those to whom Abbé Carpentier lent these permits – sometimes several travelled together – handed them over to a member of the Resistance after crossing the bridge, to be returned to the priest and issued again to others who were on the run. Taffy says he gave his to someone who awaited him in a café.

Taffy and Cole went by train to Paris, where, in the *quartier louche* around Les Halles and the rue St Denis, they stayed a few days in a *maison de passe*, a brothel where tarts and their clients rented rooms by the hour or the night. In these establishments the police did not check the register of who stayed there, as they did daily at conventional hotels.

Although he secured his door with the safety chain every night, Taffy slept with his few hundred francs tucked into his shirt, and checked the possessions in his attaché case when he woke – spare vest, pants and socks, and his identity card. On the morning of their departure, having put his money in a trouser pocket, he 'thought it would be sensible to go to the lavatory before leaving'. This was of the primitive variety that was then universal in cheap hotels and cafés and is still found in country places. It consisted of a hole in the floor, over which the user squatted and was known as a *toilette turque*. The Turks have conferred many benefits on the world, not least Turkish baths, carpets, a pungently aromatic tobacco and that wonderful rose-flavoured sweetmeat known as Turkish Delight, but this malodorous device was no delight in any way, not least in the matter of comfort.

A pilot's life depends on the care with which he carries out his cockpit checks before take-off. With this habit ingrained in him over many years, when Taffy returned to his room he inspected the contents of his attaché case once more before leaving. Everything was there, except... 'I found to my horror that the money had disappeared'.

The only place he had been was the lavatory, so back he went. 'And there, lo and behold, was the money, in the hole.'

A *toilette turque* could not be described as a 'W.C.', for water did not figure in the disposal of its contents. Primitive and nauseating though this was, it proved, this time, to be a boon. 'I had no alternative but to extract the notes and go back to my room, wash my hands and the money, and spread it on the window sill to dry in the sun which was, luckily, shining in.'

Belatedly, they caught a train to St Martin-le-Beau, a few miles south-east of Tours, where they were to meet someone at the Post Office. He would tell them when and where the Germans patrolled the demarcation line between the *Zone Occupée* and the *Zone Libre*, which they had to cross. A road to the south of the town constituted part of the border. To reach it they had to cross the River Cher. This was a short distance north of the actual line, but more convenient than the road to patrol.

'For some reason, possibly because of a holiday, we were unable to make contact. Rather than wait around for another day, we decided to attempt the crossing without any assistance.'

If stopped by a patrol, their story would be that they were strangers to each other who had met for the first time on the train. They made off down the road towards the Cher, but saw, before they reached it, that the bridge over it had been destroyed. So they left the road and crossed a field that led them to the trees lining the river bank. They hid for some time to see if any patrols appeared, but there was no sign of life at all. Their patience and caution were rewarded when at last they saw a woman leave the far side in a boat and row over to near where they had taken cover. They asked her if she would row them across, and she agreed to do so. On landing, they gave her some money, then rejoined the road on which they had previously been by walking through a copse and another field.

'Of course we felt very elated that we had, as we thought, eluded the patrols. But as we reached the road we were met by a German officer and a sergeant who had been watching our approach from a roadside café. The officer asked us where we were going and what we were doing.'

Under interrogation, 'Paul Cole took the offensive and challenged them to take us to the German Kommandantur, where he would report them for drinking in his aunt's café instead of attending to their duty.' Cole's outrageously impudent charge could have led to him and his companion being marched off under arrest.

The small café that he alleged belonged to his aunt stood near the Vichy end of the bridge over the Cher. His quick thinking was the product of nearly twenty years' living on his wits. The German, taken aback, foolishly and weakly allowed himself to be dragged into an altercation. Cole repeated his threat to report him for drinking on duty and said he would call 'his aunt' to give evidence. His audacity and, on this occasion, courage, were lethally dangerous. He had in his briefcase a list of trains running from the Pas de Calais to the Russian Front. Germany had attacked Russia a couple of weeks previously and these trains could be carrying troops and military *matériel*.

'Also,' Taffy says, 'there was a revolver in there and drawings of what he said was the first German Schnorkel submarine.' He had remained silent. The sergeant, who had been watching him suspiciously, turned to the officer and said, 'This man's not speaking. I'm sure he's not a Frenchman.'

'Show me your identity card,' the officer ordered Taffy, scrutinized it, then turned to the sergeant: 'This is perfectly in order.'

Cole, changing his tone, intervened: 'Don't pay any attention to this chap. You can see it says on his identity card that he's not right in the head.'

But the officer was still suspicious.

The sergeant's gaze had not moved from Taffy. He interrupted again: 'Look, sir, this chap is not saying a word. I'm sure he's an English soldier.'

The officer, exasperated by his wrangle with Cole and by the NCO's obstinacy, rounded on Taffy and told him to turn out his attaché case.

On the journey, Taffy had bought a slab of plain chocolate, dark brown, and, he remembers, unpalatable to boot. He put the small case on the road and opened it. The heat had melted the chocolate, which had spread over the articles of clothing and, in his own words, 'looked absolutely filthy'.

Cole's lightning-quick wits immediately took advantage of the revolting spectacle. 'I told you he was a half-wit. Look what he's done in his attaché case; he's defecated in it.'

The officer stared down at the mess, grimaced and uttered an exclamation of revulsion. But this second scatological incident of the day rescued them from their predicament, for his final words to 'the idiot' were: 'Get away from here.' But, for the moment, he did not release Cole.

Five decades after the event, Taffy comments: 'On reflection, I think their reason for letting us go was that, from the outset of the German occupation, the Army had been ordered to make a good impression on the French people.' Hitler had decreed that, for the good name of Germany and Nazism, all ranks were to be polite and as friendly as the situation allowed.

Others, in various sections of the British Intelligence Service, have put a different interpretation on their release, instead of rigorous interrogation at the local German Headquarters, after Cole's outrageous manner of confrontation with the border patrol. Further, if he and his companion had never met until they chanced to travel on the same train, how did Cole know that the other man's identity card stated that he was an imbecile? Were the Germans too thick for that to have occurred to them? Or, as British Intelligence suspected with hindsight, had the German frontier guards been told that Cole was a double agent?

'I picked up my attaché case and walked down the road, rounded a corner and hid in the hedge until Paul joined me a few minutes later.' Nobody knows what passed between Cole and the German during Taffy's absence. 'We had to make sure that the road which was the actual line was not patrolled also, so we hid and watched for a few hours. In the evening we ventured as far as the road, where we were met by somebody with whom Paul had obviously had previous contacts, and continued southwards more or less all through the night.'

On the second day they again took to the railway, this time for Marseilles. They arrived without further molestation and were taken to the large flat of Dr Georges Rodocanachi, one of the most valuable members of the escape organization.

'This was the last I was to see of Paul Cole,' Taffy says, 'although I heard a lot about him later. He was enormously helpful to me and I doubt very much whether I would have been able to do what I did do without his help.'

Garrow, O'Leary and an Australian wireless operator, Mason, were already in hiding with the Rodocanachis. O'Leary had volunteered to stay and work for the escape organization. By means of the usual Morse transmission, this request had been passed to London. Taffy was present when the reply came, '*Patrick doit rester* [Patrick should stay].' He did so as Garrow's chief assistant. It is on record that he mistrusted Paul Cole from the moment that Garrow introduced them to each other.

Now that Cole had reliable helpers in northern France who would accompany evaders and escapers to the south, he had taken to dallying in Marseilles after each trip he made himself. There, with money to burn — provided by the escape organization for a totally different purpose — he was frequenting bars and dance halls and picking up women.

He could not conceal his profligacy from O'Leary, who moved confidently about the city, where he had numerous contacts who supplied him with information. The day would soon come when he would see for himself how Cole was misbehaving.

For more than two months, Taffy's wife, Shan, had been without news of him. The Society of Friends, the Quakers, being a religious body, were able to send a telegram to their community in England reporting that 'Captain Basil Bennett' was safe and well. Shan received this on 12 August, 1941, 56 days after her husband was shot down.

After Taffy had spent a few days under the Rodoconachis' roof, O'Leary arranged for a Spanish guide to accompany him to the Spanish frontier and on to Spain.

'About the fourth or so of July we set off by train for Banyuls. There were not many people getting off the train there. As they were going through the ticket barrier their identity papers were being checked by Gendarmes. My guide had gone ahead on his own. As a gentleman, I decided to join the end of the queue.' This made him conspicuous because he was not jostling for a place near the front, as everyone else was doing, and, as he was the last to leave, the Gendarmes were in less of a hurry to get done with him than they had been with the throng.

'When it came to my turn I handed my card over and was asked where I was going.' His accent and command of French were inadequate to deceive the guards and he did not know Spanish. 'In a few minutes I was arrested and taken to the local Police Station.'

Aircrew, particularly pilots, were the most highly valued prisoners. Because their training took so long, the Allies wanted them back as soon as possible. The Germans and Vichy French were determined to prevent their escape, or repatriation on medical grounds, more than that of any soldier or sailor, because they would soon be in the air again and bombing Germany or shooting down Luftwaffe aircraft. Flight Lieutenant Higginson therefore called himself Captain Basil Bennett of the Royal Army Service Corps and 51st Highland Division, captured at St Valery-en-Caux.

'I was then interrogated again and it was decided that they would bring in an English-speaking lady – question mark lady – to interpret. I explained to her that I was trying to get back to the U.K. to continue fighting against the Germans and asked her please to use her influence to help me.

'She looked at me and said, "I would prefer the Germans to win,' then spat in my face and walked out of the room."

He was then put into a dirty cell, in solitary confinement, where he spent the next few days. After twenty-four hours or so he started scratching: he had become host to bedbugs, fleas and lice. The bedbug, or *punaise*, was a blood-sucker with a white body that slowly became red as it gorged on his blood. But it was not as agile as the ordinary jumper or the lice that burrowed in one's flies and other creases, so it was easy to catch.

Presently he was moved to a military prison in Montpellier, then after a while back to the civil prison. He learned later that the reason for these moves was that the civil authorities were reluctant to try him as he was a serviceman and the military authorities were equally reluctant. Eventually he was tried in a civil court and sentenced to six months in prison at Perpignan.

'This was a dreadful experience.' The building was very old, built of stone. The accommodation downstairs was a large room with no furniture, so everyone sat on the floor or on slab seats that were built into the wall. 'The first day I was there, there were I suppose about a hundred of us, most of whom were Catalans. There were a couple of Poles and I was the only Briton. They were criminals of every variety, murderers, smugglers, thieves and burglars among them. The punishments were strange to understand. One man was serving a life sentence for stealing the golden candlesticks from Nîmes Cathedral, whereas another prisoner had got only seven years for knifing a girl with whom he had been sleeping in a brothel. It was difficult to communicate with any of them.' If one had money one could arrange for special food to be brought in daily. 'The normal ration was 250 grammes of bread a day – one thick slice – and a plate of hot water which they called soup, but there was nothing in it at all. During the four months or so I spent in this prison my weight went down from about eleven and a half stone to seven.'

Daily, at about noon, 'There would be a hammering on the door and we'd all rush to get into a queue. Then the piece of bread and soup was passed through a little grille in the door to everyone in turn, and we went back to sit on the floor. There was an exception to this: one individual, who, I was later told, had a fair amount of money. In addition to his prison ration he was allowed to have fruit and so on sent in. So at the end of our queue his special parcel of fruit was pushed through the window. I was surprised to see him, the first day, sitting down with about half a dozen of these Catalans squatting around him in one part of the room. His parcel contained peaches. After he'd eaten one he would flick the stone in the air and these chaps would fight for this like animals. Apparently, inside the stone was a little nut which was very pleasant. The other odd thing was that we were given a packet about a couple of inches square of French tobacco that was black and horrible to look at. If you were lucky you could trade your tobacco for an extra bowl of soup.

'At the end of the day there was a rap on the door again and everyone would form a queue. On the first night I found myself on the end of it. The door opened, the guards were waiting and we were marched upstairs to a similar sized room, also completely bare of any furniture. Being the last in, I had difficulty in finding somewhere to lie down. I noticed there was a space around a metal drum, so I lay near it. It got dark and I tried to sleep. I felt wetness on my legs, opened my eyes and there was a chap urinating, theoretically, into the drum. That explained why a clear space had been left around it. From then on I made certain that I was not at the end of the queue.

'Imprisonment in these vile conditions made me realize that my previous life had been very privileged; but it was in the past, it had gone. The future looked very uncertain indeed. But a lot of it depended on my actions and I was fit and healthy and there was therefore no cause for despair.

'I had been making progress in French ever since I arrived in France, and my proficiency improved considerably after my stay in prison. I can recommend this method of learning a language as first-class. Get oneself locked up for twenty-four hours a day for four months with people who speak no other language and you will soon get to know what they are talking about and to speak to them.'

He endured this harsh confinement until the beginning of November, when he was called to the Commandant and told that he had been granted a pardon by Marshal Pétain and was to be sent to St Hippolyte-du-Fort, an internment camp where there was a large number of English-speaking prisoners.

Meanwhile, Garrow and O'Leary had begun to suspect that Cole was guilty of even worse offences than stealing money entrusted to him. It was in October, 1941, that O'Leary heard from an acquaintance that Cole, who was supposed to be on his way back to Lille, was still in Marseilles and that he was going to spend the evening in a certain dance hall. He told Garrow about this and they both went to confront Cole. He brazened it out and declared he was returning to Lille the next day.

Without telling O'Leary, Garrow decided that Cole must be killed for embezzling funds and suspected treachery and that he himself must be the one to do it. He asked O'Leary to go to Lille and investigate Cole thoroughly.

Under a false name, so that Cole would not get wind of his enquiries, O'Leary travelled north without delay. Among other facts, he learned from François Duprez that some of the evaders who left for Marseilles with Cole did not even get as far as Abbeville, where Father Carpentier was ready with travel permits for them. These men had disappeared without trace. O'Leary asked him to come to Marseilles and repeat this evidence to Garrow. Roland Lepers contributed equally damning information and agreed to arrange for Cole and himself to conduct a batch of evaders to Marseilles and make sure they all arrived there.

O'Leary was away for ten days. On returning to Marseilles he was shocked and grieved to find that Garrow had been arrested by the Vichy French Security Service and was in prison awaiting trial. So, as Garrow's chief assistant, he was now in command.

'Most of the occupants of St Hippolyte-du-Fort were soldiers, with a dozen or so aircrew, including Whitney Straight,' Taffy Higginson recalls.

Straight was a thirty-year-old American millionaire and racing motorist, resident in England. He was a pre-war pilot in No. 601 Squadron of the Auxiliary Air Force, in which all pilots were commissioned, unlike the R.A.F. Volunteer Reserve, which was not organized by squadrons. In the VR, pilots became sergeants on qualifying for their wings, and formed a pool from which they were allocated to squadrons when war broke out. Whitney Straight ended the war as Air Commodore, CBE, MC, DFC. Known as 'The millionaires' squadron', 601 justified the appellation with typically flamboyant opulence. At the outbreak of war, its Commanding Officer gave one of his pilots the day off with orders to ensure that, with petrol rationing, they would all have an adequate supply with which to run their large cars. The officer returned to report that he had bought a petrol station for the squadron.

In his new prison, Taffy found that, 'the food was fairly good and we also had Red Cross parcels, so I began to recover some weight. The place was guarded by French troops and Gendarmerie. Shortly after I arrived we started to talk about ways and means of getting out of there and back to the U.K. I was told that there was a plot by which we might be able to get repatriated, under the Geneva Convention, on the grounds that we were unfit for further military service. A number of us hit on the idea of claiming that our ears had been damaged by shellfire, and decided that this claim would be substantially improved if we could arrange for some discharge from the ears. We thought a mixture of French soap, a sandy sort of material, plus, I think it was margarine, stuffed into our ears daily, day after day, would do the trick. What I didn't know was that the doctor who had been given the task of signing the certificates on behalf of the Vichy Government was Dr Rodocanachi.

'This plan went very well and in January, 1942, we were given notice that we were to be repatriated on medical grounds. It was not until March that we left for Perpignan, expecting to cross into Spain and continue the journey to England. However, the train didn't reach the frontier, because the Vichy Government had decided that, in reprisal for the R.A.F.'s bombing of the Renault factory in Paris, all repatriation was to cease; so we were returned to St Hippolyte.'

After a short stay all the internees were moved to Fort de la Revère, a French fortress on the Italian frontier, above Nice. Unlike St Hippolyte, this was a real fortress, with a moat and drawbridge, and patrolled by French soldiers with Italian inspectors.

On crossing the drawbridge over the moat, one entered the fortress itself. There was a building on the left for officers and another on the right for other ranks, each with a separate entrance and gate. The guards patrolled the semi-circular courtyard and the drawbridge, under the archway where the entrances to the buildings were situated. Immediately inside the entrance gate to the officers' accommodation there was a chute which went down to the kitchen and was used for delivering coal and other kitchen supplies. It was protected by barbed wire to prevent prisoners from entering the kitchen.

'Round about July, Whitney had gone into hospital and disappeared from there. The rumour was that he had been able to escape. We in the fort were still looking at ways of doing the same thing, but so far were undecided about which was the best. As senior British officer, I set up a committee which consisted of Flight Lieutenant Hawkins and Flight Lieutenant Barnett, a New Zealander, and Sergeants Nabarrow and Hickton, another New Zealander, who were all RAF air crew, to try to devise a plan of escape. We finally decided that the best thing to do was to get into the moat from the kitchen. It seemed, from where we used to overlook the moat, that there was a metal plate underneath the first vertical concrete post that held up the drawbridge. We supposed that that might be the sewer, which might offer us an exit.

'We started to make and collect the equipment we required. For example, we plaited Red Cross string, which, even if it did not make a rope by which we could slide down from the kitchen into the moat, would at least take some of the weight. To protect our hands, we made gloves out of forage caps. By giving Red Cross cigarettes and other things to one of the guards, we managed to get hold of a magnet. We forced the legs of this over a piece of wood, in which we then burnt a hole, to form an instrument with which to lever off part of the iron bars that covered the exit from the kitchen into the moat.

'To enter the kitchen via the chute which had the barbed wire in it, we got hold of pullovers and other garments, so that we would be able to drop through without too much damage to ourselves. One thing that remained to be done was to distract the attention of the guards who were patrolling the drawbridge. This we thought we could do by getting the sergeant in charge of the other ranks to run a concert and make enough noise to attract the guards at a particular time to the entrance of the O.Rs' building, so that they would be looking through the gates, and, we hoped, joining in the general noise. The entrance gate to the officers' accommodation would be covered by a couple of our chaps who were not in the escape party, while we slid down the chute.'

While these preparations and discussions were going on, they were receiving visits from a Polish priest called Padre Myrda, and from an American employed in Monte Carlo, who was given permission by the Commandant of the fort to visit from time to time as a physical training instructor. Taffy was able to talk to them and they organized some helpers, who were on the O'Leary organization, to meet the escapers when they got outside and take them to a safe house while the heat was on.

'On 3 August we got into the kitchen, broke the bars on top with our improvised jemmy and dropped one by one into the fort, then rushed quickly into the shadow of the drawbridge, next to the big concrete pillar that supported it. We lifted the metal door; sure enough it was the junction point for the sewage coming from the fort and was three-quarters full of sewage of the most unsavoury kind. It was big enough to allow us to get inside and close the door, then set about getting through the exit pipe and out of the fort. Unfortunately, there was a blockage at the far end. I went down to try to clear this with a hacksaw blade we'd been given. Then the others had a go. We found that we were filing on different sides of the bars and making no difference. We had a hurried conference, after which I said to Nabarrow, who was a fairly substantial chap about six feet tall, with big feet, "Nabs, you go down backwards and see if you can kick it". So Nabs disappeared backwards, up to his head in you-know-what. There was a pause, then suddenly the level in the exit pipe dropped dramatically. We knew then what had happened. The sewage had flowed out and Nabs had gone with it.

'We crawled down one by one as quickly as possible until we were all on the outside. We then ran down the hill, but unfortunately the helpers who were supposed to be there to guide us into Monte Carlo had themselves been arrested. We made our way down to the railway line, and, as we were not pretty sights and smelled rather badly, we decided to hide in some bushes overlooking the Cap d'Ail railway station and spend the rest of the night there. After discussion, we dressed Brian Hawkins, who was the least damaged and dirty of us all, and sent him off to Monte Carlo to see if he could make contact with the safe house there, where we were expected. This we did in the morning. After a while a train arrived and there was a wave from somebody who got out of it and was looking in our direction. We waved back and a few minutes later Patrick O'Leary arrived with a change of clothes for us all. We changed and followed him by train into Monte Carlo, where we were taken to a flat belonging to a Mr Turner, a British hairdresser who had returned to the U.K. shortly before war started.

'We were visited every day by a Madame Guitone, wife of the Court hairdresser, who was Mr Turner's employer. She provided us with food that she was given daily by the Scotch Teahouse in Monte Carlo, whose owner, Miss Eva Trenchard, had also gone back to Britain. We continued to be contacted by Patrick O'Leary, new identity cards were made for us and a plan was devised for our escape. This was organized by Patrick and on the morning of 2 September I left Monte Carlo disguised as a Catholic priest, accompanied by Father Myrda.'

They were going to Marseilles, but on the way there was a moment of unexpected embarrassment that might have raised an alarm and led to his being arrested again. A lady seated opposite Taffy leaned across and asked him to hear her confession! He turned and gave Father Myrda an appealing look, but the genuine priest was alert and aware of what was happening. He interposed as though by right, being the elder, and duly heard the lady's whispered catalogue of transgressions.

'We arrived safely in Marseilles, where I was taken to the flat of a marvellous Frenchman called René Nouveau, on the waterfront, and waited there for the others to arrive before starting off again for the Spanish frontier. The Nouveau flat was used extensively by Patrick O'Leary and previous to my coming there Airey Neave had also hidden there during his escape. On the 17th or thereabouts of September I left the Nouveau flat with a new identity card, accompanied by Madame Nouveau, who was a super person, and was escorted to Perpignan, where I was put into a hotel to await the arrival of the rest of the boys.'

From there he joined other evaders crowded into a small villa at nearby Canet-Plage, belonging to Madame Lebreton, who owned l'Hotel du Tennis. Here they waited for the small vessel, due at two o'clock in the morning on the following day, 13 September, which would evacuate them from France.

On the night when they were to be fetched, O'Leary arrived at the villa and told them to start out for the beach, in single file, at one-fifteen. This was perhaps the moment of greatest tension in the whole long adventure that had begun fifteen months ago, but Taffy Higginson talks about it calmly. 'I asked Patrick what we should do if anyone hostile appeared. He said we must lie flat in the sand and stay there until the situation had been dealt with.' Evaders and escapers being essentially men of action, this advice was irksome to the whole party. Lying prone and immobile while perhaps a fire fight, in which they could not take part in their own defence, raged over their heads would be the ultimate frustration in this moment when they were about to be snatched from a hostile shore.

The vessel had arrived on time. 'When Patrick flashed the Morse signal with his blue-shaded torch, it was answered at once by a flash from out at sea. Presently a rowing boat came in and took us all off in three trips to a small ship. She was crewed by Poles and purported to be a Spanish fishing boat. During daylight she did hoist a suit of red sails, but after dark she ran her diesel engine instead, which added several knots to her speed.

Passengers were accommodated on deck, and covered by a tarpaulin whenever an aeroplane was heard.

'Next, we were picked up off the Balearic Islands by an armed yacht *Tarana* and taken to Gibraltar. We were virtually under arrest until we had been interrogated by Intelligence in London and established our identities.'

A destroyer took him to Glasgow. By now it was October and the Scottish autumn made a chilly contrast with the shores of the Mediterranean. 'I was in the Police Station, waiting to be taken to London under escort. It was cold. I managed to slip out unnoticed and went to a shop to buy some warm garments, not knowing that I would need clothing coupons. When I said I hadn't any, the shop assistant said, "Well, hang on a second, I think we can arrange it". What she did was telephone the Police, who promptly appeared and led me back. Under escort, I travelled to London, where, like all returned evaders and escapers, I was interrogated at Air Ministry. And there we are.'

That last dismissive phrase about the culmination of an extraordinary series of dangers and hardships endured through toughness of character and physique, and overcome by resourcefulness, ingenuity and intelligence, sum up the whole man. Airey Neave rightly described him as 'one of those modest, efficient people who made the Royal Air Force what it was'.

That is not the end of Taffy Higginson's story. The formative years that preceded his parachute descent into the Forbidden Zone of Occupied France, the experiences of those sixteen months at large among the enemy, then in captivity, and finally outwitting his hunters, carried him on to further successes in many spheres during the years ahead.

Flight Lieutenant Higginson was safely home with his wife and sons. 'Captain Paul' Cole was still at large in France, carrying on his nefarious practices.

It was known by now to the Secret Intelligence Service in London that he had been born Harold Cole, in the East End of London, in 1906 and had served his first prison sentence at the age of seventeen, his second five years later. Immediately before the war he had been perpetrating confidence tricks in France and was wanted by the Police there. But, as long as he was proving a useful member of the escape line, and despite suspicions voiced by Garrow, O'Leary and others that he was a danger to them, British Intelligence was willing to let him continue in its employment.

In 1939 he had managed to slip back to England, and, on the declaration of war, enlisted in the Royal Engineers. By the time he returned to France with the Expeditionary Force he was already a sergeant.

It was not long before he stole the Sergeants' Mess funds and planted evidence that appeared to incriminate a comrade before disappearing. The wrongly accused soldier managed to prove his innocence. Cole was found and imprisoned, awaiting court martial. In the chaos of the retreat and evacuation he was set free, put on civilian clothes, changed his rank and first name and set about living on his wits again.

At the end of October, 1941, Cole arrived in Marseilles as O'Leary had arranged with Lepers. A trap was set for him. He came to the Rodocanachis' flat, where O'Leary, François Duprez and two other members of the escape line held a drumhead court martial. At the verdict of guilty Cole grovelled for mercy in a sickening display of cowardice.

They locked him in another room while they discussed whether to kill him or send him back to England under escort for formal trial. Cole climbed out of a window, jumped across an air shaft at the risk of killing or seriously injuring himself, and got away.

O'Leary sent one of his colleagues to Lille to warn their comrades in the north about the proven traitor.

From Marseilles Cole had bolted to Paris, but returned to La Madeleine after two or three weeks. A Dutchman working for the Gestapo suspected him of helping British fugitives. His arrival was reported to this man, who arrested him on 6 December, 1941. To save his skin, Cole agreed to turn informer for the Germans. François Duprez was arrested the same day. He later died in a concentration camp in Germany while awaiting execution. Father Carpentier was arrested two days later and imprisoned at Loos. He managed to send a message out through a guard, describing what Cole had done. He was later beheaded in Germany.

Cole next began to give the Germans the names and addresses of his former colleagues in Paris. In May, 1942, his new function took him to Lyons, but his freedom was not to last long. A French official in the Vichy Government reported to the Vichy Security Police that a well-known German spy was in the Free Zone, and where to find him.

O'Leary arrived in Lyons the next day, armed with a pistol with which he intended to shoot Cole. He had been told the name of the hotel at which his quarry was staying, but Cole had already been taken away by the Vichy authorities.

Cole was tried by a Military Tribunal and sentenced to death for espionage. The Germans took over what had been the Free Zone in November, 1942, while he was awaiting execution. His sentence was commuted to life imprisonment and he was presently moved to a prison near Paris. The German Intelligence Service released him to resume working for them. He betrayed more of his former comrades and inveigled himself into intelligence and evasion groups. Soon after the Normandy landings in 1944 he left Paris in German uniform, on the staff of a senior SS officer and eventually reached Germany. Adrift for a while, he tricked the Americans into accepting him as a British officer on the run and worked with them, wearing American uniform, in Intelligence. After the armistice he was hunted by the French Police, who traced him to a bar in Paris in January, 1946. It was, of course, run by a woman. And, naturally, he had prevailed on her to let him rest in a spare room, where he remained alert, with a pistol in his hand. When two police officers burst in, he wounded one. The other shot him dead.

Cole betrayed some three hundred British and French men and women. All of them were tortured and at least half either died as a result or were executed.

In November, 1942, after some leave, Flight Lieutenant Higginson rejoined 56 Squadron, which was now equipped with Typhoons and stationed at Matlaske, near Colchester, a satellite of Coltishall, a famous fighter base near the Norfolk Broads. The Squadron welcomed him back, but, like all aircrew who had recently escaped from France, he would not be allowed to resume offensive operations for some considerable time. Knowing so much about the escape organization, they might, if captured, give away information under torture.

'The Typhoon,' he says, 'was proving to be a very difficult aircraft. There were several crashes and engine failures, which the manufacturer attributed to the pilots, while the pilots invariably blamed the manufacturer.' The Air Ministry decided that it would be a good idea to start an engine-handling course at Napier's, the engine manufacturer, as the Sabre engine was of an unusual design. Taffy was offered the job of running the course at the Acton factory and arranging a programme for pilots destined for Typhoon squadrons to attend it before going on to their squadrons. He accepted and in early January, 1943, was attached to Napier's.

It was also in this month that his DFC was gazetted.

'My job involved not only desk tuition, but I also visited the squadrons to talk to the pilots and see how the pupils who had been with me were getting on. I had the use of a Magister and various other light aircraft to fly myself around in. After a time I got rather bored with this and went seeking help to get back onto an operational squadron.' Without success.

Later that year Flight Lieutenant F. W. Higginson, DFC, DFM was promoted to Squadron Leader.

On 31 March, 1944, he was posted to form and command No. 83 Group Communication Squadron. This group had been established to support the invasion of Europe. 'My logbook shows a very busy period, flying Ansons and Proctors and I had my own Spit IX.' The Air Officer Commanding, Air Vice Marshal Harry Broadhurst, DSO, DFC, the youngest officer of his rank in the Service, had just relinquished command of Desert Air Force. He was later Air Chief Marshal Sir, with KBE, CBE, AFC to add to his other decorations. 'The A.O.C. also had his own Spit IX, which it was my responsibility to look after. We also had about 20 Austers, which were to be used for Army co-operation work. Another interesting aeroplane was the Fieseler Storch that Harry Broadhurst had had sent from Italy in a crate. We reassembled it and serviced it from then on. Only he and I were allowed to fly it. It was an incredible aeroplane: it could land and take off from a cricket pitch. I could now understand why I had so much difficulty, and failed, when trying to shoot one down.

'On 15 June I flew the Storch to France, to landing field B2. It must have been a scary sort of trip, because there was still a lot of air action at the time and although we had British markings, it was an aircraft that was easily identifiable as not British, so I flew it out at about twenty feet above the water.'

He was still banned from flying on offensive operations, but found this appointment the best possible alternative and greatly enjoyed it. 'Not only for the variety of aircraft that I had under my command but also because of the other pilots on the squadron. Most of them had done one, if not two, tours of operations either on fighters or bombers, mostly on the latter. Many of them were from Commonwealth countries. They were indeed a super bunch. Our task was to fly people over from the U.K. to the beachhead. And then, as the Army progressed through France to Belgium and Holland, we followed fairly closely behind, providing the necessary communication services for the Army and Air Force Staff. The last strip on which we landed was B76, at Eindhoven, where we came to a halt for the winter of 1944. This was the end of my operational service. The total amount of operational flying in my logbook is 419 hrs 15 mins.'

He relinquished command of the Squadron in February, 1945, and after a short administrative course was posted to HQ 11 Group, where he stayed for approximately two years. This was followed by a short posting to the Air Ministry before going to the R.A.F. Staff College at Bracknell for the year's course.

Work included a joint study with the students at the Royal Naval Staff College at Greenwich. The present Duke of Edinburgh, then Prince Philip Mountbatten, was on the course there. Squadron Leader Higginson 'was involved with his group' and was one of four students from Bracknell who were invited to dine in the Painted Hall at Greenwich. After dinner the R.A.F. guests played the Navy at bowls in the basement and won. When they were leaving, after a highly convivial evening, some of their hosts, including Prince Philip, accompanied them to their car. Taffy started the engine to farewell cheers, but the car did not budge. It had been raised on bricks. The Bracknell party toiled in their tight mess kit to put it back on the ground, surrounded by noisily encouraging Naval Officers. Perhaps there is warning in that never to dare beat the Navy at Drake's own game.

In 1946 Taffy joined London Welsh Rugby Football Club. But the captain, a famous international, was too staid for his ebullient spirits. Next season, Taffy transferred to Richmond, for whom he played until 1952. During these years he captained Fighter Command and led it to victory in the inter-Command championships. He also played for the R.A.F. in all its inter-Service matches, for Combined Services and for Surrey.

In 1947-8 the Combined Services XV played in France. Their fixtures, two of which were in Marseilles and Perpignan, included one against the National B Team, a very high standard. During the entertainment after the Perpignan match, some of Taffy's friends, who knew of his wartime experiences there, encouraged him to ask their host, the Mayor, if they could visit Perpignan prison where, he explained, he had been locked up during the war. The Mayor 'was very reluctant to agree, since he couldn't believe that any Frenchman could do that to a British rugger player, but after much pressure he gave us a letter to the prison Governor authorising the visit.' When they called on the Governor next morning he showed them the record book with the fingerprints and personal details of 'Captain Basil Bennett'. They were also given coffee and a long apologia stressing that, 'If *we* had been here, of course, we'd have set you free'. Taffy comments, 'You can believe that if you like, but I'm afraid I never shall.' The Governor would not allow his visitors into either of the rooms in which the prisoners spent their time.

In 1952, after graduation from Staff College, he was promoted to wing commander and posted to HQ Technical Training Command as Personal Staff Officer to the Commander-in-Chief, Air Marshal Sir John Whitworth-Jones. The special interest in this job lay in the R.A.F.'s reorganization to a peacetime force with the necessary technical schools and highly trained technical personnel to maintain modern aircraft. 'I had plenty of opportunity to write papers of many sorts and was in close contact most of the time with the Senior Air Staff Officer and travelled extensively with the C-in-C.'

In 1954 he was sent on the year's course at the Army Staff College at Camberley, another valuable experience, particularly as there were only two R.A.F. officers on the course.

From there he was posted to the Operational Requirements Branch at the Air Ministry, with responsibility for preparing recommendations and writing papers on the future requirement for R.A.F. transport, maritime and Army co-operation aeroplanes, and helicopters. This highly responsible job involved not only visiting all the Commands and Groups that were operating these types of aircraft, but also dealing with the aircraft manufacturers who were competitors in the production of them. Specifically, when a jet-engined long-range transport aircraft was required, Whitney Straight happened to be Chief Executive of British Airways. At Wing Commander Higginson's suggestion, B.A. joined the R.A.F. in inviting Vickers to present an appropriate design and Rolls Royce to provide suitable engines. Finally, the R.A.F. decided on the Bristol Britannia, which met its specification in all respects. Out of the Vickers design the VC 10 ultimately emerged.

In order to write papers on the helicopter requirement with authority, 'I had no difficulty in convincing my superior that I should be given a helicopter course and learn how to fly them. This I did at Westland's.'

During his tour at the Air Ministry there was an episode that brought the cold war with the U.S.S.R. unpleasantly to his attention. At a cocktail party at South Africa House he and Shan met the Russian Assistant Air Attaché, who spoke very good English, and his wife. 'They were quite charming people and in the course of our conversation we gave him our telephone number.'

Shortly after, Taffy and Shan were invited to the Russian Embassy. He asked whether they should attend and was told that it was up to him, but to let Intelligence know what happened. The entertainment included 'a magnificent film and some marvellous music. This was followed by a superb meal and a very jolly evening altogether. There was of course no business talked.' He duly reported this.

'A week or so later, at home at about seven-thirty in the evening, the telephone rang. The caller was the Russian Assistant Air Attaché. He asked me if he could come and talk to me and I agreed. I told him I'd be at the office at nine-thirty in the morning. But he said he wanted to talk to me outside the office, so we arranged to meet in a pub at seven o'clock. The next morning I told the Intelligence people exactly what had happened. I asked what I should do and was told to make my own decision but report what happened at the meeting. I thought long and hard about this. It was pouring with rain when I finished at the office, so I decided to go home.'

He had been home an hour or so when the Russian telephoned. Taffy suggested an appointment at the Air Ministry for the next morning. 'He then almost burst into tears and said, "*Please* can you come and meet me". I repeated my refusal and said I'd see him at the office in the morning. A week or so later I was told that he had been recalled to Moscow, and I often wonder whether he was prepared to defect. At that time he would have been very useful indeed from the Intelligence point of view.'

After he had been at the Air Ministry for four years, which was longer than the usual tour, he asked to be given a flying job and was told that he had been selected to attend the American War College, 'which didn't please me at all, having done two Staff College courses and altogether nine years on Staff appointments. I decided that the possibility of my getting another flying job was so remote that, all things considered, it would be better for me to go and try my luck in civvy street. So I resigned from the R.A.F. in 1956.'

Shortly afterwards he was offered the appointment of Military Liaison Officer for the Bristol Aeroplane Company at their base at Filton. He and Shan bought an attractive house within twenty minutes' drive of the factory, with two acres and − perhaps its most important feature − a view over the Severn to Wales. This property proved a great asset to his work, for entertaining potential overseas customers whose visits to the Company he had arranged.

'My introduction to the Company was very much helped by the fact that Peter Masefield, the Managing Director, was an old friend of Whitney Straight, with whom I had continued a very close relationship.'

Work on guided weapons at Bristol had been in progress for a considerable time and now attracted his special interest. The company was designing a new defensive system called Bloodhound, which was expected to replace the fighter in the defence rôle. This was being sponsored by the R.A.F., whilst the Army was sponsoring a similar defensive system called Thunderbird.

He was one of a team that was instructed to study the marketing aspects of the projects on which the company was working. Mr F. W. Higginson, calling on all he had learned in Staff appointments, suggested that Bloodhound would be of interest to 'our friends and neighbours overseas'. In consequence he was made Sales and Service Manager of the guided weapons section, with responsibility for assessing the sales potential in Europe. It was decided to concentrate on countries that were not yet being subsidized by America, yet had the financial ability to buy without any political strings, and had the political means to do so. The two most prominent in all respects were Sweden and Switzerland.

'After many visits and discussions, I decided that in both countries the success or failure of our efforts would depend to a great extent on personal contacts with the individuals who would take decisions. Emphasis was on creating confidence in what we told them and providing evidence of feasibility and technical competence. Here Bristol were most fortunate in having Ferranti to work with them on the guidance side of the system, since their reputation for reliability and integrity was outstanding. It was most important also to get the co-operation of the R.A.F. and Ministry of Supply.' Again, his recent Service experience proved invaluable. In 1961 contracts were signed with Sweden, Switzerland and Australia − the first overseas sales of a guided weapons system by a British manufacturer.

Taffy was then invited to join the board of Bristol Aircraft and in 1963 he was awarded the OBE for services to industry.

As a result of extensive reorganization of the aircraft and aero engine industries, involving also companies that manufactured the radar and other components for Bloodhound, there was some relocation of manufacture. He now had to visit Stevenage and London frequently. The prospect of having to continue doing so, while his home remained in Gloucestershire, did not appeal. In 1964, he resigned.

'At about that time I had the good fortune to meet a member of a famous Middle East Arabian family, Abdullah Alireza, who was living in Kuwait and had already established himself in the civil engineering and construction business and in the oil services industry as well as other spheres of commerce and trading. He had operating companies in most of the countries in the Gulf area and was intending to establish himself in Europe and in London, where he already owned properties in the West End. He was looking for a senior executive to open a main office in London to run his European affairs and to be involved in the management of his overseas companies. It seemed to me to be an interesting assignment of a diverse nature, with promise of an expanding future and working with a charming family whom I grew to like very much both at work and personally as friends.

'In addition to becoming the Managing Director of his European company I was also involved at board level with many of the operating companies in the Gulf, including the establishment in Saudi Arabia of a hot strip steel rolling mill in collaboration with the Japanese, which was intended to produce pipes for the oil industry and for other purposes in Saudi. Work involved a fair amount of travel to the companies of the Alireza Group, which was once described by an American industrialist as "a very aggressively run outfit". I found it to be very efficiently run by Abdullah and Tamor, his son. I was provided with a flat in London which Shan shared with me as often as she could get away from Bristol. When this was not possible I used to travel back to Bristol on the Friday night and return to London very early on Monday morning.

'I enjoyed the work, but towards the end of the sixties my family and I felt the urge to return to Wales. In the family discussion which followed, it was decided that the best way to do this was to farm. At that time farming land and property generally was at its lowest price and I decided that by realizing various assets I could buy the 250-acre Pen-y-Coed farm, which included a 17th Century mansion with seven bedrooms, enough to house us all [Taffy and Shan have four sons]. This was recommended by my eldest son, Paul, who as well as being an ordained priest in the Church of England, had decided that he would like to manage the farm. None of us had any experience of farming, so we bought some books and set about reading everything we could about the subject. It was agreed that I would continue working in London until we had got the farm established. We stocked with sheep and beef and left the decision about whether to buy cows for milk until we had a little more experience. We also decided to grow barley, which would help in our aim of self-sufficiency.'

Taffy's commercial experience was of constant help in making farm-business decisions. 'It became obvious that we would have to have a dairy herd to support a farm of this size. So in 1972 we bought our first in-calf heifer, began milking cows the next year and built up a herd of nearly two hundred Friesian/Holstein animals.

'Some time after this I ceased full-time work in London and became consultant to the company, which required only infrequent visits to London.'

In 1990 they sold the farm. Three of the boys had married and were living in their own houses. Wing Commander F. W. Higginson, OBE, DFC, DFM, RAF, Retd, and his wife bought a bungalow, where the garden now replaces their 250 acres.

It has been a long, happy, varied and successful career from R.A.F. apprentice, through decorated senior officer and highly placed businessman, to farmer. The same qualities that had enabled him to evade capture, survive when ill-luck betrayed him, and escape from incarceration served him throughout. Some were innate, some acquired as he went through life: fortitude in adversity, determination, unobtrusive Christianity, sense of humour and the ability to identify the salient objectives in any situation and pursue them with total concentration until he achieved them.

Francis Bacon found the words for it: 'Merit and good works is the end of the man's motion; and conscience of the same is the accomplishment of man's rest.' Taffy says, 'whatever I have achieved would have been impossible without my wife, Shan.'

In retirement, Taffy Higginson continues working on the land and in his spare time raises funds for the R.A.F. Escaping Society by lecturing on his experiences as an evader, prisoner and escaper. The society was formed immediately after the war to help, in time of financial need, those who had risked their lives so that hundreds of aircrew eluded the enemy and returned home.

CHAPTER FIVE

LEADING AIRCRAFTMAN
STEPHEN HALL DFM

IT WAS 10 MARCH, 1939, when Stephen Hall set foot on North Africa for the first time. He was twenty years and one day old, a Leading Aircraftman Flight Rigger/Air Gunner in the Royal Air Force. He had spent most of his life on the sea coast of Devon and its gently rolling farmland. The Egyptian landscape made a monotonous and arid contrast with the red soil, the green fields and woods, the low hills, the rivers and streams, of the West Country. The sunlight, intensified by its reflection from the desert sand, made his eyes smart.

Two thousand five hundred miles away Hitler was ranting and Europe was moving quickly towards the war that Britain had accepted as unavoidable. From Egypt the barking of the dogs of war sounded like a faint yapping. The new arrival did not suspect that the conflict would spread all round the globe and some of its most critical battles would be fought on the deserts of Egypt and Libya and in the air above them. For him, there was no perceptible hint of the dangers, the captivity and the escape from it that awaited him.

Stephen Hall had the heredity, upbringing and, at just twenty years old, already the mental and physical toughness to survive the most frightening and physically demanding trials of character. He also exemplified that ironical sense of humour in extreme adversity that is intrinsic to the British airman, soldier and sailor.

'My father was a Chief Petty Officer in the Royal Navy, a Regular, demobbed in 1920. He enlisted in His Majesty's Coast Guards and was posted to Ilfracombe. Then, about 1923, he applied for, and became, the first Coastal Preventive Officer in that area. It was his duty to guard the coastline from Barnstaple to Ilfracombe. We lived in the village of Braunton. Our home was adjacent to a horse-breaking farm, which meant I spent my early years with horses. The Tupper family, who owned the farm, had three sons, one aged twenty, one my age and one younger. Tragically, the eldest was thrown from a wild horse he was breaking in and killed. Mr Tupper was a real tough character, but an excellent horseman, very thorough in teaching us to ride and control horses.'

When he was twelve, Stephen's parents bought a bungalow at Vellator, where vessels moored and discharged their cargo. 'Hence,' he says, 'I have salt water and horses in my veins.' And a lot of guts to go with this infusion, as we shall see.

When he was fourteen and a half, his father 'arranged with the captain of a three-masted motor schooner, the MV *Resolve*, that I should join the crew. She was a beautiful vessel and fast under sail. During World War One she had been a Q-ship and received a direct hit amidships.' She sank one U-boat and was credited also with one possible. On a visit to Plymouth, the Navy presented her captain with a brass plate commemorating the ship's valuable service. 'It meant a little more brass for me to clean.' The life was hard, he says, yet he would not have changed it. 'I was taught to cook and seamanship, which benefited me in later years.' Seamanship was to save his life in circumstances that could never have occurred to him even in the worst of nightmares.

Another of his father's duties was to visit the newly formed Atlantic Coast Airways. In 1935, aged 16, Stephen joined the company as an apprentice. 'At the same time, I took up boxing. I was taken under the wing of a manager/trainer who ran a boxing stable, and became a licensed boxer under the British Boxing Board of Control. In addition I had to attend night school, in accordance with my apprenticeship. My first twelve months I received nothing, then my second year it was five shillings (25p) per week.'

It was now that he had his introduction to the R.A.F. An aircraft, which he thinks was an Audax, a variant of that lovely and versatile light bomber the Hawker Hart, was detached for photographic duties to the aerodrome where he worked. In those days one could not get an aircraft servicing licence before the age of twenty-one. He became friendly with the R.A.F. ground crew, who suggested that he should apply to join the Service. He did so, and, on passing two educational and medical examinations, 'On May 10th, 1937, I reported to R.A.F. Uxbridge, was sworn in, given a shilling, and I promised to serve for seven years.' He was eighteen years and two months old.

He was posted ten months later to No 216 Squadron in Egypt, which had been flying the Vickers Valentia since 1935. This dear old biddy of a twin-engined transport biplane cruised at 117 mph and could be fitted with under-wing racks to carry a 2,200 lb bomb load. In September, 1939, the Bristol Bombay, a twin-engined high-wing monoplane bomber/troop carrier, with a cruising speed of 160 mph with 2,000 lb of bombs aboard, replaced it. All the air gunners were also skilled tradesmen, which meant that the crews could service their own aircraft.

1. 'Patrick O'Leary': "One of the toughest, most gifted and versatile members of the escape organization" (p.3).

2. Guy Harris—"an excellent pilot, quiet, modest and sociable" (p.5).

3. "Sergeant Philip Wareing ... the only pilot shot down over France during the Battle of Britain who succeeded in escaping from a prison camp and making his way home" (p.18).

4. Taffy Higgingson outside the Mess at North Weald, Essex.

5. "The Secretary of State for Air, Sir Kingsley Wood, informed the assembled fighter pilots ... that their average life would be three weeks" (p.19). Taffy Higginson nearest the camera.

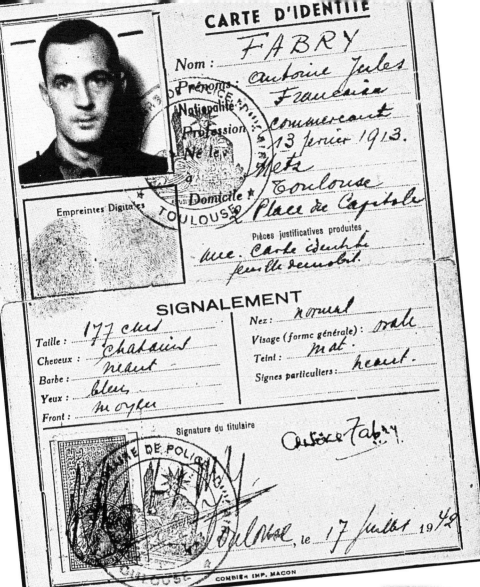

6. "'Show me your identity card'', the officer ordered' (p.31).

7. "Whatever I have achieved would have been impossible without my wife, Shan" (p.48).

Britain declared war on Germany on 3 September, 1939. Italy entered the war on Germany's side on 10 June, 1940. In Egypt, the 166 R.A.F. aircraft of all types, including flying boats, faced an Italian Air Force strength of 282, all but a few of which were bombers and fighters based in the adjoining country of Libya, which was an Italian colony.

LAC Hall's first operational sortie was on the night of 24/25 October, 1940. His description of a particular night bombing raid is typical of them all. Each drew deeply on the reserves of courage and endurance that he had accumulated, the inherent qualities that came from his disciplined, seafaring father, the character-building experiences of his youth on the backs of unbroken horses, at sea and in the boxing ring.

The target was the port of Benghazi. He recalls his sardonic thoughts at the time. 'Think, lad, of the privilege of sitting in a lovely cramped turret with the beautiful moon and stars and all hell let loose, while someone down there is intent on killing you.' His was a lonely post, the gun turret in the tail of the aircraft. 'Suddenly the nightmare of all nightmares: the whole heaven above illuminated by some twit dropping a parachute flare whose brilliant glare silhouettes us. Seconds ago we had a 50/50 chance of survival.' The unwelcome illumination had abruptly shortened the odds. 'We're climbing as we've never climbed before. Too late. Bangs, lights, flashes, tearing of metal. We are still in the air. It's dark, then one solitary stream of tracer, exactly our height, is following us. It's a hair's breadth from my turret, so we're reasonably safe. My parachute harness is ripped, there are two massive holes in the fuselage, our tail wheel is missing, my turret is hanging on well and my guardian angel is working overtime.' His fortitude, calmness and self-discipline were to endure through many dangerous enterprises, to save his life and to obtain his freedom in worse challenges that lay ahead.

By the time he finished his tour, in August, 1942, he had won the Distinguished Flying Medal. But, although an Air Ministry Order of December, 1939, laid down that all air gunners were to be of at least sergeant's rank, this was not honoured universally. Stephen Hall, with 1,300 flying hours in his logbook, was still a leading aircraftman. And despite his efforts to obtain the back pay that is due to him for the years when he should have worn three chevrons on his arm, it has not been granted to this day.

On 18 August, 1942, he embarked on HMT *Stratheden* at Port Tewfik. 'Short stay at Aden, continued to Durban and Cape Town, a most enjoyable cruise with a good ship's company.'

At Cape Town he transferred to another troopship, *Laconia*, a 20,000 ton Cunard White Star liner, which was under Army control. Her 3,000 passengers comprised 1,800 Italian prisoners of war, their Polish guards, Service families, nurses, and Navy, Army and R.A.F. personnel. 'Trouble seemed to erupt from the moment we stepped on board. Bad food, unnecessary bull, ill-feeling from day one. September 10th, farewell Cape Town. Having tasted the ship's mood in port, the prospect of a long sea voyage seemed daunting. The small contingents of Navy, Army and Air Force were allocated duties accordingly. The Navy boys took over the six-inch gun aft, the Army the Bofors guns midships and forward, leaving the R.A.F. submarine watch on the bridge. In addition to this, the powers that be, thinking of our welfare and a preventative to boredom, ordained foot drill, early morning P.T. (all ranks) and boat drill.

'I hit on the idea of approaching a couple of flight lieutenants to become their batman, which they agreed to. So I excused myself from early morning P.T. through pressure of work. Naturally there was an Orderly Room notice board. Imagine my surprise: there in bold letters, leaving me in no doubt, was my name. Absent from early morning P.T., report to Ship's Warrant Officer 9 a.m. sharp, 13th Sept. Ah, well, you win some and lose some.' In a way, he did win that one: fate intervened to prevent him obeying the order.

Two days out from Cape Town, the Navy fired a few practice rounds from the six-inch gun, 'which frightened the living daylights out of all the seagulls for miles around and nearly made the R.A.F contingent permanently deaf. R.A.F. bods lived in specially built wooden accommodation immediately below the gun platform.

'I was not concerned about being housed at the tail end of the ship. I had spent many flying hours in a similar situation and the extra up and down motion of the ship didn't worry me. My lifeboat station was the last boat on the port side, which was conveniently forward and above our deck house.'

There was a small ship's canteen that was opened in the evening to sell tea, cigarettes etc. The date was still 12 September. 'Having passed the day in boredom, I had bought myself a cup of tea and returned to my quarters. The lads were sitting around, chatting, and I sat on the floor and joined in the general conversation.

'Suddenly the ship seemed to give a shudder, followed by a terrific jolt. There was no mistaking what had happened: we had been hit. The lights went out, came on again, went out once more and remained out, plunging everything into darkness. I picked up my life jacket and, with ease, crawled up the ship's side to my lifeboat station. One did not not need a Master's Certificate to see there was no chance of launching it or any of the other port side boats, due to the acute list to starboard.

'Then, without warning, a submarine is there below us, ordering us not to shoot or he would put another torpedo into us. I crawled back to my original level on the stern, where I met a fellow Devonian, who came from Newton Abbot. He had mislaid his lifejacket and I helped him find one. The ship's list was increasing. He stood on the rail and wanted me to jump.

I tried to reason with him. He shouted "Cheerio", and jumped. I watched him sliding down that perilous journey, knowing he would be torn to pieces by the barnacles. I never saw him again.

'I looked at my watch. It was 2030 hours, twenty minutes since we had been hit. Time to leave. I tried to stay dry and clambered down a rope ladder. There was commotion, shouting. Slowly I felt the cold water creeping up my body. Finally I was fully afloat. I said a silent prayer. I wondered how deep the sea was here. I had to get away, to avoid being sucked down. I swam to a lifeboat and was dragged aboard. It was well overloaded. Among those in it were two ladies and two officers, one R.A.F., one naval. I believe the naval officer later died. There was one Italian with a nasty leg wound. The whole calf muscle had been torn out; by a barracuda, I thought.'

They heard cries for help and tried to pull people aboard. The lifeboat was one of several that were tied one behind another. The one at the head of the line was secured to the ship. An axe was found and Stephen Hall's boat was cut loose.

'There were people clinging to the side. We gradually moved away from the ship, then stopped, fascinated, to watch the dying moments of this huge vessel. During my flying days I had witnessed many horrific sights, but to witness this was probably the longest half-hour of my life. The great black stern seemed to balance in mid-air, then slowly disappeared from sight, swallowed up by the sea. Then came a tremendous under-water explosion and a huge bubble of air. We were cold and suffering from shock. Cries for help from people in the water went on throughout the night.

'The submarine glided between us, calling for the captain. He had gone down with his ship. When daylight came we could see only a vast expanse of ocean with an occasional raft or lifeboat. Sharks and barracudas? Barbaric. Not really, we humans don't set any good examples.

'U156 beckoned to us to come alongside. It endeavoured to take on board and feed everyone. The Italians were segregated in the bows, while we remained around the conning tower. When it came to my turn, the German crew were hesitant. They asked in English if I were British. "Of course I bloody well am." I was then helped aboard. The reason for asking this was that when the torpedo hit amidships it exploded where the P.O.Ws were and they tried to rush their guards, but were held back, some receiving bayonet wounds. Eventually weight of numbers had forced the Polish guards to let the Italians free. We were given hot soup, then filed back aft to give our name, rank, number and Service to a sailor who spoke good English and, according to him, knew London very well. We were then put back in our lifeboats, save the ladies and Italian wounded.

There were other lifeboats also, and some redistribution of passengers was made, so our lifeboat was a bit more seaworthy. We were told the nearest land was 700 miles away, on a compass bearing of N.N.E.'

Each night the U-boat submerged. After two days, while it was on the surface and flying a Red Cross Flag, a U.S.A.A.F. Liberator flew over. 'This cheered us up no end. Soon help will come, we thought. Not on your Nelly. About half an hour later, bang, crash, wallop, the fool had returned and was dropping depth charges and bombs. What a confusing war it was turning into: the Germans helping us while the Americans were bombing us.

'We decided to make a break for it and I volunteered to be helmsman. There were no officers. There were several sergeant air crew who had just completed their training in South Africa. A couple of them were put in charge of the water and food. We hoisted the small lugsail and had the oars ready. The sail hung limp and our four oarsmen were catching more crabs than a French crabber off Land's End. It was hot all day and chilly at night. The following afternoon we sighted an object on the horizon, which caused great excitement. When it approached we saw it was a U-boat. It took us in tow, but told us that we must have an axe ready to cut the towrope, as the U-boat would submerge immediately if an aircraft appeared. Presently there were three or four lifeboats in tow. Eventually we were cast adrift and told that the Vichy French Navy would pick us up.'

That night a searchlight shone on them and the French cruiser *La Gloire* took them aboard. She landed them at Casablanca, where, on 23 September, they were taken to No 3 Compagnie, Mle 725, Internment Centre, Mediona Camp.

'Conditions were rough.' He was issued with items of French Foreign Legion uniform. They had no soap for the first two days, then were given half a stick of shaving soap that also had to serve for washing. The camp was surrounded by a double fence of barbed wire and guarded by Moroccan troops. The prisoners slept on a straw mat over a straw-filled palliasse laid on a concrete floor. They scratched a draughts board on the floor and used stones as men. One of the sergeants, a teacher, arranged lectures by various of the prisoners, on sundry topics. They played baseball with a pickaxe handle as bat and a ball made of rags. They had to do their own cooking with rations supplied by the French Army.

The 8th of November brought a surge of optimism to brighten the gloom of a wretched existence and its uncertain duration: Operation Torch, the Allied invasion of French North Africa, began. In Morocco, the landings were made at three places on a 200-mile front around Casablanca.

The first signs of help at hand were seen and heard when 'some American Wildcats [Grumman F4F/FM fighters carrying two 250 lb bombs] put on a good show dive-bombing near the camp. We felt a little apprehensive, knowing how trigger-happy they [the American Armed Forces] are, but all was well, they missed us. (This confirms that they probably were aiming for the prison camp!) A roll call was held and we were told to be ready to move out after lunch.' Not to be surrendered to their allies, but to a prison further from the advancing front.

That afternoon they boarded lorries. 'My friend, Tom Black, a sergeant observer, and I always had escape in the back of our minds. We wondered if this was our chance. There were so many guards and it was daylight, so we would bide our time. We had travelled a long way, it is difficult [after half a century] to put a mileage or time to it, before we reached a big railway siding. We were ordered off the lorries and marched to a goods train. Our guards had now taken up positions circling the siding and train. Things still looked against us.'

It was late afternoon by now and Stephen suggested to Tom that they walk casually along the track beside the wagons and study the situation. They had become detached from the main party and stopped to look at one of the wagons. 'What do you think, Tom?' Stephen asked. 'Shall we jump into it and watch for our chance to escape?'

He recalls: 'Everything was going well, then some clot shouted to ask where we were going. Guards moved in and bundled us into the wagon, then went back and grabbed the two who had called to us. Their blankets and ours were also thrown in. Some very naughty words were exchanged!'

Day became dusk and dusk turned to darkness. The goods wagon had no windows. There was a sliding door on each side. Stephen and Tom sat down, downhearted, backs to the engine. The other two sat opposite. Eventually a door opened and two Moroccan guards with rifles and fixed bayonets got in. They settled down with their backs to one of the doors. The train set off.

'Tom and I had thought of making a surprise attack on the guards. We had another think. I was not content to sit and let miles roll away. It was dark, the guards were quiet and, I hoped, lulled into a sense of security. I felt the door around the latch and realized it was possible to open it from the inside.' He eased it open a few inches. 'And to my horror noticed the difference between the darkness inside the wagon and the lesser darkness outside. I reported back to Tom on my finding and the problem.

'Then I had an idea. I went back to the door and found that the wheels on the top of the door moved along rails. I got my blanket and, with my knife and fork and Tom's, tucked one edge of the blanket along the rails and secured it there. By doing this I ensured that no light would enter the wagon when we opened the door. I asked Tom if he was still willing to go. He agreed that we had better tell the others. When we did so, they were worried stiff about what would happen when the guards found us gone. Too bad, we're on our way. I told them the door would be open and they could come if they wished. The one who had caused all the trouble by calling out to us gave us half a loaf of bread. Tom and I stood at the door watching the telegraph poles flash by. We both realized it's not like this on the films. Let's get on with it: every mile is a mile further to walk. Which of us will go first? Tom suggested that I did and he'd follow. I hung there with the wind in my face, counted to three, shouted "Cheers", and was flying through the air, hoping I wouldn't hit a telegraph pole.

'I hit the banking and saw stars, rolled to a halt and lay there watching the train's tail lights disappear.'

Bereft of his companion, forlorn in a strange wilderness, he wondered if the guards had woken up and seized Tom before he could jump. Had there been a scuffle, in which he fell from the train and was killed or badly hurt? Had he jumped, but broken his bones? 'My worry now was whether Tom had made it. My shoes had been torn off. I walked along the track for what seemed like miles. Then I saw a figure. Was it Tom? We embraced and shook hands in sheer relief at having succeeded in the first part. Now to put as many miles as possible between us and the railway before daylight. Tom insisted that I wear his shoes. I tried them and was glad that they were too small.

'We came to an understanding that if there were any disagreement about which direction to take or on any other matter we would spin a coin to settle it. We never had to. Tom trusted my judgement and I trusted his knowledge of the stars.'

In its own way, this night was as uncomfortable and fraught with as many uncertainties as the nights at sea in an open boat. Were there French Army patrols in the area, seeking the invaders? Were there Arab tribes around who would capture them and hand them back to the Vichy troops? There were hunger and thirst to contend with. There was the tiredness of legs unaccustomed to hours of walking, after weeks at sea and in confinement. Stones and rocks lacerated Stephen's feet; Tom's shoes gave small protection.

'When daylight came we hid in some hills.' But there was no point in resting for long. They must press on, find food and water, make progress towards the coast and increase their chances of being found by Allied troops. At last, they saw a small encampment and approached cautiously. They had 'Come upon a small group of Arabs. I spoke Arabic and Tom spoke French. We told them we were aviators. They were very friendly and gave us delicious omelettes and mint tea with lots of sugar.'

They left the Arabs and tramped on, still uncertain. Could they really rely on the Bedouin not to betray them? Was there a reward for information leading to the recapture of escaped prisoners of war? It was a long, worrying day and even more painful for their feet as they covered the miles. At nightfall they found a sheltered place and slept, hungry again and weary.

When they woke early in the morning Stephen had the feeling that they were being watched. This was confirmed when an Arab youth appeared and told them that the war in Morocco was over. They asked where the nearest Allied troops were and he told them which way to go. They met an American patrol, who took them to their camp where other escapers had already arrived.

Stephen and his friend Tom were taken to Casablanca and put aboard an American ship, where they had baths, their feet were bandaged, they were given a thorough medical examination and well fed. They were also kitted out with U.S. Navy uniforms.

The object of escaping had been to get home by, Christmas if possible. In an American naval ship they crossed the Atlantic to Norfolk, Virginia. Before being allowed into the United States they had to change into American Army uniforms. Next, they were sent by train to the Overseas Staging Area, Casual Section, in New York, and put into Royal Canadian Air Force blue. Thence they sailed aboard the SS *Westernland*, which put them ashore in Scotland on New Year's Day, 1943.

The stress of Stephen Hall's operational flying in North Africa, of being torpedoed, the hazards and near-starvation on the lifeboat voyage of more than 700 miles, the hardships of prison camp, the perils of his escape from the train, left him physically and mentally fatigued to the limit of endurance. He was posted to a Coastal Command station in Devon, sent on a Fitter's course, and awarded a 25 per cent disability compensation. He was promoted to corporal and served on until 1946.

Between leaving the R.A.F. and retirement, he made a career in engineering. He devoted his spare time to Red Cross work, helped in the local cottage hospital and commanded the Berkeley and District Red Cross Detachment for twenty years. He is now 'very much involved with charity work, driving an ambulance for the local Day Centre'.

Stephen Hall DFM's indomitable courage, cheerfulness and efficiency not only enabled him to survive a variety of vicissitudes but were also an unfailing support to his comrades in wartime and have been at the service of his fellow beings ever since.

CHAPTER SIX

SERGEANT ERIC MOSS

If, WHEN WAR WAS DECLARED, Eric Moss had been content to wait to be conscripted, few would have blamed him. There seemed no reason why he should volunteer, for his native land had done him no favours. There were eleven children in the family, of whom he was the seventh. Three of his brothers were unemployed. His father, a former Regular in the Grenadier Guards, who had fought in the Boer War and the Great War, was now earning forty-seven shillings and sixpence (two pounds and thirty-seven pence) a week. Eric had intended to be a teacher, to which end he had studied with the aid of scholarships and exhibitions worth £20 a year. He had to abandon this ambition when he wished to enter Loughborough Engineering College, was required to pay half the £300 fee, and could not find the money. He became a carpenter.

Even under the torpid premierships of Baldwin and Chamberlain, both bent on appeasing Hitler at whatever cost to Britain's pride, it became apparent in early 1939 that war with Germany was probably imminent. All British males were ordered to register for military service at the age of twenty-one. Eric Moss did so on 30 April of that year, his twenty-first birthday. Because he had the impression that only university men were eligible for R.A.F. air crew, he applied to join the Service in a ground branch. He was refused. Summoned to an interview for the Army in December, he passed the medical examination. Eager to get into uniform, he kept applying to be called up. After six more months' frustration he volunteered for R.A.F. flying duties and was accepted as a Wireless Operator/Air Gunner. He joined in July, 1940.

After his wireless and gunnery courses and promotion to sergeant, he arrived at an Operational Training Unit in June, 1941, to be trained on Blenheim bombers, which carried a crew of three: pilot, observer (as navigators were then called) and WOP/AG.

'The Blenheim turret was a cold, cramped, miserable place to be in on a cold day or at altitude. We had not yet been issued with electrically heated clothing and boots. My toes would just go numb with the cold. Those fleece-lined boots, having been worn some time, gave no warmth at the soles or toes. Any attempt to wear extra socks only made matters worse, as the bulk of them restricted the circulation unless you were lucky enough to get oversized boots.'

Here he had his first experience of the many hazards that attend those who defy the law of gravity. 'The tuning of the transmitter and receiver and the use of the Morse key had to be done with the head down. Alongside my knees were two metal open-topped boxes, each holding 1,000 rounds of .303 belted ammunition.' One day the crew were flying over the Welsh mountains in stormy weather when the aircraft suddenly dropped 400 feet in an air pocket. 'Not nose first, but flat. Two thousand rounds of ammunition jumped out of the boxes and landed on my lap. Cor blimey! The pain! When we landed, the pilot came to my hatch to see why I had not got out.' Eric had to put all the ammunition back before he could move. 'At the hospital no permanent damage was found, but I was given three days off flying duties. I spent these on my bed, as I walked like a crab and my unfeeling friends would roar with laughter as they sang, "No balls at all" [a ditty well known to rugger players and the R.A.F.] when I shuffled about.'

He had his first crash when, after bombing practice, the undercarriage would not descend. The crew did not know that one 25 lb smoke bomb had hung up. The pilot made a belly landing and it exploded, filling the aeroplane with acrid smoke. 'I thought I would bring my lungs up with the constant retching.'

Not long afterwards his aircraft stalled on the approach at a height of 60 ft and landed so heavily that the undercarriage collapsed. He hit his jaw on the gun butts and his head on the turret roof.

The course ended in October and the crew were posted to Burma. They left in November for Portreath, in Cornwall, where they would refuel before continuing to Gibralter. While waiting for suitable weather at both the place of departure and the destination, Eric Moss was found to have jaundice and sent to hospital. The crew acquired a replacement and left without him. He was lucky: 'They landed on a Japanese-held field and disappeared.'

Six weeks later, after sick leave, he set out from Portreath early in 1942, with a different pilot and observer. Their first take-off was aborted by an oil leak that forced them to turn back. On their second attempt the pilot, a heavy drinker, fell asleep over the Bay of Biscay at 12,000 ft and had to be roused by the observer before the aircraft dived into the sea. After several days' delay at Gibralter they flew to Malta, where they arrived in an air raid. The following day they landed in Egypt. While the aircraft was being prepared for its onward flight, Sergeant Moss went down with a high temperature and sandfly fever. Again, the others of the crew flew off without him, accompanied by his replacement.

Following twelve days in hospital and a spell in a transit camp near Cairo, he again found himself at an O.T.U. This time he was in a crew of four, two of whom were air gunners. Their aeroplane was American, the Glenn Martin Baltimore: 'An aircraft I had never heard of, and I doubt anyone in England had either.' The Mk IV had four .303 guns in the wings, two or four in the dorsal turret, two in the ventral position and four fixed, downwards- and rearwards-firing. It carried 2,000 lb of bombs and was 40 mph faster than the Blenheim.

His pilot, Sergeant Brian 'Jumbo' Ekbery, had been a Civil Servant. The observer, Sergeant Roger Bates, was 'a sincere, intense workaholic. The fourth member was "Jock" Johnson, a nineteen-year-old Scots lad'. They were posted to No 223 Squadron and operated from various desert landing grounds. An accident when landing, which tore one wheel off and dug a wingtip into the ground, set them back while their pilot underwent some dual instruction and other crews drew ahead of them in operational time. In the desert, Sergeant Moss had met several of his friends from his training days. 'My mates still had their original crew, but this was my third and I seemed jinxed.'

On 9 October, 1942, he had just returned from a few days' leave when the crew was called to briefing. There had recently been heavy rain and seventy-two German aircraft were bogged down at El Daba. The R.A.F. was about to pay them a visit and further increase their immobility. Ekbery and his crew had barely taken off when oil squirted over the windscreen and they had to return to base. Eric killed time by lying on his bed reading. He was soon disturbed: the crew had been allocated another aircraft.

'There were 28 U.S.A.A.F. Mitchells with us who had orders to open their bomb bays when we did and bomb when we did. As the bombs were painted yellow they were easily discernible leaving the aircraft, and one of my jobs was to count them as they left us, to make sure there was no hang up.'

This was the second raid on El Daba that day. Enemy reaction to the first one had been slow, probably because the Germans supposed that the R.A.F. was also bogged down. 'This time, however, he was waiting for us, the muck from his 88 mm coming up thick, fast and accurate as soon as we came into range. We were also much lower than we should have been, which helped us not at all. After the first few black puffs exploded outside our aircraft the next gigantic cracks of the explosions seemed inside the fuselage, so close were they.'

There was a loud metallic clang, the aircraft lurched and lost altitude with its port engine stopped. 'About this time the bombs were released and we rose like a bubble in water. I was looking at the ground and the tiny aeroplanes which were our targets. Suddenly they disappeared. The ground took on the look of a freshly drawn pint of bitter or a bowl of soapsuds, as about 500 bombs burst in the space of less than a minute. For a few seconds the A.A. fire wavered, then started again until we passed out of range.' They were going the wrong way and had to turn about. The other aircraft also did so, climbing at the same time.

'We had to turn on a dead engine and go back over the target still losing height. The Ack-Ack started again as we came into range.' He looked down and could see the flashes of flame from the gun muzzles as they fired at the crippled Baltimore. 'I pointed my two guns down and fired four 100-round belts at those flashes, watching my tracers bounce amongst them. I threw the empty belt crates down at them.'

The flak ceased. The second engine stopped. 'Those stinking black gobs of smoke floated away, leaving the air clear for me to watch the multiple streams of tracer coming up towards us. Invisible drills perforated the fuselage about me. With no engines, Ekbery held her as flat as he dared, hoping to get us over the lines – but no luck. Jock suddenly called, "There's a fighter on our tail," and Ekbery had to put her nose down to get extra speed.

'The small arms fire intensified. Why our floating sieve wasn't blown out of the sky I don't know. My fingers closed on the triggers of the four machine guns fixed two each side of me, to fire backwards and downwards, and I held them down. I hoped they were putting the enemy off aim: 1,400 rounds per minute each is a lot of flying lead, and I didn't have to bother about saving my gun barrels. So long as Jerry was firing I kept the triggers down, until I could see stones and foxholes and sand within feet of my face.

'We hit the ground and skidded along on our belly, the interior of the aircraft filling with sand and dust. We had come down right amongst the enemy.'

The danger of fire is the first thought that occurs to the crew when an aircraft crashes. Eric Moss released himself from his parachute harness and forced his way out from under the Baltimore.

He saw that the observer was seated on a wing that had broken off, tearing up his log and maps. The pilot was looking at the wreckage, his revolver in his hand. The second thought that enters a man's mind when he has been shot down among enemies at whom he has been shooting is about the treatment he will receive for having killed and wounded some of their number. Brian Ekbery had his revolver extended at waist height. Eric Moss recalls, 'I shouted, "No Ekbery, no," and threw my gun as far as I could. Ekbery hesitated. For one horrible moment I thought he would make a futile stand. Then he shrugged and tossed it away.

'Odd bullets hit the ground near my feet and I put up my hands, watching the enemy advance.' They were Italians, carrying light rifles with fold-over bayonets. He kept his eye on the small soldier nearest to him, who was having trouble with his bayonet hinge; it kept flopping down. 'I asked him for a cigarette. His face lit up as he said *"Sigaretta? Si"* and gave me one, lighting it for me.'

Within minutes German troops arrived in a motor vehicle. They showed no more animosity than the Italians had. They took their prisoners aboard the vehicle and drove off, stopping occasionally at a foxhole to exhibit them to their friends. The airmen were thirsty. Eric Moss nudged the young NCO in charge and said, 'Water?' The German stopped and called to someone in a foxhole, who tossed him a water bottle. Eric drank: 'It was fifty per cent cognac.'

They stopped at an anti-aircraft gun site, where there were four newly dug graves. Bodies wrapped in blankets awaited burial. 'My blood froze. Were they mine? They had to be; no other gunner would have opened up with all those Kittyhawk fighters of ours milling about us. Our mates had been flying thousands of feet above us. I looked at the faces of the enemy. But there was no hatred, no nothing; it was all part of the job; it was war.'

Their captors delivered them to a cluster of tents, most of which bore a red cross. Wounded men lay on beds: evidently British or allies, for the camp was surrounded by barbed wire and guarded by armed sentries. They were pushed into a tent and told to lie on rush mats. Eric tore pages out of his pay book and buried it. In the evening other prisoners were brought in. German soldiers came and went, taking no notice of them, until one youngster appeared with an accordion and played familiar songs, 'Tipperary', 'Lili Marlene', 'Pack Up Your Troubles'. 'A sour-faced corporal stopped him.'

They were made to take off their boots and trousers, which were returned next morning. Breakfast was a slice of black bread spread with meat paste, and half a cup of coffee. A lorry took them to a shattered town, probably Mersa Matruh, where they were herded into a small wired-in compound and sheltered under the top half of a dirty, rotting tent.

One by one they were led away, Eric Moss the last to go. Ekbery slipped his silk escape map to him under pretence of shaking hands, and Moss buried it under a mat. There was the noise of a scuffle by the gate and two Italians dragged in an apparent British soldier, who said he had been caught in barbed wire for three days before being found. Eric offered him his tin of bully beef and the spoon the Italians gave prisoners in place of a knife. The putative Tommy said he was not hungry. This made Eric suspicious. A true countryman is sharply observant, and he was born and bred in the Oxfordshire countryside. Moreover, the fellow's hair was well brushed and oiled, his face was smooth, there were no blisters on it or his lips after allegedly being in the sun for three days. His boots, under a thin coating of dust, were polished, the toecaps unscratched. The imposter produced his pay book, which looked brand new, and asked Eric where he kept his. He asked questions about the squadron, about Eric's view of the enemy, his opinion about the outcome of the war. Eventually, having received no answers, he gave up and went to speak to the gate guard, who let him out.

The German officer had a disturbing amount of information, such as the name of the squadron commander and the fact that Sergeant Moss had recently been on leave. To his questions, Eric repeated his rank, name and number. At last he was taken to another tent where he rejoined his crew and others. In the morning the same officer informed them that all prisoners taken in the desert were handed over to the Italians.

Another lorry ride, to a camp where there were some hundred prisoners. They were fed: two hardtack biscuits and a tin of meat. Eric kept the empty tin to drink from. They slept on the ground, with no blankets. They moved every couple of days, in huge Italian lorries with a guard in the cab and accompanied by German troops on motor cycle combinations, armed with machine pistols. Every day the rations were the same, hardtack and tinned meat. Still no blankets. Lice began to infest their clothes.

After two or three weeks they arrived at Barce where they lived under shelters made from groundsheets supported on short lengths of aluminium tubing. There were large contingents of Australians and South Africans there. The latter were lavishly equipped with clothing, which they bartered for food. There was intense hatred between these two nations, and 'Generally the Aussies had even less time for us than they had for the South Africans. Nonetheless, I know of no fist fights between the Brits and Aussies.'

There was so much rancour that a fight was arranged between an Australian and a South African in the hope that this would damp it down. The Italians set up a ring of posts and ropes, and neutral seconds and a referee were appointed. Both men were large and moved like experienced boxers. It was a bitterly fought contest, the culmination of the anger that weeks of taunting had created between the two nations. Eric Moss cannot remember whether the fighters wore gloves, but he does recall that a great deal of blood was spilled by both. At the end of the tenth round both men, poorly nourished for many weeks, were exhausted and had to clinch to avoid falling. The referee announced a draw and henceforth there was a noticeable improvement in the relations between the nationalities involved.

The brutality of the prisoners' code was as depressing and demoralizing as the lack of food, the discomfort and the vermin. A South African Regimental Sergeant Major stole a small piece of bread. His comrades strung him up by his thumbs, his feet off the ground, for two hours.

The 8th Army was approaching Barce and the prisoners were hurriedly moved. After many halts they reached Tripoli towards the end of December and were put aboard a ship for Sicily, confined to the hold. 'It was not long before men started to complain of stomach pains and after a few hours we all came out in gigantic rashes. The white blisters were as big as a thumbnail. Men became ill and some South Africans climbed the stairs and shouted *"Male"*, which means "illness", but no one came and we had to endure the pains. Soon the air became foul as men defecated where they stood. There was a dip in the floor on one side where all the urine and excreta gathered. Every time the ship rolled the noisome filthy torrent swept over them. Men still slept by this nauseous mess, their existence so miserable that they no longer cared.'

The next evening they arrived at Palermo during an air raid, with bombs falling near the ship. They left there by train, crossed the Straits of Messina and continued by rail to Capua, where they spent Christmas in a transit camp. It was very cold and each man slept on an armful of straw and one blanket. In January, 1943, they were transferred, once more by train, to Camp 70 at Monte Urano, near the east coast of Italy, about thirty miles south of Ancona.

The camp, which had been a jute factory, held 8,000 prisoners. Their quarters were cramped. They slept in three-tiered bunks with only thirty inches of headroom, on either side of an alley four feet wide. The camp was surrounded by barbed wire and a ten-foot wall along which there were sentry towers. A few yards beyond the wire a row of pines grew beside a ditch.

The only British officer was a Medical Major. There was an average of six deaths a day from malaria, dysentery, beri beri, malnutrition and suicide. Eric Moss's pilot was a Catholic. The priest who attended the camp sent the names of his congregation to the Red Cross in Geneva via the Vatican radio. Through Ekbery, Eric was able to have his name included. Two months later he received his first letter from home. Meanwhile, his mother had presumed him dead.

Working parties of POWs went every day to work on farms and at various labouring tasks. Sergeant Moss joined a party of senior NCOs who were taken by train every day to the nearest town, Fermo. As a carpenter, he was employed on making wheelbarrows. The members of the party were able to do some bartering on the black market and were given extra food. 'More than double rations of thick macaroni cheese and tomato puree were putting flesh back on our bones and soon we were able to take surplus food back to the camp to be reheated and eaten by our friends.'

Eric had made friends with a private soldier, John McHugh, who had been taken prisoner on the day he landed in Algeria on Operation Torch, 8 November, 1942. He had caught malaria and been treated in Italian hospitals for several months, during which he had acquired a good knowledge of the language. The two men decided that 'If we got half a chance, we would get out of camp, and we made up our minds that it had to be via the movable section of the wire fence', where one of their fellows had been shot. This was the last ten feet of the tall barbed wire, abutting the wall, which was pulled aside to allow rubbish carts and other essential traffic to pass through. 'Since our armies had landed in Sicily and were sweeping north towards Messina and the toe of Italy, the attitude of the guards had changed. They would often call down to the prisoners for news of the war, as it seemed that we were better informed than they were. Some even admitted the possibility of the Axis losing the war. None seemed over-concerned now if anyone strayed over the warning wire [a two-foot-high fence six feet within the main barbed wire] for a ball, or to get closer to talk to them.'

The two men saved as much chocolate and as many biscuits as they could from the Red Cross parcels, which, with their shaving kits, they kept in John McHugh's small pack. This did not rouse suspicion; many carried a small pack or a Red Cross cardboard box with a string sling wherever they went, to avoid theft of the contents. These two intending escapers kept a close watch on the movable section of the wire.

After the Salerno landings on 9 September, 1943, of which news reached the prisoners, there was a noticeable reduction in the number of Italian troops about the place. The caged men became restless. The Medical Major passed on an order reputed to have come from General Montgomery, that anyone caught trying to escape would be tried by court martial. The war in Italy, it was said, would be over in twenty weeks.

There were anti-aircraft guns close to the camp and another on the guard tower nearest the movable section of wire. U.S.A.A.F. P38 Lightnings, easily identifiable fighters with twin tail booms, were seen every day and fired at.

'We were close to our bit of wire one day early in September when a number of American aircraft flew over. The gun on the tower opened up and then stopped − a blockage. The prisoners, no longer ordered back to their barracks, collected by the gun. Soon they were barracking the crew, who became more flustered and unable to get the gun going. The crowd of POWs became larger and more vocal. I looked at the wired trestle, put my hand on the wooden cross-member and pushed. Surprisingly it moved − not much. I gave John a nudge, glanced at the gun crew's feet above me, and gave the trestle another harder push. It moved enough for me to wriggle through, pushing as I went. John followed me, and we were out. I remember someone calling me back in English, saying, "You'll be for it!" But I was over the few yards to that line of pines and into the ditch behind it.'

In that swift rush to freedom it was not only the sudden, unaccustomed violent physical effort that made their hearts race and lungs labour; it was also the expectation of a burst of machine-gun fire or single shots from sentries' rifles, aimed at their backs. The first few hundred yards in a daylight escape are enough to make any man's bowels deliquesce as he wonders if legs, heart and lungs, long unexerted, weakened by lack of food, will carry him to cover before the bullets start to fly.

But there was no outcry and there was no shooting. They were through the trees and over the ditch, onto a dusty road. They kept up their frantic pace for a full minute... two... three, then were forced, panting, to a slow walking pace, their ears pricked for sounds of an alarm and pursuit. None reached them.

They tramped on and presently a farmhouse came in sight. As they got nearer they heard a dog barking and saw a woman come out to stare at them. Warily, they looked for telephone wires, although the house seemed too shabby for its inhabitants to afford such a convenience, but there was none. No danger, then, of a telephone call from there to report their presence.

They continued until they came to another house and a boy loitering outside asked who they were. John interpreted and Eric told him to say they were Germans. The boy was not convinced: 'You are prisoners.' But he gave them some green apricots − which they threw away when out of sight − and his mother came to join them, carrying a jug of wine and some beakers, and offered them a drink. At first, Eric did not care for the rough wine. 'I am not a wine drinker, and had only ever tasted port, which this stuff certainly was not. But by the time I'd finished the beaker I was taking a different view. The stuff wasn't Best Bitter, but it was certainly better than nothing. We had a second glass...' but he had his wits about him '...before the unwelcome thought occurred that the woman might just be killing time while her husband was getting help with a reward in mind. John had been talking to her and she had asked him whether he was hungry. I told John to say no and thank you, and let's go on.'

So on they went and 'as the day wore on we began to enjoy our wonderful new freedom, together with the beautiful countryside, and so far friendly natives. With the help of the vino this grew to euphoria.'

At another house where they were offered food they stopped to eat bread and garlic sausage and drink wine. Their host gave them bread to take with them, and unripe apricots that they again threw away for fear of stomach upsets.

This was a region of smallholdings, each perhaps of twenty hectares (50 acres). It was hill country, whose slopes were favourable to viticulture. Wheat was sown between the ranks of vines, and vegetables grew in plots adjacent to the houses. They saw no livestock; the only animals apart from dogs were bullocks between the shafts of farm carts. There were no hedges or fences; the properties were divided by uncultivated strips about half a metre wide, to mark the boundaries.

On that first night of freedom they slept in a haystack until the barking of his dog brought the owner out. By the light of an oil lamp he held, they saw that he carried a gun. Searching for intruders, he stopped near the rick and they could see that he was barefooted and elderly. In answer to his 'Who's there?' John said 'English prisoners,' and the old man turned away wordlessly to return indoors with his dog.

Dawn woke them, stiff and cold, to a morning of heavy mist. Hungry and tired, with the prospect of many more long days of tramping and nights of hard lying, of depending for food on the generosity of poor peasants who themselves had to exist on a scanty diet, it was a discouraging moment.

Eric asked his companion how he felt.

'Awful. I reckon we should go back to camp.'

'This,' he says, 'jolted me for a moment. Then I said, "If you feel you can't go on, John, then you must do as you see fit. But I shall carry on alone. Why not wait until the sun has warmed us through, and give it another go, just for today, before you decide?" ' That persuasive 'just for today' was the operative phrase and reveals Eric Moss's innate understanding of psychology. It is also further evidence of his strength of character and purpose.

'He reluctantly agreed and I persuaded him to indulge in a brisk "mark time" for a minute to get our blood moving. Then as we moved off we ate the bread given us the night before and after a few minutes, with the sun getting up, we both felt better. We were, we hoped, heading south, with the rising sun giving us a bearing. We took care to avoid walking through crops so as to avoid antagonizing the people.' There speaks the countryman again.

Their march was slowed not only by fatigue but also by the frequency with which farm children spotted them and dogs barked. A parent would emerge onto the road bearing bread and wine and invite them to stay a while. They discussed these invitations while they walked. 'It was tempting, especially when the house and people seemed cleaner and more to our liking. But there was a risk to our freedom, and I suspect also to theirs. Anyway, I wanted to get home. This war lark was not at all what the novels made it out to be. We had seen enough black-edged photos of young men, each with its cross, to know that *"Morto in Russia"* was just as heartbreaking to these people as our own "Killed in action".'

They remarked on the fact that all the adults they had met were middle-aged or old, with the exception of the young women. All the young men were in the armed forces or deserters in hiding.

Many of the men they met had fought on the British side against the Germans in the last war, and regarded the British as 'less of a menace to them and theirs than the Fascists' tax collectors and their landlords'.

That night they again slept in a haystack, reassured by now that they would be safe among these people. In the morning they came to a stream that they had seen several times during the past thirty-six hours, and decided to follow it. It flowed along the valley bottom and the riparian shrubs would give them cover.

At noon they were invited into a house near the stream, for pasta with tomato puree and grated sheep's cheese. Eric learned later that at haymaking and harvest they ate every three hours but, in winter, only once a day.

John gave him the gist of his conversation with their host: the King of Italy had removed Mussolini from office as Prime Minister and Dictator and signed an armistice with the Allies, but the Fascists were continuing to fight on the German side.

On leaving the farm they took to a main road and, on rounding the first bend, met a tall, heavily-built man with grizzled hair coming towards them, carrying half of a pig's carcass. He called, 'Get away from here! The Germans took over Monturano Camp this morning.' They all paused while the Italian confirmed Mussolini's dismissal and told them at Camp 70 the British Major had armed some of his troops with Italian rifles and set them to guard their comrades. The Germans had arrived soon after. Of the 8,000 prisoners, few had escaped. The rest were entrained for Germany. Eric Moss and John McHugh had broken out with only a few hours to spare.

They moved on, but were in a dilemma. If they continued on their way they might run into Germans or Italian Fascists. If they hid, someone might betray them. For a moment even Eric's resolution faltered. He was tired and confused and suffering from mental stress. All he wanted was a bed to sleep in. The road ahead curved again and three houses came into view. A man emerged from one, looked up and down the road, and stood watching them draw near. When they were within earshot he and John exchanged a few words. 'He asked where we're going and he's invited us inside, because it's dangerous to keep to the road,' John explained. 'His name's Pio Remmio.'

They had met the benefactor they so badly needed. They trusted him from the first. He had an honest face and a manner that instilled confidence. In time they were to learn that he had once belonged to the Fascist Party but had been expelled when he disagreed over matters of principle. His fellows had given him a thrashing and forced him to swallow a litre of olive oil. He was now virulently opposed to Fascism.

The farmhouse floors were of brick, the ceiling consisted of wooden joists that bore the brick floors of the upper rooms. The brick walls were covered with dingy, chipped lime mortar. The windows had shutters but no curtains and some of the panes were broken. In the living room stood a long table with stools around it. A big black cauldron hung from a chain in the fireplace.

Pio brought out a bottle of white wine and his wife, Rosa, produced a ham. It was covered with dust, cobwebs and bird droppings, but Pio wiped it clean and it tasted delicious. Ham was served only on a special occasion; Eric did not taste it again during his stay in Italy. There was also bread and sheep's cheese.

There were some other men present, but they were not asked to share the food. There was discussion about Eric Moss, whose fair hair and blue eyes looked dangerously German and execution was the penalty for sheltering a German deserter. 'Rosa, who did not appear too keen to keep us, wanted to dye my hair black. Instead she dyed my clothes.' It was decided that the two Englishmen would stay for the time being, while the situation was reappraised and other plans were made.

In the 1940s, Italian peasants lived in almost medieval poverty and squalor. The two fugitives slept on the living room floor, on straw with a shared blanket. Each morning they gathered the straw in the blanket, ready for the next night. The vine prunings were saved for baking bread, which was done every twelve days. The latrine was a small circular enclosure made of plaited maize stalks, which was used until the stinking mound it contained grew so high that the fence had to be moved.

Ten days after their arrival, Pio and two other men took Eric, all of them on bicycles, to another house, where he spent a few days. He stayed with two more families for a week or two, then returned to the Remmios. Wherever he lodged he did his best to repay his harbourers by making wooden soles for their sandals (but they worked bare-footed), helping with the grape harvest and pollarding trees. Despite this practical demonstration of gratitude, he upset Rosa. Served with a helping of what looked like black beans, he was about to eat them when he discovered that they were the eyes of an insect the size of a housefly. 'I only just reached the window in time before I vomited.'

Eric, revolted by the latrine, preferred to use the bullocks' stall, which was laid with deep straw. The son of the house reported this and 'Pio was angry with me for the first time ever. The bullocks and their stall were sacred.' After that he took a mattock with which to dig a hole some distance away.

One of the local landowners had an illegal wireless set, listened to the BBC and passed on the news at the wine bar in the village. This in turn was borne daily to the Remmio home by Pio or one of his friends. The Italians, characteristically, were over-optimistic. Every time Eric said he ought to start moving south, they asked why. The Eighth Army would soon be here. But the Eighth Army, advancing along the east coast, was held up seventy miles away and the American Fifth Army was stuck equally far down the west coast.

He was rescued from this stagnation by a farmer named Panicha, to whose house he had been invited for a meal. Panicha told him he had heard there was someone at a village called Porchia, four or five hours' walk away, who perhaps could help him. They set out that night. Their journey ended at a small farm, where the farmer told Eric to spend the day sleeping in the bullocks' stall while he was out with the beasts. When it was dark the farmer took him to a nearby house where two men were talking in Italian. One of these, who was obviously British, and 'had a certain air of authority and confidence', looked him over before asking, in Italian, what he wanted. In English, Eric asked if he knew of any way by which he could pass through the lines to the south. There was a brief, rapid Italian exchange between the two men, before the Briton replied, 'I know of no such person, and if I did I would say no. Have a drink and then go. I can't help you.'

In dudgeon, Eric refused the drink and left. That night he trudged back to rejoin Pio.

It was late October, just over a year since he had been shot down, and by now there was active opposition in the district to the Germans and Fascists. There were several Partisan groups, with escaped Allied prisoners of war among them. One night an aircraft flew over and dropped a container filled with food, clothes, cigarettes and leather for soling footwear. The Italians who found it took it to a British ex-prisoner, from whom Eric, some days later, got two pairs of boot soles and a little food.

This delivery by parachute was soon followed by the arrival of a Parachute Regiment officer accompanied by a small party of troops, whose mission was to make contact with the escaped POWs in the region. A meeting was arranged, which Eric attended. John did not; he was suffering a bout of malaria and had, moreover, acquired an Italian girlfriend. The paratroop officer gave orders that everyone present was to keep silent about what was afoot. They must be ready to move at an instant's notice. He reminded them that they were under military discipline and he would tolerate no insubordination.

The reaction to all this was typical of the scepticism of British Other Ranks who have been in battle. Eric Moss says, 'I was not over-impressed, and only a dozen POWs were interested. That container drop must have been known to the Germans. And that officer seemed altogether too "gung-ho", too much a "macho" man of action.' In whichever of the armed forces he is, no ordinary man likes to serve under someone who is hell bent on winning medals.

When word came that they were able to assemble for a final briefing, it was cocooned in cloak-and-dagger precautions. They were to make their way to the Manocchia River and follow its bank towards the sea. Somewhere along this route paratroops would challenge them, they would give the password and the paras would escort them to the river mouth. Eric distrusted the whole business. Most of the local inhabitants were aware of what was being planned. Gossip about the meeting had spread. There had been no need for the briefing; instructions could have been passed by messenger. People were already asking him when he was leaving. Among them was Pio, to whom he had replied, 'I don't know. Remember Porchia?' John had decided not to accompany him.

On the appointed night, he left without saying goodbye to anyone. He met some of the others and they moved on in a group until at last they heard the expected, 'Halt! Who goes there?' and gave the countersign. There was a wait now for others to appear. Then they set off for the coast. After ninety minutes they joined another column.

Rifle shots suddenly broke the silence, followed by sub-machine-gun fire and grenades exploding. Bullets swept through the undergrowth around them. Men turned and ran. Eric ran too, but uphill away from the river. He was brought to a violent stop when one of the wires along which vines were trained caught him across the throat. All around there was the sound of stumbling, pounding boots and of men blundering through maize and vineyards. He wondered how many of them were Germans. It was nearly two o'clock in the morning when a man carrying a lantern came out of a cowshed.

'Prisoner,' Eric said.

'Manocchia?' the man asked.

'Yes. No good. Some wine, please.'

The man gave him a piece of bread and a glass of spirit that took his breath away. He regained Pio's house shortly before first light.

Two days passed before he learned why the plan had gone awry. The R.A.F. had bombed the road and rail bridge over the river mouth and halted a German convoy, which had been forced to stop there for the night. Hence the encounter with the escapers, thirty-three of whom were reported killed.

Autumn gave way to winter and, before Christmas, snow fell. No word came of further plans for rescue. Life returned to its former tenor on the Remmios' farm, where Eric and John were still hiding. In the late spring news went round of another meeting to organize an escape. This time there would be no more meetings. Twenty-four hours later, accompanied by John and again without saying farewell to Pio, Eric made his next bid for freedom. The various parties followed each other in single file, to minimize their trail. Shortly before the sun rose at 4 am they arrived at some buildings in which they hid and were given a hot meal. They slept until 10.30, then were sent out to hide in a maize field under the hot May sun.

When night fell they continued the march. The previous night's events repeated themselves; stop for shelter and a hot meal, a few hours' sleep, then out to hide among the tall, standing corn. They spent a second night in the same place, a delay that caused worry lest escape were to be foiled again.

All day they lay in the cornfield once more, not daring to move because any movement of the body would cause the maize to move too, and the enemy was at hand.

Towards midnight they moved out on the last lap that took them down to the beach. There they could just discern a large Landing Craft lying bows-on with her ramp down. On either side of the ramp stood soldiers wearing stocking caps and carrying sub-machine guns, waving at the escapers in urgent signs to hurry aboard.

Eric says, 'No words were spoken except my whispered, "Thanks, mate," as I patted the shoulder of the first soldier I passed.'

Hardly were they aboard when the engine note quickened, the ramp rose and clanged shut and the ship began to move. Three men had arrived seconds too late. They plunged into the sea. Two caught ropes that were thrown to them and were hauled aboard. The third drowned.

On that night, 24/25 May, 1944, for which Eric Moss had waited more than twenty months, 98 escaped prisoners of war were picked up — a record for the three Adriatic Marine Evacuations that were successfully carried out.

When the sun rose, Spitfires appeared to escort them in relays until they were put ashore behind the British lines. Thence they went by train to Naples and from there Eric Moss was flown home via Gibraltar.

He was promoted to warrant officer on return to Britain. The rest of the war he spent instructing at an Operational Training Unit and on Flying Control duties. He was demobilized in April, 1946 and spent the rest of his working life in the building trade.

CHAPTER SEVEN

FLIGHT SERGEANT R. MACLEOD
AND FLYING OFFICER N.T. FAIRFAX

Daylight low-level bombing?

'We could get a time check from the church clock as we pinpointed each village and map-read our way in and out,' recalled Rod Macleod, a navigator in 107 Squadron, on Bostons.

Bostons? American, the Douglas Boston was. A cigar-shaped aeroplane with an upward tilt to the last fourteen feet or so of its forty-seven-foot fuselage, which gave its tail a jaunty look. The Mk III, with which this story is concerned, was rated with a top speed of 303 mph at 13,000 feet. At 50 feet, the squadron's operating height, Rod Macleod reckoned it as 330 mph. It was well armed, too; four fixed .303 guns in the nose and twin .303s in dorsal and ventral positions. The bomb load was 2,000 lb.

No 107 enjoyed a reputation that took some living up to. It had flown its first operation in May, 1918, when seven of its DH9s (two-seater, open cockpits) dropped 1,400 lbs of bombs on their target. By the war's end in November, 1918, the Squadron had unloaded forty tons of bombs on the enemy; no small effort, with each aircraft carrying no more than four 112- or two 230-pounders. It was a brief existence though. The Squadron was disbanded in June, 1919.

In 1936 the R.A.F. Expansion Scheme was introduced in response to Nazi Germany's and Fascist Italy's growing bellicosity and manifest desires to overrun Europe and Africa respectively. Two years later, 107 Squadron was re-formed and equipped with the Blenheim Mk I. When the Second World War was declared on 3 September, 1939, it was flying the Blenheim Mk IV. On the next day, ten of these aircraft from 107 and 110 Squadrons made the first bombing raid of the new war, on the German Fleet in Schillig Roads.

By the time Flight Sergeant Rod Macleod joined the squadron in April, 1943, it had won ninety individual decorations for gallantry. He was twenty-two years old, a Canadian who had been a policeman in Oxford.

The wireless operator/air gunner, Flying Officer Norman Fairfax, who was twenty-eight when war broke out, had spent the four preceding years in Colombia as Assistant Accountant at a gold mine. Before going to work abroad he had served in the City of London Yeomanry, a Territorial Army regiment. He was a trained soldier and now he wanted to go home and join in the fight; but only the R.A.F. was accepting volunteers from anywhere in South America. It was February, 1941, by the time he set foot in his native land again to train as a pilot. He did not qualify, so became a WOP/AG, was commissioned at the end of the course and posted to 107 Squadron.

Flying Officer Jim Allison, the pilot with whom they both flew, was a South African who had been a banker in peacetime.

On Friday, 27 August, 1943, the crew was one of six that were briefed for a low-level raid on the electrical power plant at Gosnay, the only supplier of electricity to the whole of northern France. It had to be put out of commission at all costs and the attack had to be made at 1900 hrs precisely, the time at which the day and night shifts changed over.

On this trip they were taking a passenger with them: 'Skeets' Kelly, a well-known newsreel film photographer, with his four cameras. This was his twenty-fourth operational sortie in bombers.

'At all costs' was a phrase used only too literally to emphasize the importance of the target. An unnecessary exhortation; the crews took for granted the terms of the service they had volunteered to give. Sitting through briefing was a febrile enough experience without any embroidery. The way men wriggled on hard chairs and forms, the craning of necks to see the wall map that showed the route to target, the sudden brief flurries of unamused laughter and muttered comment were evidence of that. 'You may have fighter escort covering your withdrawal,' the crews were told. Rod Macleod's comment many years later was, 'This statement was a considerable boost to our morale, but we still had to get there and be on our way back before we could hope for any relief from attack.' Even 'You *will* have fighter escort' would have implied the same proviso.

They crossed the enemy coast at 50 feet, cruising at 250 mph in echelon starboard. High overhead they saw a large formation of U.S.A.A.F. B17 Flying Fortresses. In hostile air space it was always heartening to see one's friends, even though there was no radio contact with them and neither formation could help the other if fighters attacked — which was what happened. Allison's crew spotted, dead ahead, 'several Focke Wulf 190s, the best fighter the Germans had.' These were climbing to intercept the Fortresses, 'but, on seeing us, they decided we were easier prey [the B17 had ten .5in guns distributed all round, above and beneath it] and broke off to attack us.'

Allison's aircraft, 'S' for sugar, was positioned immediately to the right of, and slightly behind, the leader, Flying Officer George Turner. All six were widely spaced, to allow for individual evasive action. The tactic was to stay low and avoid being silhouetted, because, when a fighter broke off after its first attack, a second attack was very difficult, for there was comparatively little difference between its speed and the Boston's when flying so low.

'Therefore from the coast to the target all six Bostons were flying *around* forests, instead of over them and literally *along* the roads and streets of the small villages that we passed.' Hence the comment about reading the time by church clocks. 'On previous low levels we had brought home yards of telephone wire, leaves and small branches, usually collected in the actual target area.'

It was a drill that worked well this time. All six got through to the target. Under fighter attack they could, at least, retaliate. There might be the spang of FW190s' bullets and cannon shells punching and bursting holes and rents through the Boston's airframe, but the gunners had the satisfaction of shooting back and the pungent smell of cordite drifting about excited the senses with that peculiar stimulation that men have experienced in battle ever since the invention of gunpowder. But over the strongly defended Gosnay power installation the light bombers were as vulnerable as game birds driven over the butts. From the Bostons, almost brushing the buildings with their bellies amidst a concentration of heavy machine guns and 20mm cannon, it was impossible to shoot effectively at the enemy gunners.

Their bombs were fused for eleven seconds' delay. 'Turner bombed first, we were second to straddle a large target area at only rooftop height. Three others got in and released. One took a direct hit and just disintegrated. Another flew into the explosion and also went up.' The sixth could not get in before the first bombs would have exploded, so was forced to go for one of the numerous secondary targets.

Despite having been hit many times, 'S' was still airborne, but the port engine was barely turning over. They emerged from the target area to find more FW190s waiting. 'They pounced on us and shot away one aileron and a big piece of our rudder. Flat out, our aircraft was able to do only about 230 mph.' So the three other survivors soon left them far behind, under attack by three fighters and taking what little evasive action was possible on one engine. 'Got into a port turn and could not straighten out. As our aircraft was going over on her back, out of control, our pilot put her down in a grain field for what felt like a perfect belly landing. The time was 7.25 pm and three Bostons out of six had failed to return from another low level.

'I, sitting in the nose surrounded by glass [perspex, actually], certainly owe my life to a very good pilot. There was a belief among navigators on Bostons that in a crash landing they would not stand a chance, so no one ever strapped themselves in. Besides, it was most uncomfortable and made map reading more difficult than ever, it already being quite a task at 50 feet and 250 mph. Consequently when we hit the dirt, I too was not strapped in my safety harness. However, we all got out without a scratch, except that I had a very small cut on my right forearm.

'I was first out through the emergency exit in the roof, the pilot was next, closely followed by the two gunners, our own wireless operator/air gunner, Norman Fairfax, and Skeets Kelly, who said he had got some of the best action shots he had ever taken.

'Quickly we took off our harnesses and Mae Wests and threw them into the aircraft. Someone got the one-pound incendiary bomb and threw it into the fuel tank. We all ran as fast as we possibly could for a mile or so into some shrubs that were growing in a ravine. Four farm workers in the field just ignored us except for gazing in amazement. Naturally, we avoided them.'

They reckoned it would take the German troops about half an hour to arrive, unless there were any stationed in a village about a mile away, whose church tower they could see. The aircraft was burning fiercely, sending up showers of sparks and billows of smoke and causing the ammunition to detonate intermittently. They decided to wait until dark before going on.

Describing his emotions, Rod wrote, 'Hiding in a ravine a mile away from a burning aircraft in a hostile country, not knowing when, if ever, one would get home again is a sickening feeling.' The first moments of escape from a crashed aircraft are infused with the shock of the event and the terror of fire breaking out, before the realization that one is safe from injury or a particularly unpleasant death has sunk in. On top of that, there was the demoralizing knowledge that the odds must surely be in favour of them all being caught by the enemy. At least, this time, the aircraft was burning because the crew had set it alight. Nonetheless, it was a beacon guiding the enemy in their direction.

Norman Fairfax recalls his feelings clearly: 'There was no time to think but just to get away from the aircraft. On arrival at this copse and after a cigarette, for me at least, one was able to collect one's thoughts and put our extraordinary situation into perspective. We realized how extremely lucky we were to be alive and unhurt, especially after seeing two of our aircraft crash in flames and the loss of more members of our squadron (a loss was quite a regular occurrence after an operation). Naturally we were breathless and very shaken but I do remember it was a lovely summer evening and, on a personal note, I remember lying back squaffing blackberries, smoking with thoughts of no more 'ops' tomorrow and regrets that I wouldn't be able to keep an assignment I had with a WAAF that evening. But my situation was different from the others, in that I was single and the others were married and Rod's wife was pregnant. But then, of course, one had to get back to reality and what happens next.'

They decided that to stay together or each to make his own way would be too risky. They agreed to pair off, travel by night and rest by day. 'The question was, who was to go with whom? Our crew had been together for over eighteen months, but Skeets Kelly was, to all intents, a stranger with us. Sensing this suggestion, Skeets suggested we draw lots. It turned out that he and Jim Allison would go together, while Rod Macleod and I would make the other pair. We all shook hands, wished each other the best and hoped to meet again in England some time, maybe not until after the war, but we all hoped it would be much sooner. We shared the last cigarettes before parting company. It is a funny feeling saying goodbye to a pal in enemy territory and then going out into the unknown. We were now all wanted men and liable to arrest at any moment.'

An hour and a half after they had crashed it was dark enough to press on without inviting attention. They set off south-east, pausing often to listen for sounds of movement that would warn them of enemies out hunting them. Keeping off all roads, Rod and Norman walked for six hours, frequently impeded by tall fences that necessitated retracing their steps to find a place where they could climb over. There were herds of cattle in many of the fields, and, as Norman had become very thirsty, they stopped to do some milking. This should not be difficult, as the cows were used to being milked at pasture. Rod described it: 'I had milked previously many times. However, as Norman could not milk, it was rather difficult for him to get the benefit, so he lay on the ground and I squirted milk down into his mouth.'

Norman Fairfax adds that on this and subsequent long tramps they both suffered from a nagging thirst that they also quenched from cattle troughs.

By 3 am they calculated that they must have made six or seven miles across country, but had probably covered twice that distance on account of their frequent back-tracking. They lay down to sleep in a haystack.

Two hours later they woke to the sound of people talking and laughing and knew they must be close to a village. Creeping near to the backs of the nearest houses, they saw what appeared to be telephone wires. This they had not expected in a small country community, so concluded that the occupants were comfortably-off collaborators, and withdrew. They learned later that the cables carried electricity.

The best thing to do, they now thought, was to find an isolated farmhouse and ask for food. They had the usual emergency rations, but intended to keep these in case they could find no other means of feeding themselves. At 6.30 am they came to a farm standing on its own and approached warily, keeping out of sight. Eventually an old farmer came out to feed the chickens. Norman whistled and drew his attention.

'On seeing us he became very afraid, as he suspected that we were Germans trying to catch any Frenchman who might be helping Allied airmen. This explained his great resistance to assisting us at the time. I asked him for a drink in my best schoolboy French. He told us to come into the house and gave us a glass of wine and a glass of beer, but did not offer any food. The old man and a girl of about sixteen seemed to be the only occupants of the farmstead. They both treated us with great caution.' Even after the fugitives explained that they belonged to the R.A.F., neither seemed convinced nor disposed to help.

'As there appeared to be no future here, we decided to move along and hope for more assistance from the next contact. However, we did get a map of the Pas de Calais from the farmer, which he had on the wall. It was the back of an old calendar.'

The map was rich in detail and they were able to lay out their route. They left just after 7 am and went to the next farmhouse, some half-mile away, where smoke was rising from the chimney. They were still hungry but the weather was fine and their optimism was high.

When they drew near to the second farmhouse they saw a woman milking in what Rod described as 'the little corral'. They told her who they were, that they were very hungry, and asked for food. She also became highly suspicious and questioned them searchingly about where and when they had crashed and where they had spent the night.

'I might say that we both looked like anything but airmen,' Rod wrote later. 'Tired, dirty, hungry, cold and shivering as well as suffering to some extent from shock, even though not injured. After the trek through the fields at night we were mud up to our knees; our hair was standing on end as we had lost our caps in the aircraft.' But these, surely, were the very details of their appearance that should have dispelled suspicion. Even the most stolid and unimaginative French peasant could hardly expect them to look clean and rested after the ordeal they claimed to have suffered.

There was a rapid conversation between the old lady and her daughter. 'They had to take the big decision about whether we were real or just stoolpigeons, as had already been suspected by the man on the previous farm.'

Both women impressed on the fugitives how dangerous it was for them to help Allied airmen in any way, and that, if caught, they would be shot on the spot as an example to others.

'This we fully realized and appreciated, but we were getting more and more hungry. After some time they brought out a bowl of coffee which was very cold and some bread which was not brown and yet not quite black either. This was the famous black food that the Germans were supplying to the French. It was much worse than the worst quality of cattle feed. It was in long rolls about three inches across and a foot long and very hard. They were most anxious that we leave as soon as possible, and goodness knows they had every right to be, too.'

A nearby wood gave them exiguous shelter while they gnawed the sour-tasting bread and rested. Rain began to fall. They gathered fallen branches, on which they lay among fallen trees and stumps, but sleep would not come. Towards noon they left, hoping to find more effective shelter in a larger wood they could see. They were walking across open ground when a FW190 swept over no more than 500 feet above their heads. They expected to see it bank steeply and turn back to dive at them, but the scare was quickly over as its pilot gave no sign of having noticed them. 'After that we stayed close to cover in daylight.'

After three hours of wandering from one wood to another, 'not getting anywhere or accomplishing anything,' their morale sinking, they were determined to keep trying to obtain help. 'No one wanted to have anything to do with us at all,' Norman says. 'We were fed up, I suppose, and resigned to it and hoped our luck would change.' Their predicament was all the more galling when they visualized what the three crews who had got back from the Gosnay operation would be doing now. As Rod put it, 'The rest of the Squadron on a wet afternoon would be in the mess, enjoying a beer. For us it could have been very much worse, but at that moment it did not seem likely.'

From lectures they had been given on the escape organization in France, they had tended to form a falsely roseate picture of what normally befell shot-down aircrew. It sounded 'just a piece of cake. In fact many almost looked forward to this wonderful experience of being in enemy territory, where you would be welcomed with open arms, and be in civilian clothes spending the same evening in a local estaminet drinking beer. This was quite possible, but such was not our luck, because so far we were unable to convince anyone that we were not Germans posing as Allied airmen.' The man who had given them wine and beer and the woman who had given them coffee and bread might just as well have sheltered them. By the mere act of giving them food or drink and not reporting them to the enemy, they had committed offences that carried the death penalty.

'The next milkmaid, who was much more amiable, gave us some milk which we drank and enjoyed and promised to get us some clothing by that evening, so a rendez-vous was made for seven o'clock.'

It was an appointment they did not keep. They were sitting under a hedge 'wet through, exhausted and disgusted with our misfortune', when, at about five o'clock, they noticed a man slowly approaching them. He was elderly and carried a pitchfork. Because of his age, they were not too much afraid of him if he decided to use it as a weapon. When he was close enough they saw that he had lost a hand and had an iron hook in its place. At once it flashed into their minds that he had probably been wounded in the Great War and would therefore be disposed to help them. When he stopped in front of them, Rod bid him 'Bon jour'.

'Are you Germans?'

The question pushed Rod Macleod, weary, famished and soaking wet, into momentary impatience, although he did not show it; he and Norman had asked for nothing. But he quickly realized that the old man's caution was justified. He produced some English currency, but the doubting Thomas was not convinced. Then he pulled from a pocket a two-day-old copy of the *Daily Herald*. He always carried the day's copy of a British newspaper on ops, following a tip he had been given at an escape lecture. 'Some joker said if you have a very recent issue of an English paper with the date, generally you will convince them that you are not a stoolpigeon masquerading as a shot-down airman.'

It proved a good tip and one wonders why he had waited so long to resort to it. 'This did the trick and the old man, Monsieur Lavite of the village of Fief, changed completely. He took us to his little cottage, where we had a good meal and eventually slept the night in his bed, while he slept on a chair in the kitchen. He lived with his mother, a very old lady, but still able to potter about the house. They made us very welcome. He went out and killed a tame rabbit and boiled it, making a large pot of soup for us. We took off all our clothes that modesty would allow and dried them by the open fire as the rabbit was cooking.'

At about ten o'clock, after they had eaten and were feeling sleepy, 'many of the trusted friends and neighbours had to come and actually see the *aviateurs anglais*, wish us luck, bringing old clothes, caps etc., anything that would be of any use to us in our efforts to make good our escape and so to fly another day against a cruel, ruthless enemy. This no one knew better than these very same peasants. This was the France we had heard about and expected.'

By midnight a large pile of jackets, trousers and caps had accumulated and they were able to fit themselves out adequately before at last getting to bed. At 5 am they were roused, given coffee, a packet of food to take with them and led to a forest before the locals were up and about. It was raining again. They had intended to rest all that day and continue their walk after dark, but, with civilian clothes over their uniforms, they felt it was safe to resume their way at once.

Still following a south-easterly direction, keeping to the fields and avoiding main roads if possible, despite their confidence in their disguise, they trudged all day until nine in the evening, when a river barred their way. From their map they saw that the river, a road and a railway line converged, so they reasoned that there must be a bridge, and it would probably be guarded. There was a bridge and they crossed the river safely. But on climbing the embankment to the rail tracks, they stopped in sudden fright. Norman thought he saw a cigarette glowing in the dark. They remained motionless, eyes and ears searching for the armed sentry who was enjoying a surreptitious smoke. Then they realized that they had been alarmed by a glow-worm.

They quietly crossed the river, railway line and main road at Anvin, went down a lane that led them out of the village, and carried on until midnight. They worked out that they must have travelled fifty miles by now, found a pile of straw and fell asleep on it. At 3 am the cold woke them but they lingered for another hour before taking to the road once more. Six o'clock found them in a small village, Croisette. It was raining again and they were hungry. They decided to spend the day there.

At the first house on whose door they knocked, the old man who answered and whom they asked for a drink wanted nothing to do with them. Their kindly thoughts about the French seemed premature. They tried again and their trust was justified. They were invited in and well fed. While their clothes dried, they washed and shaved for the first time since leaving England, then spent the day asleep in a hayloft.

All the men in the family were engine drivers, 'and all happy to entertain us, even though one of them had been shot up five times by R.A.F. train-busting aircraft, and in one attack his fireman had been killed, he still felt he was honour bound to do all he could for us.' His brother had been on the receiving end of two attacks. Asked about the nature of their duties in the R.A.F., the two airmen were in trepidation about their hosts' reaction when they revealed the facts, 'and we were prepared to make a hasty exit. When they learned that we belonged to these low-level train-wrecking outfits, they were all still willing and thrilled to have us.' Instead of being bundled out of the house by wrathful trainmen, 'When we left that evening we had had another huge meal, were refreshed and each of us was given a large package of boiled eggs, boiled potatoes, bread and a large bottle of wine. Real hospitable people, these French!'

This time their intended destination was Fillièvres, some thirty kilometres away, which they expected to reach easily by the next morning, as they were well rested and had plenty to eat. 'We just milked a cow whenever we wanted a drink, using our water bottles (rubber, aircrew for the use of) as containers.'

Despite the improvement in their welfare, the mental stress of being in danger of discovery by the enemy at any moment kept turning the screw on their nerves. Tension brought disagreements. 'Norman and I would get into terrible arguments over which way we were going. More than once we parted company, each to go his own way, only for me to hear some ten minutes later a call in the night air, "Mac, Mac, where are you? Wait for me." So I waited, feeling much better for having him to argue with. After all, who ever heard of an air gunner being able to find his way anywhere, anyway? His nickname was "Tracer", not only because of the ammunition in his guns but also because his second name was Tracey. A good fellow, even though he would argue about things he knew nothing about!'

They were walking along the roadside after leaving Croisette when a German staff car, carrying four officers, passed them, going in the same direction. It slowed. Their heartbeats raced with expectation that the car would stop, to reverse with the driver's foot hard down on the accelerator and the other occupants drawing their sidearms. Their stride faltered to a slower gait. They peered around in the darkness for a place where they could scramble away from the road and bolt. But evidently the Germans decided that they were either locals or tramps and drove on.

At one o'clock in the morning they came to the outskirts of Fillièvres, where they bedded down among sheaves of corn. On waking four hours later they made a reconnaissance, skirting the village, which was larger than any other they had yet encountered. They were 'happy to see a total absence of military personnel'. But a main east-west highway ran through it and they could see long convoys of troops passing on their way to defend the Western Wall. They again found that the large-scale map they had been given on their first morning was of great help. It gave much more useful detail than any escape maps with which aircrew were issued.

Twice, they had been told of a British parachutist who was operating in the Fillièvres area. Hence their decision to come there. 'Now that we were here, we had to be very careful not to be caught or betray any saboteur who might be operating unknown to many people. So we stayed in some bushes all day and kept watching the people and the happenings of the district. From our vantage point on top of a little hill we could see all the village pretty well. We watched the farm workers as we lay in the sun on this our fifth day in France, thus far undetected. About 11 am we watched a formation of Mitchell bombers [U.S.A.A.F. B25s] passing overhead and being attacked by enemy fighters. Later in the afternoon two Mustangs flew right over us at low level. It gave us quite a thrill to see our own aircraft do a beat up in enemy territory while we watched from the ground.'

During the day they discussed how they should approach the British parachutist, to whom Rod refers as 'this spy chappie'. They came to the

8. Stephen Hall in 1943.

9. Norman Fairfax, René Gerrault, Rod Macleod, Fillièvres, September, 1943 (p.83).

10. Eric Moss enjoys "a spell in a transit camp near Cairo" (p.60).

11. Pio Remmio: "the benefactor they so badly needed" (p.68). This picture, taken in 1989, shows him holding a certificate of thanks from General Alexander.

12. Stanley Munns "with his nineteenth birthday behind him and three ops in his log book" (p.104).

13. Bill Eddy "gave his own parachute to the man whose 'chute had been burnt" (p.120).

14. (*left*) Alan Matthews during his time with the *Maquis* (p.133).

15. (*below left*) Maurice Smyth, who made it home after crash-landing in the sea off the coast of Jugoslavia (p.146).

16. (*below right*) Franz von Werra "rivalled Baron Munchausen with the lies he told about the enemy aircraft he claimed to have shot down" (p.153).

conclusion that 'if such a fellow existed around these parts', then the local saboteurs and patriots would surely know him. 'If we could get in touch with one of them, they in turn could contact this spy for us.'

How to get in touch with the right people? They made up their minds 'to chance our luck again and hope it would hold out and we would avoid running into a collaborator'.

Accordingly, after dusk fell they entered the village, hoping for the best. The first people to see them were three women bringing home a can of milk from the fields in a dog cart. To open a conversation, they asked the name of the village. The women told them, but did not linger. 'We waited a little longer and then decided we would call at the nearest farmhouse and, putting our cards on the table, hope to be received by a sympathetic family.'

A large farmyard looked inviting. They crossed to the house door and knocked. A voice called, '*Entrez.*' They did so and realized at once that they had made a mistake. They should have waited until somebody came out to them. Three men, five women and several children, were in the kitchen, having their evening meal. '*Nous sommes aviateurs anglais,*' they announced.

'The effect was alarming, as all these folk were immediately scared out of their senses and semi-panic broke out with all and sundry talking at once and gesticulating, until one man, a young fellow about twenty-three, took us outside and asked us various questions on the way to the barn. He asked us to prove we were Allied airmen. Here I produced my currency and my *Daily Herald*, now six days old, and our regular identification discs. He seemed satisfied and said he would help us.'

This young man, René Gerrault, lived with his wife, Paulette, and two small children in this big farmhouse with his uncle, who owned it. René had been a sergeant in the Army, evaded capture when France signed an armistice with Germany, and took himself off to the Unoccupied Zone. Homesick, he did not dare return to his family for fear that the Germans would deport him to forced labour in some Ruhr factory making war materials, or, as he was a bricklayer, to repair bomb damage. But the Germans were equally concerned to ensure that the farms in France produced as much foodstuff as possible, so those who worked on the land were virtually exempt from being shanghaied to manufacture munitions or restore blasted factories. René changed his description to 'farm labourer' and returned to work for his uncle, where his elderly aunt, his mother and unmarried sister and two small cousins from Lille were also living under the same roof.

He had the courage and audacity also to join what Rod MacLeod describes as 'a local German-sponsored auxiliary police', and received 200 francs a night for a two-hour patrol. 'Needless to say this patrol was never able to capture or find any of the local saboteurs, of whom the chief was a fellow of absolutely reckless courage, at times almost foolish in his bravery in deceit and double-cross. A fellow they called René Gerrault!'

Having satisfied himself that these were genuine evaders, he took them back to the house. The children, who were the most likely to let slip an incautious word about the new arrivals, had gone to bed. 'He introduced us to everyone and, although the womenfolk were still very shaken and not too happy with our being there, the rest accepted us, asked numerous questions and seemed quite interested and helpful. We had a marvellous meal of steak, eggs, potato chips and plenty of fresh home-made bread and butter. We enjoyed it immensely and for the first time learned how inadequate our French was, now we were being asked all kinds of questions by nine or ten different people. However, we made ourselves understood and could understand them quite well. That night we would sleep in the barn and René would call for us at five and take us out into the forest before the village awoke. We would spend the day there and await his return in the evening. We were to take a fishing rod and spend our time pretending we were just out for a spot of fishing in the river running alongside the forest.'

The next morning, after coffee, they duly made for the river, victualled and provided with two bottles of wine and a pack of cards. The weather was fine and they felt both mentally and physically at ease. They were confident that, although René was not a member of the escape organization, he would get in touch with someone who was. His wife, sister and mother had come round to the view that he would not run the household into any danger, and their attitude to the Englishman and the Canadian became cordial. At noon on that first day of simulated angling, Paulette and Yvette brought them more food, and cigarettes for Norman.

Towards 8 pm René came to fetch them to the house for another abundant meal. They slept in the hayloft again and in the morning went 'fishing' once more. So far nobody outside the farm family knew of their presence in the village, save a Monsieur Emile, who had been present when they arrived at the door and asked for help. René assured them that this friend of the family was a good patriot, which was borne out when he brought them two bottles of beer while they were picnicking and let them sleep in his barn that night because it was not wise to bide too long in one place. That same evening they had supper with René's parents. During the next few days they were also mealtime guests at other houses. Whenever they moved about the neighbourhood someone went ahead to scout for a German patrol. He would give warning of the enemy by whistling 'Lili Marlene', whereupon they would retreat. However confident their hosts were, the atmosphere was never totally relaxed; while they were in anyone's house the women were tense with fear of a sudden incursion by the enemy, despite all precautions.

Rod Macleod comments, 'All these suppers which we had at various homes were banquets and we began to realize that the French people really lived, their staple diet was wine and steaks or chicken. Wine was only two francs a litre. All during our time in their country we lived like kings as far as food was concerned, especially in the rural areas.' Food throughout the country was rationed and these farmers fed far better than the general population.

After their night in Monsieur Emile's barn he roused them early with a jug of hot milk and two slices of bread and butter each. That day they spent in a different wood. Care had to be taken not to establish an exact pattern of behaviour; there were families in the village who could not be trusted. German troops had been stationed there from time to time and a searchlight battery site lay quite near. On the other hand, in addition to the active members of the Resistance, there were many who could be trusted implicitly. One of these was the priest and another was the shopkeeper. The latter subtly indicated to Yvette that he was aware of the evaders' presence by offering her a French-English dictionary. It might be useful when the Allies returned to France, he said, and in the meanwhile she could start to study for that longed-for time. But it was disturbing to know that word was circulating about their presence in the locality.

They had been hiding in the new place for over an hour when they saw five men cycling towards them. Alarmed, they were tempted to make a run for it, until they recognized René among the group. It was 7.30 am and they were puzzled by his arrival in broad daylight. Monsieur Emile was another in the party, and a third, redheaded man whom they had met and been told was an active saboteur. The two strangers were well dressed and obviously not manual workers. The elder, aged about thirty, was introduced as René Guittard, a mathematics teacher at the Frévent lycée. The younger, Maurice Malo, was only seventeen, fair-haired and blue-eyed, of German descent (presumably from Alsace) but active in the Resistance and endowed with great courage and contempt for the enemy.

'These new acquaintances were very official in their method and obviously had some experience in that work. René Guittard asked to see our identity discs, took our numbers, names and ranks, the target on our last operation, the date and time of attack, the type and serial number (but not the squadron number or squadron letters) of the aircraft. He then said, "I will be coming back in a day or two. If the information is correct, you will be going back to England a day or two later by aeroplane. On the other hand, if you are stoolpigeons, you will both be shot!" '

They felt that to accept this without reservation would be stretching credulity too far. Both were aware that R.A.F. aircraft did land in France by night. Indeed they knew a pilot who was engaged in these clandestine operations. But they couldn't believe that a small aircraft would come swooping in within a couple of days and whisk them away home. René

Guittard added that their relatives would know within twenty-four hours that they were alive, well and safe in France, which they also doubted. Their scepticism was justified some time later, when they found out that this yarn was spun to all who were in their predicament as a morale-booster.

It was one week since they had been shot down. Events had moved swiftly in their favour after the first two disappointing days. 'On returning that evening to René's [Gerrault] for supper, everyone was in a jubilant mood and an air of expectancy was evident. That same evening an old man came to give us a haircut and there was also a visit from the priest.'

They had been told that they would be moving to Frévent. Meanwhile they were no longer spending their days in the forest, but in the garden of the farmhouse, which was fenced, with high bushes that gave complete privacy. Moreover they were sleeping in a bedroom at the house. Maurice Malo, who carried despatches to René Gerrault, came several times over the weekend. They saw one delivered in a waterproof cover in a bottle of milk. They listened to the BBC every day. On Sunday Yvette took some photographs, of which they received copies when they returned to France in 1944 and were stationed nearby.

At 7.30 am on Monday some Flying Fortresses flew over and were passing overhead when, for no apparent reason, since they were neither being attacked by fighters nor fired at by flak, four parachutes opened beneath them and one of the bombers blew up.

German troops arrived immediately after the accident, to hunt for survivors and patrol all roads in the area. In consequence the planned departure of the two R.A.F. men for Frévent at 10 am had to be postponed until the next day.

Three of the four Americans were captured. The fourth landed uninjured close to a large wood, a hundred yards from a road and half a mile from the village. Knowing that the enemy would swiftly be on his scent, he discarded his gloves, life jacket, helmet and parachute harness in that order while running to hide among the trees. Five men and two girls, sawing wood, waved him towards a ditch covered with long grass and briars, into which he dived. Two Germans dashed into the wood and asked the woodcutters if they had seen any of the parachutists, which they denied. Then, finding the abandoned articles, the Germans realized that they had been searching in the wrong direction. They returned to the wood and one of them actually crossed the ditch where the fugitive was hiding. At about 11 am the search was abandoned, whereupon one of the Frenchmen went to the ditch. He told the American that in an hour or so someone would come by with a horse-drawn water cart on which would be two barrels, one containing water, the other, civilian clothes. The carter would stop and leave the garments just inside the edge of the wood. On his way back, he would pick up the American's uniform. When this was done, somebody else led the American to the farmhouse where Rod and Norman were staying.

He explained what had happened. Their bombs were fitted with a new type of fuse. The engineer, who should have been instructed in their use, knew nothing about them. When, therefore, an incendiary bomb caught fire and filled the aircraft with smoke, the pilot ordered his crew to jump, but only four were able to do so before the aeroplane exploded.

The Germans buried the dead and the locals heaped flowers on the graves.

The move to Frévent intended for Tuesday morning was also aborted, this time because a heavy attack by U.S.A.A.F. Marauders (Martin B26s) devastated the marshalling yards at St Pol, twenty kilometres north of Frévent. All motor vehicles were commandeered to remove injured civilians — 600 were killed — from the town. Aboard a train, 400 German troops were killed and 1,000 injured.

Macleod and Fairfax both felt it was high time they moved. The house was crowded and René was inclined to be reckless in his bravery and contempt for the Germans. They felt the situation had become too dangerous. They stood on the brink of catastrophe twice on Tuesday afternoon. They were in the room off the kitchen when there was the tramp of jackboots and a peremptory knocking on the outer door. One of the women opened it and they heard German-accented voices. But the two Germans had not come to search for them, they were seeking billets for troops of the Hermann Göring Division, which was coming to the district from Russia, to re-form and take its place on the Western Wall. In the afternoon they were in the garden, shelling beans and feeling secure with the bushes around it to hide them, when the local gendarme appeared unannounced. He could not help but see them. However, he gave no sign of having done so, said he had come to deliver a radio permit and took himself off without comment. These two near-misses not only came as a salutary warning to the fugitives, but also deeply disturbed Paulette and René's mother.

At last, on Wednesday, at one o'clock in the afternoon, carrying a small bag containing articles of underwear they had been given, they left, feeling deep gratitude and admiration for their helpers and sad at parting. They gave René Gerrault their battledress blouses as souvenirs and their silk escape maps to Paulette and Yvette. René Guittard had come to fetch them in a butcher's van that was waiting beyond the village, to which René Gerrault accompanied them. Guittard's wife, known as *La Fleur* on account of her petite prettiness, had come with him for the ride. Overhead, a dogfight was going on, in which they saw a Me109 shot down. It hit the ground and burst into flames. They took this as a good omen. They climbed into the back of the van and at 3 pm were delivered to the Guittards' house.

As they entered, the radio announced the news of Italy's surrender to the Allies. This was exciting for the French, who at once began to talk of an Allied landing on their Mediterranean coast. The ban on listening to Allied broadcasts was ignored everywhere and within ten minutes the news had gone round the town.

'The first act on entering a house was to toast the Allies, *La France* and, the most popular one, *l'Invasion*. We again had a good meal and a visit from the parents of René who was a local boy and had a very good reputation in the little town. A cousin, Pierre, and young Malo also paid us a visit. This time Malo brought his mother and sister.

'René arranged to get us identity cards that evening. These were more detailed than the British counterpart. They had a photograph and gave age, build, height, colour of eyes, trade, place of birth and address. I remember I was Maurice Dubois, a school teacher by profession, born in Dunkirk in 1916, who normally lived in Lille.' Their signatures had to be witnessed by an official in the Town Hall. How it was done, they had no idea, nor did they ask. It was better not to know too much.

'That night we spent in René's house and the following morning four of us played cards for a couple of hours as we watched convoys of troops on their way to the Western Wall. This was the first good leisurely look that we had at German troops, and they were a dejected-looking bunch and had old and battered equipment. Their trucks were in need of repair and paint. Their uniforms were shabby and old. The men appeared fed up and had not the usual sprightly appearance which we had been led to believe was characteristic of the Wehrmacht. During the inevitable delays that all convoys encounter, the troops stood around seemingly uninterested in the whole affair. None made the usual whistles or catcalls as the local mademoiselles passed by, so characteristic of troops the world over.'

That afternoon René Guittard told them they would be billeted in the town. Norman would stay with his parents, who kept a café, and Rod with a couple who owned a hardware shop and whose son was doing forced labour for the Germans.

'I arrived at my new abode at 3.30 on Thursday September 9 with René,' Rod wrote, 'who left stating he would be back later with some old English books and some pre-war magazines.' His host and hostess were introduced by the name of Ancet. A year later, when the Squadron was based in France, he learned that their real name was Guyot. 'They made me very comfortable and we became good friends. I lived in the room off the kitchen during the day and had a radio there, so I listened to the BBC all day. It was always tuned very softly, but at least was a good pastime. I slept in their son's bedroom and had the use of his bicycle. I used it on a few occasions, once I became accustomed to rubbing shoulders with German troops. Once confidence is acquired there is nothing to it.

'I was given a black Basque beret, which all the Frenchmen wore, more especially all patriotic Frenchmen, as to them it was a symbol of Free France. I also got a pair of trousers, a much better fit than any I had had so far, and with a blue jacket I could pass very easily as a Frenchman. I went out one afternoon for a walk with young Malo. Then another day I took the bicycle to Fillièvres where I spent a very enjoyable afternoon with the Gerrault family. On a few occasions Monsieur Guyot took me for a walk, usually in the company of a young Frenchman or two, and we had a few drinks in the local cafés, places where the licensee was known to be *"un bon patriote"*. On one occasion I took part in a card game I had learned from René Guittard. The licensee did not know I wasn't a Frenchman until informed by Guyot. Then out came the wines and special drinks. I remember it was on Sunday and after locking the door we all sat there and drank most of the afternoon. Old Norman was living in a tavern; I was just visiting one!'

One evening the American who had baled out and was staying at Malo's house was brought to visit him. The next day he returned the call and the two of them, with Malo and his brother, went for a walk in the country and stopped at a café for a glass of wine. This account of freedom of movement and easy sodality with the locals sounds casual and carefree, but every minute was fraught with the realization that the Gestapo or SS could descend on the fugitives and their helpers at any moment and without warning. The off-hand manner of narration masks a special brand of courage.

René Gerrault came sometimes from Fillièvres to take Norman and Rod out for a beer. One evening a barmaid became inquisitive about why Rod was not talking as much as René, to which René replied that his friend was Belgian and did not speak French well.

'I'm Belgian too,' the barmaid said. 'Where do you come from?'

'Ostend,' Rod replied. Whereupon she began speaking to him in Flemish.

'As the situation was getting very awkward,' he recalls, 'we decided to leave. Outside I heaved a sigh of relief; she was probably dating a Stormtrooper.'

On the way to Fillièvres with Maurice Malo one evening, they met René Gerrault coming into Frévent, and stopped at a café for their usual vin blanc. A German NCO entered, recognized Gerrault and wanted to buy him and his friends a drink. 'Because of his special patrol work, René came in contact with many Germans and they treated him with the greatest respect. The German sat down for an amiable chat, but after wishing him good health we drank ours down quickly, said we were on the point of leaving when he had come in, and were in a great hurry. If only he knew how great a hurry!'

During their stay at Frévent they were frequently told they would be leaving by night in an aircraft that would land in a field close to the village of Coughy, about three miles away. The time and date would be given in code on the BBC's French programme. Mac was shown the field where the aeroplane was to land, but time passed and the message did not come. Now he was told that if the airlift were not considered safe, perhaps he and Norman would go by sea or over the Pyrenees to Spain. All these means had already been used.

What they did not know was that their pilot, Jim Allison, had left Frévent the day before they got there.

On Wednesday, 15 September, they were told that they would definitely be travelling by the Paris-Pyrenees-Spain route. The next day a woman came for them. She was a stranger, and as René Guittard was in Arras, his wife refused to hand them over to her. Eventually they left on Saturday the 18th, with René and his cousin Pierre, by train for Arras. Tickets were always bought in advance by the guide and given to the protégés before leaving the house.

Every rail journey was a major risk. On this one, short though it was, the risk was increased by the tremendous battering, eleven days previously, of the marshalling yard at St Pol, where they had to change trains, and other damage to the line along the route, which entailed delays that gave the enemy more time to interrogate and search passengers. Pierre was trebly at risk. He had obtained leave from forced labour in Germany on the fabricated plea of going home for his father's funeral. Not only was he liable to the death penalty for the falsehood, but also because he had failed to return to Germany. And helping Allied Servicemen was a third capital offence.

The station and its environs were infested by Gestapo agents in plain clothes or uniform, so the two fugitives had been told not to stand together or near each other, but to mingle with the natives and act as much like Frenchmen as possible. Norman Fairfax, forty-four years later, says that he always felt apprehensive on railway stations if he was too near Rod MacLeod, because he is five feet seven inches and Rod was well over six feet tall and tended to stand out among the locals.

He recalls: 'I think Rod was more impatient than myself to get back, but then he had more reason as his wife was pregnant, whereas I was still single. So he used to fret a bit if we were stuck somewhere, getting bored and not knowing when the next move would be. Sometimes we discussed whether we should go it alone, to speed things up, rather than remain in the hands of the Resistance groups, but then we thought it better to let the professionals handle matters. I suppose I was a more phlegmatic character and don't remember being particularly demoralized or in deep despair, but of course there were certain moments of unease, like when the German troops were around Frévent, Bapaume and Paris, and, of course, when travelling on trains.'

In an environment where not only a huge number of enemy soldiers and Secret Police, but also traitors in German pay, might penetrate his civilian disguise or give him away every time he ventured out of hiding or even while he thought himself safe indoors, nobody could be nerveless. But one has only to look at a photograph of the young MacLeod, with his hefty physique, or the young Fairfax, compact and sturdy, and to study their features, to see that both were endowed with much strength of character as well as muscle. They and their pilot all strike one as rugged young men who could look after themselves in a rough-house and didn't give a damn for a bunch of swaggering Jerries.

Their first experience of surreptitious travel by train was a severe test of nerve. Rod remembered it in every detail. 'The suspense was terrible. We had a half-hour wait and everyone seemed to be staring, or so it appeared to us who were very self-conscious. We pretended to read the timetables and wandered around as casually as possible, but to act like a native was impossible. They never stopped talking and all had a basket or little sack under their arms and were mostly small and elderly people. Not many young men aged twenty-five and over six feet were to be seen in France in those days, so it wasn't any wonder that we received the attention of one Gestapo fellow who had me under observation for ten minutes prior to the train arriving. He was very suspicious and making his way towards me when the train came in. I climbed aboard with him still watching me. However, he did not come aboard, but I definitely believe that I was saved by less than a minute.'

They arrived an hour late at St Pol, where they had a long wait for their connection to Arras, during which they had first-hand evidence of the effectiveness of the Marauders' attack. Although eleven days had elapsed, only one track was open, which entailed a great deal of marshalling and long delays.

While Flying Officer Fairfax and Flight Sergeant Macleod were waiting on the platform at St Pol, 'There were about three hundred passengers waiting and about fifty German troops and railway workers trying to repair the tracks, as well as the special repair squads that the Germans rushed all over the place on such jobs. All these Krauts appeared very glum and unhappy with their lot in life, scowling and looking depressed, which from what we had seen, Germans generally did. The French, however, despite the terrific damage done to their town or city, did not seem at all upset and went about quite cheerfully. They accepted the whole thing as part of the price of their liberation one day, which they considered was just a matter of time.'

The weather was poor, with cloud base down to about 500 feet. 'A wonderful day for a low level, as the visibility under was very good and the protection of low cloud cover was immediately available.'

The R.A.F. meteorologists had evidently forecast the weather in northern France accurately. 'Suddenly the air raid sirens sounded and a formation of Mustangs flew at rooftop height over the town, scattering Germans in all directions, while the natives just stood there and many of them literally cheered and threw their hands in the air in their accustomed excitable manner. We had at least to smile, but I was not at all enthused by the bravery of the French and wished that everyone had made a rush for the nearest shelter. I was not too happy about being a victim of an air raid by our own aircraft and I was not sure that they did not intend doing just that. However, my fears were unfounded and they flew on, just rocking their wings in salutation as they passed and spotted the crowd on the station platform.

'Our guides had big smiles on their faces and thought the whole thing wonderful. They explained later that a beat up did more for the morale of the French than anything else, possibly because it was something tangible.

'The enemy now appeared more disgruntled than ever and I fancied any moment they would organize a roll call and find out who cheered and who did not; with suitable reward such as an Iron Cross or a bullet hole through your head, depending on how you rated in the trial. However, the train to Arras arrived and such imagination was at once put out of my head to allow for the more urgent trial of getting aboard and safely to Arras.'

They had to make sure of getting into the same First Class carriage as their guides, and, when they reached their destination, of following them out of the station. Now began the tracing of a circuitous route that was to become familiar, to shake off anybody who might be trailing them. After going round several blocks of buildings by varied routes, they finally stopped at a house they had passed three times, not far from where they had started.

The occupants were Madame Payen, her son Albert, aged twenty-four, who worked on the railway, and daughter, Léone, 'a startling beauty of seventeen'. The new arrivals were expected and lunch was ready, with an English-speaking woman friend to interpret. René and Pierre left at two o'clock. The original plan was that a new guide would take the two evaders over at Arras and conduct them direct to Paris. This had been changed and they were to go to Bapaume, twenty kilometres away. They took a 6.15 pm train from Arras to Achiet, where they changed for Bapaume. Their guides were the lovely Léone and a remarkable old lady of sixty-four who played a highly important part in the escape line. She had several identities and numerous disguises. On this occasion her hair was snow white and she was using the name of 'Madame Blanche', which amused them by its aptness.

On the second leg of the journey a woman gave her a parcel without saying a word. Handing over a package before speaking or shaking hands was a sign within the Resistance. This time it contained butter.

Arrived at Bapaume station, Rod offered to relieve Madame Blanche of the large suitcase she was carrying, but was rebuffed. He laid hold of the handle in a second attempt and received the same curt treatment. Instead of the standard roundabout route, probably because the suitcase was so heavy, they went straight to the safe house. Once indoors, the old lady explained that if she had surrendered her luggage to him, the food inspector at the station gate would almost certainly have stopped him and searched it for black market food. Any occasion that forced him or Norman to speak French had, of course, to be avoided. But accompanying an elderly woman and letting her carry her luggage still rankled. He had not expected so many hidden snags in acting the rôle of his assumed nationality.

The householder, Madame Madeleine Duclerq, whose father was living with her, was Belgian. She had married a British soldier during the Great War and spent four years in England. Her husband worked for the Imperial War Graves Commission, but had been sent to a concentration camp in Germany in 1940. Their only son was in hiding in Normandy, to evade deportation and forced labour. The Nazis' methods of conscripting forced workers were similar to those of the eighteenth century naval press gangs, who dragged men out of taverns. Hitler's minions would arrive at any public gathering or entertainment, park their lorries outside, stop the proceedings and frogmarch every able-bodied male out to be loaded into them.

Norman and Rod spent eighteen days in Bapaume, during which, says Macleod, 'we met everyone worth knowing in the local Resistance "Who's Who".' They dined twice with the Mayor at the Town Hall and quite often at his home. All the local Resistance members brought eggs, butter, steaks, grapes, wine and beer to Madame Duclerq's. 'Never in so short a time was so much eaten by so few. We have both agreed that we had not eaten or drunk so much in any eighteen-day period, either before or since our visit to Bapaume in September, 1943.'

The Mayor, Monsieur Guidet, an active member of the Resistance, had won the Distinguished Service Medal and wore the ribbon in his buttonhole, even when dealing with the Germans in his official capacity.

The first time they dined at the Mayor's house they met a young British infantry officer, his name not disclosed to them, who was leading a life of bizarre deception. His home was in England, but he had spent every alternate year of his education at school in Lille. After the retreat of the British Expeditionary Force, in which he had taken part, he accepted the offer of a transfer to the Intelligence Corps for special duties. He returned to France in the spring of the following year to take a lead in the Resistance movement. To cover his absence and the matter of communicating with his parents, without betraying the fact that he was in France, the War Office appointed a close friend of his as a shadow. The latter was posted to the north of Scotland, where 'Lieutenant X' told his parents he was stationed. He went home regularly on fourteen days' leave, picked up by a Lysander and dropped back by parachute. When Fairfax and Macleod met him he had been on leave seven times and made a total of ten night jumps. Before each return to duty he left several letters to his parents, which were posted at suitable intervals in Scotland. His shadow there opened his mail, and, if any matter required an answer, he would type it and forge the signature.

The end of this story of outstanding patriotic devotion and bravery was tragic. He operated until September, 1944, when he was captured and shot, a week before the Bapaume area was liberated.

Their sojourn in Bapaume was punctuated by frequent visits from Madame Blanche, who was a courier between Paris and the small towns of northern France. It was she who told them the date of their next move. On their last night they had dinner with the Mayor and his family. On the following morning they went to his office for the usual pre-journey briefing. On arriving in Paris they were to follow Madame Blanche at a safe distance, Norman a few yards behind her and Rod trailing him at the same interval. She would lead them to a church, where she would kneel in a pew on the right of the nave. They were to take their places in a pew on the left side and a little behind. A man would enter and kneel beside the old lady. When he left, they were to follow him as before. The Mayor then drove them to Achiet, bought them first-class tickets and reminded them to be sure they were in the same carriage as Madame Blanche.

They were never to see the Mayor again. Before Bapaume was liberated he was arrested and sent to hard labour in Silesia, where, through torture and exposure, he died in the winter of 1944. His memory lives in a memorial in Bapaume's market square, as the man who did more to keep the spirit of France alive during the Occupation than anyone else in that part of the country.

When they got to Paris they found the man whom they were supposed to meet in church awaiting them on the platform. Madame Blanche entrusted them to him at once and he led them by a devious route to the Church of St Vincent de Paul. Here, in the sacristy, 'a very attractive blonde' took charge of them and they were given two tickets for the Métro. At ten-yard intervals they followed the young woman for half an hour until they came to a Métro station. The time was about 6 pm, the rush hour, and the place was so crowded that keeping her in view was not easy. When their train came, all three had to force their way into the same compartment.

At the end of their underground journey their guide led them to an apartment block and up to its fifth floor into 'a very modern furnished apartment'. Shaking hands, she uttered her first words to them, in impeccable English, 'How are you?' and identified herself as Madame Charmaine. It transpired that she had been educated in England. They were the first airmen to be harboured by the occupier of the flat, Madame Hochepied.

Madame Charmaine's fate was as tragic as those of 'Lieutenant X' and the Mayor of Bapaume. She was indiscreet enough to keep a diary. When the Gestapo arrested her two months after she had helped Fairfax and Macleod they learned from it the names and addresses of many Resistance members. All were arrested, tortured and either sent to concentration camps or executed. She herself died in Buchenwald.

Madame Hochepied had a married son, Robert, who had been in the Army at the time of France's surrender in June, 1940. He had escaped from a prison camp, was living under an assumed name in another arrondissement of Paris, and working as a chef in a large café. He and his wife visited his mother often, bringing food. With what seems, in hindsight, crass foolhardiness rather than an admirable gesture of confidence and disdain for the enemy, these three took the two evaders to a cinema one evening. The seats were in pairs, in separate small boxes, and Rod Macleod found himself sharing one with a German soldier, 'a fact which distracted from the enjoyment somewhat. I was scared that he might ask me for a light or start a conversation on the merits of the pictures we saw. However, he never spoke.'

One evening the married couple gave a luncheon at home in their honour at which there were fourteen guests. It began at 3 pm and ended four hours later. 'Food and drink were in abundance. They had managed to get a goose on the black market. After the last course the entertainment began with several songs in which everyone joined, and several solos by one of the girls. It was a very fine evening. We had learned the secret why Frenchmen never seem to get intoxicated because no matter how much they consume they keep eating all the time they are drinking.'

During the week they spent with Madame Hochepied, the man – a Belgian count – who had met them at the railway station came to see them, and Charmaine visited twice, to play cards and give them the opportunity to converse in English.

On Monday, 11 October, 1943, they left the flat at 6 pm to catch a train for the south. Charmaine took them to a park, where, on a bench, they met 'a small, dark Belgian girl who later became a Sabena stewardess'. While they were all sitting there, both girls suddenly threw their arms about the men and began an extravagant display of affection. They had spotted a known Gestapo agent approaching, but he passed by without pausing. This passionate public embracing was a frequently used subterfuge. It reminded the two friends of a lecture by a returned evader that they had attended, which he entitled 'He Kissed His Way To Freedom'.

Charmaine left them to the Belgian girl, who took them to a café for a meal. On emerging at nine o'clock they saw 'two fellows on the far sidewalk who looked anything but French, as we probably did ourselves'. Next day they met them: Sergeant John Buice, an engineer on Flying Fortresses, who had been shot down over Paris on Bastille Day, and Sergeant Peter Smith, a Lancaster navigator, shot down in Belgium in the first week of August.

Recounting the event ten years later, Rod said: 'With our guide, Norman and I found seats in an empty carriage to Bordeaux. We now felt relieved for some reason. We carried a collection of the latest magazines, mainly of the German-sponsored type. One in particular, called *Signal*, was always a help with Gestapo in any interview. We arrived in Bordeaux, half asleep, at 7 am and were passed over to a man without a single word being spoken or even an opportunity for us to thank our charming little brunette guide. Norman has met this girl on several occasions as they are both employed in civilian flying. I have no doubt that he has amply thanked her.'

They were now in the very capable hands of Monsieur François, known as Franco. With him, they boarded a train for Dax and took seats opposite Sergeants John Buice and Peter Smith, whom Franco's wife was shepherding.

On arrival at Dax, at 9.30 am, six bicycles were waiting for them in the station baggage store. Norman was dismayed. 'I never had a bike when I was a kid. My parents died when I was quite young and my early education was spent in an orphanage – no bikes there. To tell the truth, I had been on a bike once when on holiday – got on, wobbled a bit and then fell off.'

As Macleod says, 'This possibility had not even been considered, as it was taken for granted in France that you could ride a bicycle as soon as you could walk. However, he made a wonderful job and with a little holding up he soon became an accomplished cyclist, eventually riding fifty kilometres a day.'

Norman's account of his experience on the ride from Dax to Bayonne is modestly dismissive of what was a bruisingly torturous journey. 'I got on the bike and managed to get going after a few wobbles, but in order to stop I just fell off; the brakes on the bike I was given were not at all satisfactory. So that was quite a trip and quite an experience for me. Naturally I was generally the last in the group and must have been a bit of a headache for Franco.'

The ride was not entirely purgatorial. It was still pleasantly warm in this part of the country. Ten kilometres along the road the party turned down a lane to a field, where two girls in gaily coloured summer dresses joined them with baskets of sandwiches, fruit, beer and wine. One of these spoke English and told them that she had won the Ladies' Open golf tournament in Germany in 1939 and been presented with the prize, an engraved silver swastika, by Hitler. She was a Fleming, but had come to the south-west to work with the Resistance. She always carried this swastika with her, a talisman that extricated her from many potentially lethal situations when she produced it to dumbfound the Gestapo.

All eight of them resumed the ride, in mixed pairs. 'To all intents and purposes just a happy cycling party out enjoying this beautiful morning air in the foothills of the Pyrenees. What a ride. One has to make this journey from Dax to Bayonne on a bicycle to realize the distance and seemingly endless hills to climb, to realize it is anything but a pleasure. I had the greatest admiration for Norman. How he stuck it out all day up and down those hills I will never know. I who consider myself an experienced cyclist was very glad when the ride was over.'

Rod adds that he 'was just about all in' when, at ten that night, they stopped at the Café Pierre. He did not know exactly where this was, except that it stood a considerable distance beyond Bayonne along the highway to the frontier. The meal they now ate consisted of very small birds, which he was convinced were sparrows, bread, grapes and wine. They were to rest there for twenty-four hours. Franco, before leaving with the rest of the escorts, emphasized that they must make no noise. The café, which was normally occupied only by the husband and wife who owned it, would be frequented throughout the day. It was a matter of life and death for this couple that none of their customers should have a hint of what secretly went on there.

They slept and rested until 5 pm next day, when a meal was brought to their bedroom. Three hours later Franco and the three girls reappeared to accompany them on the last stage to the Spanish frontier. They signed the book at the café that recorded all the escapers who had passed through. Their four names made the total up to two hundred, an impressive tribute to the discretion of its owners and the guides who frequented it. Indeed 'quite a dangerous hobby for a respectable innkeeper', as Rod MacLeod puts it.

They set off shortly before dusk, again in pairs. After pedalling ten miles or so they left the main road for a lane at the base of a mountain. They rode along it for a hundred yards until they came to 'two tough-looking characters lurking in the shadow of a tree. These were our new guides, members of the Basque Maquis and this was the meeting place.'

The ten of them sat down in a field overlooking Biarritz to eat. As there was no immediate danger, 'This handover was quite different from all others, and it gave us an opportunity to thank these people for what they were doing and to say farewell in the appropriate manner.'

Their last meal in France consumed and the evidence destroyed, Franco paid the new guides and the two parties separated with the customary toast '*à l'Invasion*'.

The airmen were in the care now of professional smugglers who had been going to and fro between France and Spain for generations. They were entering on the most dangerous part of the whole odyssey. The smugglers all had a price on their heads. Capture meant death. If intercepted by a German patrol they would shoot it out. Describing events a decade later, Rod said, 'This being explained to us at the time of being placed in their hands sounds very thrilling ten years afterwards, but at the time it did not sound very healthy to us.'

This was also the most gruelling section of their long journey. Since the first few days of walking, they had taken little exercise and were scarcely fit for so severe a test of endurance. Thirst also plagued them. One of Norman's memories is of 'getting a terrific thirst and what pure pleasure it was drinking out of a mountain stream. Our guide of course had his leather bottles of wine; he shared them among us and that went down well too. So climbing, climbing and more climbing, being egged on by our guide, was a bit exhausting and I remember Rod Macleod suffered more because of his footwear and, of course, he was a big fellow. I was lucky in that I had been given a pair of shoes which were quite comfortable and really wore well, whereas Rod's were a tight fit and so this climbing was more difficult for him.'

Five hours' climbing earned them a respite. They stopped to admire Biarritz, beautiful in the moonlight. On then to close the gap that remained between them and the frontier. The area was patrolled by troops with police dogs. Near the frontier, one of the guards scouting in advance of the group thought he saw a patrol. 'Excitement and fear ran high for a few minutes in case we had been seen and a gun battle was imminent.' It was a false alarm and after half an hour they moved on, frequently on hands and knees to avoid being silhouetted against the skyline.

'By 2 am we were across and actually stood in Spain, a free country, or at least a neutral country. Or was it a neutral country? We were soon to find out.'

Under the Fascist dictatorship of General Franco, who had welcomed German and Italian Air Force squadrons and Army brigades to fight on his side against the Communists during the Civil War of 1936-1939, the British had little sympathy to expect, despite Spain's official neutrality. Early in the Second World War it had been touch and go whether Spain came in as an ally of Hitler and Mussolini.

From now on they would at least be able to communicate easily with the natives, through Norman Fairfax's fluent command of the language.

At a farmhouse a few hundred yards inside the border they fed and spent the rest of the night on some hay in a cowshed. Around ten o'clock, after breakfasting on a potato cake and a glass of wine, the four airmen continued alone, following a track which, they were told, led to a main road.

They did not know it until long after, but from the moment of their arrival in Paris they had been passed down one of the three main escape routes, the Comet Line, which operated all the way from Brussels.

They reached the road at 12.25 pm on 14 October, 72 kms north of Pamplona and 10 kms south of the Franco/Spanish frontier. There was a sentry on duty where the trail joined the road, 'but he seemed more concerned in carving his name into a tree than in questioning anyone passing by', and did not hinder them. Soon after, they passed a working party of about a hundred Spanish troops who were breaking off for lunch. These also ignored the four foreigners, whose feet were beginning to feel sore and forced them to rest from time to time and bathe them in a roadside stream.

The first town they came to was Elizondo, where they could see several of the Guardia Civil in the streets. These were evidently expecting intruders; ten of them approached and beckoned the new arrivals to follow them. They were under arrest and at 4.25 pm were in jail. 'All four of us in one small stinking room 12ft by 12ft, which contained a washbasin, a toilet and some terribly smelly blankets. That night we all curled up on the floor in our clothes as we were. The only food we got was a plate of beans and one potato. Next morning we left for Pamplona on the upper deck of a bus.'

At their destination they were interrogated, photographed, fingerprinted, given temporary identity cards and told to give the Franco salute.

That afternoon a police wagon took them to the village of Lecumberri, high in the mountains of Navarra, where they were put in a requisitioned hotel, the Ayestaran, which served as a transit camp. It was used to accommodate refugees, of whom at this time there were about thirty, mostly French. They slept in a room with four single beds 'and though only two meals a day were served, they were very good'.

During the first week there the Uruguyan Consul came to visit and Norman managed to have a talk with him. The Consul's wife took the names and numbers of the three R.A.F. men and promised to notify the British Consul. Sergeant Buice received 300 pesetas by wire from the American Consul and each got 35 pesetas a week allowance from the Spanish authorities. From some charitable fund they also received 100 pesetas.

One night Norman bribed a guard to let him out so that he could go to a telephone booth. He got through to the Air Attaché at the British Embassy in Madrid, who assured him that he and the other two would soon be fetched.

Rod wrote a letter to his wife and gave it to a French representative of the International Red Cross, who was visiting the camp, and who assured him that it would be given priority in their mail system, which operated through Portugal. It was delivered two months later. During their first week, another hundred or so internees arrived, mostly French, Belgian and Dutch.

It was a period of intense boredom. They were confined to the grounds, watched by armed Guardias Civiles, from whom small luxuries such as butter and bread could be bought at exorbitant prices. Their time was spent sleeping and playing cards or table tennis. Sunday brought some alleviation; all were allowed into the village, under armed escort. They bought soft drinks, biscuits and bananas, the last a rarity in wartime Britain. That evening Rod and his two British friends were told that they would be leaving at once and were hurried to the railway station. The train left at 9.50 pm and arrived in Pamplona at 11.15. They spent the night in 'a filthy boarding house', from which the British Consul received a substantial bill.

In the morning guards took them to the station, where they met a Spitfire pilot and an Australian from a Mustang squadron, both of whom had spent six weeks in Spain, ten days in prison and the rest in the fleabag boarding house. A Spanish Air Force officer took over the duty of guarding them all on the train to Saragossa. He was an agreeable companion, 'a good fellow and very much an air force type', who had lost an eye and had burn scars on his hands, legacy of the Civil War. Those in the flying Service of any country have a natural affinity; the R.A.F. and Luftwaffe always treated each others' prisoners with courtesy and as much cordiality as protocol and patriotism permitted. This Spanish pilot took them to his Air Force Headquarters, where they were given drinks and friendly treatment. The British Consul stood them dinner before they went on by road to Alhama, where the hotel in which they stayed was a staging post for British and American air crew. They found four of the R.A.F. and one American already there.

Thence to Madrid, where three more of the R.A.F. joined them and they were given some second-hand civilian clothes at the British Embassy. Flying Officer Macleod did well; he was lent an overcoat belonging to the Ambassador, Sir Samuel Hoare. Their party of twelve moved on by lorry to a night stop in Seville, where they picked up one more British evader, before carrying on to Gibraltar.

After the rigours and fears, the moments of imminent discovery and the bouts of inner solitude and doubt, during the twelve hundred miles they had travelled, the final stage on their road to British territory was accomplished in a mood of jubilation and conviviality tinged with a touch of farce. They stopped at Jerez to be entertained by the Manager, and his three daughters, of the English sherry vintners, Williams and Humbert. The guided tour around the premises entailed a liberal amount of tasting. By the time the Embassy official in charge of the party seated them in a restaurant for a very belated lunch, some of the liberated visitors were feeling a trifle bemused.

Macleod recalled that, 'Some character came into the restaurant peddling something and his equipment gave me the impression that he was a shoe-shine boy. A shoe-shine was just what I wanted. My shoes had not shone for many weeks, so I gave them to him. When he returned them I found that he had soled and heeled them. This was the last thing I wanted, as I had no money to pay, for one thing.' However, a whip-round yielded the requisite five pesetas.

At 8 pm on 29 October, 1943, exactly seven weeks and a couple of hours from the time they had taken off from Hartford Bridge, they entered Gibraltar.

René Guittard had arranged for the BBC to transmit a coded message, 'if and when we arrived in the U.K.' This, *'Bonjour à la fleur'*, was duly broadcast and received.

When Macleod and Fairfax got home they found that Jim Allison had beaten them by a week, while Skeets Kelly had been caught and spent the rest of the war in a prison camp. After three days together and some bad frights, they had decided to split up. Rod was emphatic that travelling as a pair was the best way. It helped to keep morale up, and loneliness and boredom at bay, every situation was judged by two minds and every possible action was discussed before being decided on.

The crew returned to operations and completed a second tour together. That was followed, for Jim Allison and Rod Macleod, by a posting to a communications squadron, and for Norman Fairfax appointment as Operations Officer on a Typhoon wing. The Armistice found all of them stationed in Germany.

The Gerrault and Guittard families survived the war unscathed. Madame Payen and family also lived through it, but Léone was arrested in September and kept in prison for six weeks, during which she was raped many times by German soldiers. Madame Hochepied was arrested, her property confiscated and, her health ruined, she was reduced to destitution. Madame Blanche came through untouched by the enemy.

CHAPTER EIGHT

SERGEANT STANLEY MUNNS

EVERYONE KNEW WHAT 'flak' meant by now, from newspapers, cinema newsreels and the wireless. After nearly four years of war, it was accepted as the word for German anti-aircraft fire. Actually, flak was short for *Fliegerabwehrkanone*, anti-aircraft guns. But the Bomber Command aircrews who operated by night didn't see the guns, they saw, heard and all too often felt, the shells. That was what the ugly word signified for them.

The flight sergeant who was addressing the newly qualified batch of air gunners had memories of long, cramped hours in his draughty, cold gun turret. Watching the stuff burst all round him in sizzling crimson flashes, his predominant thought, like the rest of the crew's, was: Which one will have *our* name on it? When fragments of shell casing hit the aircraft they made a sound like a blacksmith's hammer on the anvil. (*Not* shrapnel, as it is generally and incorrectly called. Shrapnel shells were filled with steel bullets that scattered when an explosive charge inside the shell detonated.) Through the holes and gashes that the lumps and slivers of hot steel tore in the fuselage, the wind soughed and keened and whistled.

Then there were the night fighters, Messerschmitt 110s and Junkers 88s, creeping up on you to let fly with their machine guns and 20mm cannon. Among their considerable armament was a pleasantry that Jerry, with his ponderous humour, called Schräger Musik, sloping music, consisting of two 20mm cannon firing forward and upwards. The tune these played was lethal. Guided by airborne radar, the pilot could slide unseen beneath a bomber's belly from astern and fire a fatal burst into its entrails.

The flight sergeant did not mention the night fighters, but they were as much in his thoughts as flak when he warned his newly fledged comrades that the easy part of being an air gunner was over and the reality of the job for which they had volunteered lay immediately ahead. Firing at a drogue towed behind a slow aircraft flying straight and level in daylight had been fun – competitive fun, to see who on the course could score the most hits. Being shot at by anti-aircraft guns and hostile air gunners was going to be no fun at all. There was not even the certainty that they would have a chance to fire their guns in anger. Machine guns could not retaliate against flak from a height of several thousand feet. And fighters attacking in the dark were usually there and gone before a bomber's gunners saw them.

Did Stanley Munns receive by telepathy any of these thoughts and mental pictures from the seasoned air gunner? He doesn't say. But he does tell us that during operational training he was rear gunner in a twin-engined Whitley, which carried a crew of five. His pilot, Flight Sergeant 'Shep' Shepherd, was a Canadian, as were the bomb aimer, Sergeant 'Mac' Macgillivray and the navigator, Flying Officer Gus Knight. The wireless operator/air gunner was Welsh, Sergeant 'Stevie' Stevens. They now went on to flying the four-engined Halifax and acquired two more aboard: Sergeants Mick Michie, the upper turret gunner, another Canadian, and a Londoner, Sergeant Johnny Walker, the flight engineer.

In the summer of 1943, after three weeks experience on the 'Halibag', they were posted to a Royal Canadian Air Force squadron, No 428, based at Middleton St George, near Darlington, Yorkshire; which is now Teesside Airport.

All aircrew in Bomber Command had to do a tour of thirty operations before being sent on rest. If, for some reason such as illness or injury, a man could not complete a tour with the same crew, he did so with another, or others. After his rest of six months or so he flew a second tour, originally another thirty operations, later reduced to twenty. In November, 1942, a few months before young Sergeant Munns' crew flew their first trip over Germany, Air Ministry had calculated that the percentage chance of surviving a first tour on heavy or medium bombers was 44 per cent. The chances of surviving two tours were 19½. It should have heartened heavy and medium bomber crews, if they had known the statistics, that the chances of surviving one tour on light bombers were 25½ per cent and on torpedo bombers 17½ per cent. On a second tour these fell to 6½ and 3 per cent respectively. The generally accepted figure for the whole war is that 33 per cent of Bomber Command's crews lived through 30 trips. But as 1943 wore on, losses were mounting and reached their worst during the period November, 1943, to March, 1944, when Berlin was the main target. January, 1944, was Bomber Command's darkest of the whole war: 314 aircraft, of which 136 were believed shot down by fighters, were missing. This meant between 2,000 and 2,500 men were killed, wounded or taken prisoner.

Even taking these grim figures into account, the two squadrons at Middleton St George had been suffering an inordinately rough time. Stanley Munns' crew were told that the total of crews on both squadrons who had completed a tour was six, and altogether sixty crews had been lost. The effect on newcomers' morale cannot have been exhilarating.

Stanley records that Johnny Walker, convinced that their crew would be shot down in flames, had the morbid habit of harping on 'flamers'.

The captain (pilot) of a new crew had to fly on two operations as supernumerary with an experienced crew before taking his own over enemy territory. This left the other members with time on their hands to listen to discouraging gossip. It could only have come as a relief to set off for their own first raid.

With his nineteenth birthday behind him and three ops in his log book, Stanley Munns knew what to expect when the crew made their fourth sortie over Germany: flak and searchlights were no novelty now. Lancaster squadrons, faster and with a higher ceiling than Halifaxes, were to attack Berlin, while the Halifaxes of the Canadian Group to which 428 Squadron belonged were on a diversionary raid to Mannheim, a long and tiring flight.

Next night the crew were on the Battle Order again. This time their target was Leverkusen. Two successive nights of several hours in the air with senses unremittingly on the alert seem to have proved excessively fatiguing for the pilot's or navigator's concentration. When their aircraft turned away from the target it was off course and separating from the main bomber stream. Its track took it over Aachen, which was strongly defended, and, on its own, it was easy prey for the flak gunners. Shells burst alongside the Halifax and shards of metal ripped into it.

The pilot's voice came over the intercom, telling his rear gunner that he had no control over the rudders and asking if they were still in place.

Stanley's ironical comment is, 'As I was sitting between the rudders, I was happy to say they were.'

They concluded that the control wires running the length of the fuselage must have been damaged.

'A bomber aircraft cannot be landed without rudder control, so we knew we would have to bale out sooner or later. As it happened, it turned out to be sooner.'

Shells hit the engines, which stopped. The hydraulic system was also damaged, which prevented feathering the propellers. These were windmilling and dragging the aeroplane down.

When the navigator estimated that they had crossed into Holland, Flight Sergeant Shepherd ordered his crew to bale out. To don his parachute, Stanley had to leave his turret and enter the fuselage, where it was stowed. The interior of the Halifax was dimly lit, but there was a bulkhead between him and the rest of the crew's positions. Having taken his chute from the rack, he had to clip it on in almost total darkness. Then he fumbled for the door latch.

'Panic seized me and I made no contact.'

The prospect of ending one's life at nineteen, or suffering severe burns or a crippling injury, at best being unscathed but taken prisoner, is just cause for momentary haste and mental confusion. He wondered if he had time to return to the turret, turn it round and drop backwards through its open doors. He decided to try the bulkhead door again and felt for it with his forearm, while he counted the passing seconds and wondered how many were left before the aeroplane crashed.

He found the latch, opened the door and saw that the fuselage hatch was open. There was no sign of any other member of the crew.

He checked his parachute; the wires around it were caught in the harness clips with the parachute-holding lugs. Would this cause the parachute to malfunction? It was too late to release the wires. He slid through the escape hatch.

'As soon as I felt myself falling through space I pulled the ripcord, a stupid thing to do, as the chute could have caught on the tailplane. However, it soon pulled me up with a jerk and I was floating down in pitch darkness.'

Getting out while the Halifax was still high enough to allow the parachute to open fully was fine, but where would he land? On a roof or high tree that would break a bone? On a high voltage cable? On a telephone wire that could entangle and choke him to death?

'A few more seconds and I landed flat on my back in a dry dyke, probably the only dry dyke in Holland. Because it was a dark night and I could not see the ground coming up towards me, I had made a perfect landing.'

The word 'dyke' could be confusing in this context. It means both a mound or dam to prevent low-lying land from being flooded, and a ditch. Stanley Munns uses it in the latter sense.

He unclipped his parachute and its harness and left them in the dyke. As he climbed the bank he heard aircraft in the distance, going home. 'I swore at them in the frustration of being stranded on a dark and cold evening in a German-occupied country. However, the optimism of youth prevailed and I thought the thing to do was to walk to the Spanish frontier. So I set off across the fields in a north-westerly direction, away from the Dutch/German border and heading for Belgium.'

He had to cross a ditch full of water, jumped and slipped back deeply enough to saturate his legs below the knee, chilling them and his feet. As he walked on, mud accumulated on his flying boots, which are uncomfortable to walk long distances in at any time. 'As I approached a barbed wire fence, my legs felt as though they had weights attached to them, so I just rolled over it. Fortunately I was still wearing my flying suit and life jacket, so although the wire tore my clothing I did not hurt myself.'

A haystack loomed out of the gloom. He sat down to rest on some loose straw, leaning against the rick. But the weather was so cold that despite his fleece-lined clothes he was shivering. Unable to sleep, he moved on. He had

had enough of plodding across fields, so took to a road, walking briskly. When two cyclists came towards him he jumped into a ditch. The light on his life jacket, there to guide rescuers or fellow crew members when airmen ditched or parachuted into the sea, came on, glowing orange. The men were engrossed in conversation and did not see it.

Further down the road, while he was resting beside a small river, a cyclist spotted him and dismounted. 'I sat still, hoping he would think I was a sheep or a bush. I discovered many years later they do not seem to have sheep in Holland. However, he remounted and rode away.'

His initial purpose was to keep going, putting as much distance as possible between him and the crashed aircraft and other survivors. He was sure that German troops must already be searching for him. His parachute harness with his name and number on it lay near where he had come down. He had abandoned his life jacket in a ditch. The fields he had traversed bore his footprints; he had left quite a trail. Making contact with someone who might help him would have to wait.

Late that evening he found an open barn, a roof supported on four legs, packed with hay. He climbed onto it and made himself an adequate shelter among the bales. Fairly comfortable and protected from the cold, he slept well until wakened early in the morning by voices in the farmyard. He decided to wait until darkness fell before resuming his trek. With some difficulty he broke the plastic seal of his escape kit for some Horlicks tablets. It also contained maps, a compass, Dutch, Belgian and French currency.

As soon as it was dark he set off once more. A few miles tramping brought him to a road junction where a signpost told him he was entering the village of Nuenen. An isolated house tempted him to try his luck. At his knock the door was partly opened and a man peered out at him.

'R.A.F.,' Stanley said. The Dutchman looked blank, so he repeated it.

The door was being closed, but suddenly it opened again. The man said, 'R.A.F.,' beckoned him in and led him to a dimly lit room, where he left him while he went to bring some bread and butter. As soon as Stanley had eaten, the clearly very frightened householder indicated that he must leave at once.

He had not gone far when he heard a vehicle behind him. Before the headlight beams lit him he took to a ditch again. Bad luck for him, it was full of water. He had no option but to stand there soaked up to his knees until the car, almost certainly a German Army one, had passed.

Clambering out of the ditch, it was borne in on him that, in wintry conditions, his plan of walking to Spain was impracticable. He must find help. A nearby farmhouse was the obvious place.

When he knocked on the door this time, a woman appeared.

He said, 'R.A.F.'

She understood at once, showed no fear, and said in pidgin Dutch, '*U et en drink,*' Her meaning, 'You eat and drink,' was plain. Many Dutch words resemble German, but many also resemble English: '*et*' is pronounced like the English word 'ate', and '*drink*' is exactly as in English. She took him into the living room, where her husband was sitting, seated him at the table and brought him ham and a glass of milk.

From pictures Stanley had seen of the Dutch countryside, he inferred that he must be in Holland, so he tried to open the conversation by asking the man if he was Dutch. This was mistaken for '*Deutsch*', a familiar word in an occupied country, although the Dutch for 'German' is '*Duits*', pronounced '*Daowts*'. This, the man asserted that he was not, but the conversation languished as he knew no English.

The woman indicated to Stanley that he should sit on the couch, so he took off his wet boots, lay down and fell asleep. He does not know how long he slept, but he does remember his relief when the stranger who roused him identified himself in English as a former Dutch Army officer and asked if he wanted to return to England.

'Yes.'

'It is possible, but I do not know how it can be done. Perhaps by submarine.'

Sergeant Munns had decided at the outset that he must avoid capture at all costs. The notion of existence in a prison camp appalled him. He told the ex-officer that he was willing to try any means of getting back to England.

'There are small children in the house,' this new helper explained. 'The farmer and his wife are frightened that they might talk about you if you stay here. I am going to take you on my bicycle to another farm, where you will spend the night.'

So Stanley perched on the carrier while the ex-officer pedalled down a narrow lane to his next overnight shelter. He shared the farmer's bed, while the lady of the house made shift for herself in another room. Early in the morning he woke to the unsettling sight of his temporary bedfellow crouching beneath the window with a knife in his hand. There were Germans about, the farmer explained with words and gestures. Stanley hoped that if the enemy entered the place his host would not show fight; he didn't feel that a knife was much of a match for firearms. But the Germans moved on.

That afternoon two men belonging to the Resistance organization turned up. They rode bicycles, the standard form of transportation in that flat country, in peace as well as war. They had brought him a cycle, civilian clothes that included a raincoat, and a razor. He gathered that the farmer would destroy his uniform. He accompanied the two Resistance men to the outskirts of Eindhoven, with only one anxious moment – when he automatically crossed to the left of the road when they turned a corner.

At the house to which he had been brought he met a third Resistance helper, who spoke good English and asked, 'When will the Allies land in Holland? We want to join in the fight.'

'I don't think an invasion can take place before summer. And when it does, it will be in France': a reply at which the Dutchman showed disappointment.

The same man now asked him not to give anyone away if the Germans caught him. 'I replied with bravado that they would have to shoot me before I would talk, and he replied, "I believe the word of an Englishman", which made me feel very humble and wish that I had not made such a boastful remark.' It was sincerity of intention, not boasting. Anyway, the euphoria when suddenly befriended amidst a host of enemies would have prompted a bold, if perhaps incautious, promise from any nineteen-year-old, and from most men a great deal older.

His next encounter with an English-speaking member of the Resistance was less polite. At about eight o'clock that evening, after he had eaten, a stranger came into the room and asked him bluntly if he really were English. 'Because if we find out you are not, we will shoot you. Do you understand?' To emphasize that he was ready to do so on the spot, if necessary, he drew an automatic pistol from his overcoat pocket. Sergeant Munns assured him of his genuineness. What else could his questioner have expected?

Instructions followed. 'When the clock on the wall says eight o'clock, I want you to walk out of the front door, turn left and walk down the road, and take the first turning on the right and go to the church.' The Dutchman then left.

'I guessed this was a test to see if I would run away,' says Stanley, 'but as I had no reason to run, I followed the instructions.' He would have been shot in the back if he hadn't. 'It was dark and the only thing bothering me was that I was sure I was being followed. As I approached the church I thought I might be leading a German agent to someone in the Resistance organization, so I walked past the church. As I did so, a priest came rushing out to me and said, "Did you not see the church?" I told him of my fears and he said I was only being followed to make sure I did not get lost.

'Inside the church I was given a railway ticket and informed I was to be taken for a short journey. I was introduced to my guide, who said he would do all the talking necessary and I was only to show my tickets at the barrier.

'We entered an empty compartment on the train and sat down. Almost immediately two German soldiers came in and sat down opposite. Although it was a short journey I was apprehensive all the way.' 'Apprehensive' is surely a mild understatement. 'What if the soldiers spoke to me? What if they asked for identification?'

The Germans made no overtures, hostile or friendly. At the small town that was their destination his guide took him to a house owned by a headmaster, where he stayed several days. 'The only thing of note during these days in the house was a kind of relay system that broadcast the evening news in English, I like to think it was for the escaping airmen, but more likely it was being sent to Britain as propaganda.'

Another train journey with a young girl as guide took him to Weert, 15 miles south-east of Eindhoven and within five miles of the Belgian frontier. She seemed to have no fear, for she talked to him in English throughout the journey, regardless of being overheard. He went with her to a small house where he met a New Zealand airman named Nicholas Matich and an American, Robert Sheeham.

As soon as they were left on their own, Sheeham suggested that if they were approached aggressively by one German on his own, they would put up a fight. But if there were more than one, they would give themselves up. The others agreed. Some minutes later a man wearing a long, dark overcoat and peaked cap stalked into the room. Sergeant Munns looked at his two companions. Should they launch a concerted attack at once? It was just as well they did not; another man similarly dressed was on the first frightener's heels. It looked as though capture were inevitable. But the sinister-looking intruders were Dutch policemen who were to conduct them to the Belgian frontier.

First there had to be a test of the airmen's authenticity. One of the policemen told them he played in a dance band and asked if they could recite the words of 'Stardust', a popular foxtrot in both Britain and the U.S.A. They duly did so and were soon mounted on bicycles, accompanying their shepherds, in the guise of being under arrest, to the border.

They stopped at a small village where they spent the night, Stanley Munns with a family in a 'gipsy-type caravan'. In the morning, 'I was with the man from the caravan when a neighbour said good morning to me in Flemish,' '*Goed morgen*' is Dutch, but the same in the Flemish dialect, so the man who greeted him could have been either Dutch or Belgian. Stanley replied in English. 'He did not seem very surprised and the caravan man just smiled.'

When the three evaders had been brought together the Dutch policeman walked with them into Belgium, where two Belgian policemen took over the duty of escorting them. These led them to a large detached house owned by a wine merchant.

Again, their authenticity was put to the proof. 'That evening we were plied with strong brandy until we were inebriated. We were then surprised to be given pencil and paper and asked to answer a number of questions, mainly associated with the R.A.F. If the other two airmen did not know the answers, I was so high on the brandy that I shouted the answers like someone these days on a television quiz show.'

They stopped next at Neerpelt, where the New Zealander and Stanley stayed with the cobbler. Sheeham was taken elsewhere and they did not see him again. Two days later, Stanley and Matich left separately. The former was escorted to Antwerp by a short, dark-haired man. He found out after the war that he was on a new escape route, the previous one having been discovered by the Germans. At Antwerp he was taken to a café, *De Zwaan* (The Swan, of course), where the proprietor's wife was English. A night stop there. On to Brussels in the morning with a new guide. They had to stand in the corridor. There was a momentary embarrassment when the ticket inspector spoke to Stanley, who looked to his guide to reply. 'But he didn't say a word. Apparently the inspector was only saying that I would lose my ticket if I placed it loose in my raincoat pocket.'

At the main Brussels railway station, the Gare du Nord, a young girl met them and guided Stanley to a flat where the door was opened by another girl. Her friendly but unexpected greeting, 'Hello, you fucking bastard,' was accompanied by roars of laughter in the background. American airmen were already installed in the flat. With a warped form of humour commonly displayed by mindless oafs, they had been teaching her obscenities. Schiller's *'Mit der Dummheit kämpfen Götter selbst vergebens,'* (with stupidity the gods themselves struggle in vain), expresses fitting contempt for such clods and their mischievous practices.

Fortunately for him, Stanley did not stay long in this uncongenial company. He was taken, on the same day, to a house where he would spend a few days. The occupants were an elderly lady and her two sons, one of whom had been tortured by the Gestapo. The experience had left him mentally disturbed, morose and taciturn. His brother, a Civil Servant, was active in the Comet Line, and Sergeant Munns was the two hundred and forty-third allied air crew to be handled by this organization.

'Whilst I was staying in this house I managed to get my first bath since baling out, although I had only a few inches of luke-warm water as the gas pressure was very low. After a few days a man came to see me and said he would be taking me to the railway station the next day. In the meantime I was to get my identity tags, which were tied around my neck, sewn inside my trousers. As I did not see any point in this, I did not bother. But the next day on public transport with this man he asked me if I had done as he said. As I replied "No", he then took a penknife from his pocket and cut the string holding the tags around my neck. He put the tags in his coat pocket. I thought he would give them back to me at a later date, but after seeing me to the station and meeting another guide, I never saw him again and therefore lost my only means of identity.'

The fresh guide had two Americans with him. 'One was a huge man standing some six feet three inches tall and weighing about sixteen stone.'

When they boarded the train the guide told them to get off when he did. 'I felt rather apprehensive over the loss of my identity tags and I wondered if I was caught, could I be shot for a spy being in civilian clothes and no means of identity.' Consuming fear rather than some apprehension would have been most people's preoccupation in the circumstances. And the answer to his unspoken question was 'Yes'. But young Sergeant Stanley Munns was a cool customer and well endowed with guts, as we shall soon see.

Their destination was a small country town near the French frontier. They followed their guide to a farmhouse. He told them to wait in the doorway of a shed while he knocked on the house door. The door opened and a girl was silhouetted against the lamplight from indoors.

'Immediately the big American towered over me and said, "I am first" '.

Stanley was not enjoying the company of the Americans whose society was forced upon him.

The farmer had three daughters. No sooner had the household and guests sat down to a meal than the offensive American started talking to the farmer in French. As the solitary Englishman in the company could not understand what was being said, he told the American to stop the conversation, an injunction that was ignored.

Suddenly the farmer looked at Stanley Munns and astonished him by the phrase, 'No short arm'. The vulgar Service abbreviation for the male member shocked him by its unexpectedness and incongruity in these surroundings. In the R.A.F. a free-from-infection inspection by a medical officer (FFI) is commonly called a 'short arm inspection'. In the present context, the R.A.F. man was at a loss to find any sense in the term. Then it struck him that the loutish Yank must have told the farmer that he had made some remark about having sexual relations with one of the girls.

'I was furious and picked up a sharp dinner knife and thrust it into the American's face. But he just laughed and must have thought it was a great joke.' Another lout with a puerile notion of what was funny, and a bully with it, confident that by his sheer size and weight he could impose his offensive lack of manners on everyone.

Immediately after the meal the evaders left, crossed the frontier by rail and were put in the care of separate guides for the onward journey to Paris.

The Gare du Nord in Paris was packed with enemy troops. For Munns it was a deeply agitating first encounter with the enemy at close quarters; to find himself suddenly amid such numbers of them was bewildering. Surely among this horde there would be someone whose perceptiveness was acute enough to penetrate his charade. Surely there must be a Military Policeman or Intelligence Officer who would recognize his uneasiness and arrest him. But self-doubt and fear turned to triumph when he had made his way through the press of his enemies unscathed. His woman guide took him by

Métro to a suburb, where he was placed in a flat with an old couple. Two Americans, Elton Kevil and Jackie Wiggins, had preceded him there and all three slept on the floor in a shared bedroom.

They woke next morning to Christmas Day. Members of the family turned up at the flat. Dinner began with oysters, a novelty to Stanley, and one he did not relish. When asked if he had enjoyed them, he said he had and his politeness was rewarded with a second helping − the last thing he wanted. 'The rest of the evening was enjoyable enough. After a few drinks the two Americans and myself sang songs in English at the top of our voices, which must have been heard for yards around, but we were not asked to stop.'

Shortly after Christmas they were photographed for false identity cards. When Stanley was given his, he found that his age was alleged to be twenty-six, an unconvincing deception, for he looked even younger than his true age. It was a necessary risk. Frenchmen under the age of twenty-six had distinctive identity cards that the Resistance organization could not obtain. What with this and the loss of his identity discs, he was not a happy air gunner when he set off next day on the Métro, with yet another lady guide, for the station where they would board a night train to Bordeaux. He had a further reminder of his vulnerability when striding along a Métro platform: the lady told him he must not walk like an Englishman, but take short steps like a Frenchman.

Elton Kevil, Jackie Wiggins and a third American were also on the train, each of the four airmen with his own guide and in a separate compartment. During the night Stanley thrust his way down the crowded corridor to the W.C. When he got there he met an embarrassment for which he was unprepared: the standing passengers were staring at him as he hesitated at the door. He did not know whether the sign above the lock indicated 'vacant' or 'occupied'. There seemed no option but to try the handle. Luckily, it was unoccupied.

From Bordeaux they continued by an early train to Bayonne, where his guide took away his raincoat to pass on to another evader waiting in Paris. 'I was now dressed in a light sports jacket and light trousers in the middle of winter and with a dodgy identity card in my pocket.' The Americans retained their overcoats, whether because they had not been asked to give them back, or had refused to do so, he did not know. But it didn't seem fair that he should be the only one without some extra garment at this cold season, with worse to come when they climbed the mountains.

At Bayonne a male guide took all of them in hand for the railway ride to Dax. Before showing them to their seats, in pairs, he warned them that German troops would search the train because it ran so close to the frontier. The guide isolating himself was confirmation of the danger with which this final stage of rail travel was fraught. Cannily, Stanley sat by an inner window through which he commanded a view of the corridor and would be able to see trouble coming. Elton Kevil, seated at a window at the other end of the compartment, had a view of nothing but the passing scenery.

There is a body language of eloquent stillness that can arouse suspicion even in a situation where it is restlessness that is most readily suspect. There is a casual ferocity about the demeanour of armed men in uniform, whatever the duty they are about. However self-possessed a fugitive may be, there are unconscious small movements and signs of tension that betray him to an astute pursuer. No matter how much self-control Stanley Munns exercised over his demeanour, he was in grave danger − perhaps, as he could not prove his real identity, in mortal danger. However careless or unobservant a hunter may be, to his prey who can only stay where he is and hope not to be detected, he is the embodiment of a death threat.

The sudden materialization of field-grey uniforms was made no less traumatic by being expected. 'The sight of German soldiers entering the corridor, then the first compartment, sent my heart thumping and as they came closer I began to wish I had not been able to see them, because I was sure that by the time they reached us they would be able to hear my heart jumping up and down.

'Eventually a soldier entered the compartment and, speaking French, asked for identity cards. The French passengers were the first to hand over their cards for inspection and the soldier seemed merely to scan them and hand them back. Elton Kevil passed over his card, the German glanced at him, looked at the card and looked back again at Elton, appeared suspicious and reluctantly handed the card back. He then took my card and to my horror he spoke to me in French. I did not understand what he said, but I thought he may be referring to my age, so I just sat there tight-lipped. He repeated what he had said before, more aggressively, I just looked blank at him. He realized he was not going to get an answer from me and with a look that said "I give up" handed back the card.'

It took unusual resolve not to flinch under such scrutiny and questioning. Louis Pasteur had acknowledged it long ago when he declared: '*Le hasard ne favorise que les esprits préparés.*' (Chance favours only the prepared mind.)

In the station yard at Dax the Englishman and three Americans were met by two men, one of whom told them, in English, to select bicycles from half a dozen that were propped against a wall. The weather was comparatively mild, for which Stanley was grateful in his thin clothes and without gloves; the two Basques and their protégés were faced with a long ride to the foothills of the Pyrenees. The guides rode in front. As the miles reeled by under his wheels, Stanley found himself tiring and dropping behind, until at last he could see only the back of one of the Americans, who was himself trailing behind the others.

While he was separated from the rest, his journey might have ended there and then with discovery and arrest. He was entering a small village when he saw a German turning circles in the middle of the road on a woman's cycle and chatting to its owner, who was standing at the roadside watching him. 'I panicked slightly, as I knew that if the soldier and I clashed I was finished, as I had no one to speak for me. But my luck held out and with two near scrapes I passed by.'

Stanley Munns was neglected for hours. 'I was now on my own and hoping the guides would not make a detour. Almost exhausted I eventually caught up with them outside a bungalow type of building where we were to have a meal and stay the night.'

Early the next day they began their long tramp, 'climbing ever higher and stopping only to rest for a little food and some wine from a goatskin bag'. He was acutely aware that one great danger still lay ahead: German soldiers patrolled the frontier on the French side and Spanish troops and Guardia Civil − armed police equivalent to the Gendarmerie and the Italian Carabinieri − on the Spanish side. Neither would hesitate to shoot on sight, before identifying their targets.

By nightfall they were following narrow tracks through the snow. Stanley had been walking quite well during the day and was leading the group when Jackie Wiggins collapsed. He went back to see what was happening. One of the Basque guides had been able to raise the American to a sitting position and was urging him to stand up. Seeing Stanley standing there, the Basque urged, 'Get up. Look how well your English friend is standing.' Wiggins wasted neither energy nor breath in his laconic reaction: 'Fuck him.' But he made the effort, perhaps out of national pride, and managed to haul himself upright with an arm about the guide's shoulders. Thus supported, he carried on.

Hours later they stopped beside a river which, for some distance, marked the frontier. One of the guides went alone to see if it were possible to cross by a bridge downstream. He reported that it was guarded by Spanish police, which left them no choice but to wade through water so cold that, if it were not running, would have frozen. It was a bitterly chill and clammy business. On climbing out at the far bank they stamped their feet in the snow to try to restore some warmth to their feet and legs and dry their trousers.

'At last I was in Spain, the Comet Line had done its job [He did not, of course, know this at the time.] and four more airmen had escaped from the occupied territories. But Spain at this time was no friendly haven, so our journey continued in secrecy and we were hidden in the hayloft above a stable. There was no glass in the windows and the bitter wind blew straight in as we settled down in the hay for the night, still uncomfortable in our wet clothes.'

There was a stone fireplace in a corner of the loft, but only hay to burn, no wood for a lasting fire. They had climbed a wooden ladder to the loft. One of the Americans, Thomas Applewhite, suggested that they remove every second rung and use them for firewood. This was what they did, then sat round the blaze trying to dry their clothes. The draughty loft was still cold when they stretched out to sleep, and Stanley was thankful to Applewhite for spreading his heavy overcoat over them both.

Their guides did not appear on the morrow. At midday a young man and a girl brought them food on tin plates — red beans, potatoes and mutton with sheep's wool still adhering to it, but greatly welcome. They spent the rest of that day discussing whether to venture to the closest town and seek help in getting in touch with the nearest British and American Consuls or the Embassies in Madrid. The decision was to wait until noon on the following day, and if no guide showed up, to press on without one.

An anxious morning passed before the two guides rejoined them. In sunshine they walked the lower slopes of the Pyrenees, slaking their thirst from clear mountain streams and resting from time to time in one of the small huts, built of woven branches, which are abundant in that region. In the fading last light they stopped at a farm where they were fed on corn cakes baked on the hearth and allowed to sleep on furry pelts in a chicken run.

On the next day they walked as far as a narrow road where a car awaited them. The driver gave them each a cigarette, but Stanley was so tired that 'I never finished mine. I fell asleep with the lighted cigarette still in my hand'. He woke to find they were in San Sebastian, where they were delivered to a British-owned hotel.

'We were made most welcome at the hotel and for the first time in weeks I was able to bathe in loads of hot water and to sit down to good meals. Eventually a car arrived from the British Embassy, complete with Union Jack flying from the mudguard, to take us to the Embassy in Madrid. With a Spanish chauffeur at the wheel, we set off on the long ride to the capital.'

One more hazard delayed their exit from San Sebastian. The car wheels were trapped in a tram line. The passengers could not get out to help the chauffeur to push the car free, because the vehicle was British territory; if they stepped out onto Spanish soil they could be arrested and interned. A crowd gathered around the inexplicable spectacle of four passengers apparently ignoring the strenuous efforts of their driver to release their vehicle. The occupants watched anxiously for a policeman to come on the scene, but with the help of a wooden plank for leverage and the weight and muscle of sundry onlookers, the wheels were lifted out of the jamb before the law hove in sight.

The drive of more than four hundred miles took them up and down the heights of northern Spain in falling snow, and across the plains where villagers sat outside their houses, gossiping in the sun. Not a German uniform in sight. The whirlpool of a global war had sucked the greater part of the world's population into its vortex. It was not easy to reconcile their feeling of remoteness from it with the knowledge of what they were returning to in the immediate future. The sense of unreality was all the sharper when, in the dark, they came to Madrid, brightly lit, its brilliance reflected in the sky, in contrast with blacked-out Britain and the enemy-occupied countries they had just left.

During his two days in the British Embassy Sergeant Munns learned that he was the youngest evader to pass through there. Years did not count in the life he had led for the months since he had joined the squadron. It was experience that mattered, and he was going back to the war feeling that he had become a veteran.

His conveyance on the last land stage of his journey was a British ambulance that took him and his companions to Seville. Here, on board a Norwegian ship, a party was being held to confuse the guard by the number of guests who were arriving and leaving. The airmen joined them. When the ship was searched before sailing, they were hidden in the bilges. Down the river to Cadiz, then the short run to Gibraltar, where the three Americans were accommodated in a hotel and Sergeant Munns was told to report to the R.A.F. camp.

Macgillivray, his crew's bomb aimer, had already arrived there. They were issued with new uniforms and flown home together. The two Canadian members of the crew who had evaded capture, Macgillivray and Michie, the upper turret gunner, who had returned to England before them, were repatriated; Stanely was posted back to operations with a new crew. More flak and night fighters, and promotion to flight sergeant, lay ahead.

When he returned to civilian life he joined a well-known British company and rose to be Office Manager.

Thirty-seven years after his escape he returned to Belgium for a reunion of aircrew escapers and evaders and those Belgians and Dutch who had helped them and were still alive. He met some of those to whom he owed his own liberty and he wishes their names to be recorded here for 'their outstanding bravery': Piet and Mary Kuyten, the second farmer and his wife in the village of Nuenen; Frans van Riel, one of the policemen on the Dutch frontier; Michou Ugeux, the young girl who met him at the railway station in Brussels, and Odile de Vasselot, his guide on the train to Paris.

CHAPTER NINE

FLIGHT LIEUTENANT W. E. M. EDDY

ANYONE WHO LEARNS to fly at the age of thirty-two and, four years later, is a squadron leader with the Distinguished Service Order and Distinguished Flying Cross must possess more gifts than the obvious quality of courage.

Virgil's '*Hos successus alit; possunt, quia posse videntur*' (These success encourages; they can because they think they can) accounts for Bill Eddy's achievements as much as did his natural bravery.

His own restrained and debonair account of evading capture, when shot down in German-occupied Belgium and making his way across enemy-infested France, reveals an engaging character – confident, gentle, kindly and humorous.

Much of his confidence was probably innate, but it was surely strengthened by youthful experience. Riding is an excellent inculcator of self-assurance, and he was already a keen horseman as a schoolboy. But it was an unusual and somewhat bizarre circumstance that must have developed all his latent audacity. When he was at Stowe, one of the masters was not only an accomplished trick rider, but also instructed young Bill Eddy in this esoteric branch of equestrianism. The boy acquired enough skill to perform with his mentor in public during his holidays to raise money for hospitals. The average public school beak regards horses as unpredictable beasts, dangerous at both ends and uncomfortable in the middle. To encounter one who could ride like a Cossack, a Spahi or a mounted acrobat in Bertram Mills' Circus at Olympia, was more than a trifle anomalous.

It was not, however, to horses that Bill turned for a career when his parents emigrated to Argentina and he joined them there on leaving school. His father, Sir Montague Eddy, who was Managing Director of the Southern Railway in England, retired to the Argentine, where he bought fruit farms. It was on these that Bill was employed.

Ronnie Sheward, a wartime pilot on Hurricanes, Spitfires and Typhoons, who was born in the Argentine and educated in England, knew him well. They met when Ronnie, having forgotten Spanish during his eight years in

England, went back to his native country and was sent to work on an estancia (farm) to re-learn it before beginning a career on the Stock Exchange. The manager was an Australian whose step-daughter 'Blackie' Bill was courting. The two young men were compatible and their friendship quickly grew.

For Ronnie Sheward, who enjoyed outdoor life, the prospect of being immured in an office had no appeal. 'Having done a couple of years on the estancia and had the time of my life, Bill easily talked me into fruit farming.' He then did some talking of his own, to his parents. The consequence was that they sent him to an experimental farm to learn fruit farming, after which he worked for Bill Eddy for a year. It was during this time that Bill's daughter, Jill — now the Countess of Radnor — to whom Ronnie Sheward is godfather, was born. Ronnie also learned trick riding, and when Bill and he formed a polo club they gave displays to earn money for it.

But Sir Montague Eddy sold his farms, Bill took a job on a big sheep estancia, and Ronnie made a second trip to England to join the R.A.F. Bill, who was a few years the elder, followed, although by then he was married and had three children. After being awarded his wings he was retained in Training Command as an instructor, so it was not until 1943 that he was posted to No. 103 (Bomber) Squadron at Elsham Wolds and began operations against the enemy, flying Lancasters.

At an operational training unit, he had formed his crew on 2 July, 1943: Flying Officer Reggie King, navigator; Sergeant Ossie Fry, wireless operator/air gunner; Sergeant Reg Styles, bomb aimer/air gunner; Flight Sergeant Woodward, flight engineer; Sergeant Jackie Emerson, of the Royal Canadian Air Force, rear gunner. 'My crew and good friends,' he wrote of them a decade later. They lacked a dorsal (mid-upper) gunner, so this position had to be filled by casuals.

On 24 February the crew flew their fifteenth operation, on which Wing Commander Nelson, who commanded the Squadron, went with them. 'The target,' Squadron Leader Eddy recalled, 'was the ball-bearing works at Schweinfurt. The trip went like a charm, check points bang on time, target likewise, good run in — good run home. Congratulations for efficient and well co-ordinated crew. It had been an honour and a pleasure to have the Squadron Commander with us, and we were all very pleased with ourselves.'

In heavy bomber squadrons, two of Longfellow's most familiar lines, 'Something attempted, something done, Has earned a night's repose', were turned on their head. The crews flew by night and did their best to snatch some repose by day. It was not always a long one, but at least to operate on two successive nights was rare. In the Nissen hut they shared with Bill's black labrador, Traque, which means pal in Araucano, the language of a South American tribe, Bill and Reggie King were untimely roused with the order to report to the Flight Office. They were on the Battle Order again for that night.

All was haste and there was no time to do an air test. As usual, an air gunner, this time Sergeant Churchill, was added to the regular crew to man the dorsal guns. Pilots beginning a tour of operations had to fly two sorties with a crew that had done at least fifteen. Accordingly, they had one of these aboard: 'A delightful chap, Flight Sergeant Andrew Miller,' Bill noted. The aircraft they were allocated was 'P' for Peter as usual. 'It was our eighth consecutive op in her and we loved her dearly.' That night's target was Augsburg, thirty-five miles west-north-west of Munich.

They slipped easily into the normal routine. Dusk was falling by the time they left the Briefing Room and went to fetch their parachutes from the Parachute Section. Bill recalled that there was a lot of joking 'and eighteen-year-old Jackie Emerson getting a big kiss from each of the parachute WAAFs. I only got a "Good trip, sir" !'

The next step in the habitual order of events was to hand Traque over to 'Chiefy', as the flight sergeant in charge of the ground crews was always known, at the flight hut out at the dispersals, before doing the external checks around the aeroplane and going aboard.

'Just as I was about to start up, a car came round the perimeter and stopped in front of us. Wing Commander Nelson [the squadron commander] got out and waved a telegram at me. He read out the contents to the effect that my wife, "Blackie", had just had a son and that both were well. I called back down asking him to send her my love and congratulations and to tell her I would be with her in Kettlewell, Yorks, next evening, with a week's leave!

'There was just time before start up to enroll Reggie, Ossie, Reg, Jack and Jackie as Godfathers and name the child Peter (of course).'

Even after an air test a few hours before taking off on a sortie, aircraft often developed faults while standing at their dispersal points. But P for Peter was as reliable as ever. Starting and running up her four engines revealed no snags. Bill was even keener than usual to get airborne and finish the night's work, then dash off to see his wife and new son. There seemed no reason why he should not be back punctually at his estimated time of return. His was a seasoned crew and only last night had earned their Commanding Officer's praise. The weather was good. Augsburg was a lot less uncomfortable than Berlin. Bill was not a man to feel apprehensive at any time, and tonight there were only good things to think about.

Over France, the first sense of something being not quite right intruded. The sophisticated navigation equipment, G and H2S, began to misbehave. 'We missed Reggie's usual concise and confident instructions as regards course and turning points.'

Still there was no disquiet among the crew; Reggie could navigate without these refinements. And they were in a stream of bombers, so the night sky would presently be lit by searchlights and the exploding bombs dropped by those in the van would show them the way to their objective.

Eyes searched ahead for signs of the attack going in. There was none; instead, it was on the port side that the darkness was awash with the glow cast by a burning target and bursts of flak. They altered course but were ten minutes late in starting their run in. 'The result was that we got a lot of individual attention from searchlights and flak.' But, undeterred, they finished a steady bombing run. As soon as the bombs were away they set course for home.

They were still deep in Germany, with Luxembourg and Belgium to cross. The whole route was vulnerable to flak and night fighters. There was moonlight to help the anti-aircraft gunners on the ground and the night-fighter pilots and radar operators in the air.

The Vosges Mountains, rising to three thousand feet, lay across their track and it was while they were near these that a shell burst at the forward end of the navigator's cabin, which was immediately aft of the pilot's seat and level with the port inner engine.

Amidst the stench of cordite and smoke, flames were raging. Flight Sergeant Andrew Miller, who had gone along for the ride, to learn how an experienced crew did their job, burned his hands fighting the fire. He and some of the others managed to extinguish it, but found that one crew member's parachute had been destroyed.

This was not the end of their problems. Bill was dismayed when he checked the fuel gauges. The tanks had been holed and all four engines were losing petrol. One engine stopped, but the Lancaster maintained its height. Another ran dry and it began to lose altitude. When he was left with only one engine, and a mere two thousand feet above ground, Bill ordered the crew to abandon the aircraft and, against protests, gave his own parachute to the man whose 'chute had been burnt.

They all demurred. They were a crew, not a random group of individuals, and if he had no recourse but to land their aeroplane, they would stay and share the crash. He told them they must go at once. The others reluctantly baled out, while Ossie Fry paused to urge Bill yet again to share his parachute. The captain ordered him to jump without delay and there was no option but to obey.

The gentle slopes of the Vosges foothills were beneath. Bill Eddy chose to make a belly landing in the snow on a large, flat-looking area near a belt of trees. P for Peter slid forward like a monstrous sledge until a small hummock rose in front of her. Her nose dug into it and she came to an abrupt halt. The fire had burned through Bill's straps as well as his chute, so he was hurled head-first against the front of the cockpit and knocked out.

When he regained consciousness a few minutes later he set about doing his last duty as captain before departing the scene. 'For the last few rather hectic minutes (on the ground) in P for Peter I was working against time, convinced that the enemy would arrive at any moment, but I finished my chores without sight or sound of anyone.' Some chores! He had to set fire to the wreckage, not easy when the petrol tanks were almost dry. 'It was now about 2 am on 26 February. As I walked away from the burning aircraft many rounds of ammo from the belts to the guns were going off and making a terrific din.'

One can imagine the excited shouts he must have expected to hear: '*Da es brennt ... schnell kommen ... aber vorschtig, die Munition explodiert.*' But there was not a voice to be heard.

Despite his own predicament, he spared a thought for his crew and how they were faring. In particular he reflected wryly on Andrew Miller, who had accompanied him to see how things were done by a practised crew. Flight Sergeant Miller had transferred to the R.A.F. from the Army, in which he had been a warrant officer. Badly wounded during the fighting in June, 1940, he had been left behind at Dunkirk. As Bill Eddy put it, he was 'looked after by French peasants and eventually found his way back to the U.K.; how I never found out. When well again he remustered to the R.A.F., completed pilot and operational training, joined 103 Squadron and came flying with us; and in a few hours was back on the wrong side again! Really too bad.

'The snow was about eighteen inches deep, and much deeper in drifts. Feeling shaken and depressed [the distance between him and Kettlewell, Yorkshire suddenly to be measured in weeks instead of miles and hours] I started walking downhill. I stumbled over the snow-covered edge of a shallow pool in a stream, a flight of wild duck got up in a fright with much quacking. Shades of duck shooting at dawn along mountain streams in Patagonia, with Blackie my wife and Jet, my labrador bitch. Morale suddenly up a hundred per cent, I now thought how fortunate I was to be alive and unhurt, and determined to evade if I could.' He discarded his forage cap and pulled his trouser legs down over his flying boots instead of tucked into them, so was not immediately recognizable, in poor light, as a fugitive airman. Only his Irvine jacket, with its distinctive large fur collar, might arouse suspicion. At the bottom of the valley he came to a road and followed it westwards. He passed a few people who were either up betimes or going very late to bed, but none took any notice of him.

'As dawn was breaking I looked for a place to lie up for the day and finally settled on an old-fashioned earth and brick oven. I spent the day there and ate some sandwiches and drank coffee I had brought from the aeroplane. It was very cold but I stuck it out until dark, when I started walking again. I saw several signposts with French-sounding names on them, but couldn't identify them on my escape map.'

He passed through several villages, but still nobody paid him any attention. The cold was increasing. He had trudged westwards all night and as the second day was dawning he saw the dim lights of a small town in the distance, where he decided to seek help. Sensibly, he chose an isolated farmhouse. For some minutes after his knock there was no response. He was about to leave and try elsewhere, when a woman's voice asked who he was and what he wanted.

In his narrative there now comes the phrase that occurs in almost every account of evasion and escape: 'In my best schoolboy French...' It is a lamentable revelation of the standard of language teaching in even the most expensive or academically distinguished British schools that their products should be so inarticulate after many years of classroom study.

He asked if there were any Germans about, to which the answer was 'No'. He asked if he were in France and was told that he was in Belgium. He explained that he was a British airman in need of help and asked her please to open the door. Silence followed until 'an elderly grey-haired lady and a very young girl with fair hair came round the corner of the house.

'I showed them the wings on my battledress and the old lady opened the front door and took me into the dining room. I then did my best to explain that I, as an R.A.F. pilot, would be sent to a prisoner-of-war camp if captured, but if they were found helping me the consequences for them would be very much more serious.

'She understood, smiled and brought me bread and hot coffee and told me to wait.'

She went to a nearby farm and returned accompanied by her son Emile Schmidt, who welcomed Bill warmly and told him that he had fought in the last war with the British against the Boches.

'He brought me a pair of tweed trousers, a brown pullover and a good leather coat that he must have badly needed. He then wrapped up my battledress and flying jacket with care and buried them, to be recovered after the war!'

The sun had just risen when Emile Schmidt took Bill to a small house beside the railway line in a small town where his elder brother, Léon, lived. He had to rouse the sleeping household. As soon as they were admitted, Bill gave them the same warning as he had given old Madame Schmidt: 'and was told again that they realized the risks they ran, but were pleased to accept them as one of the few ways left open to them to continue the war against the common enemy.

'Léon, a tall, thin engine driver with a long grey moustache, his charming fair wife and two teenaged daughters made me welcome and gave me more hot coffee, bread and cheese. Meanwhile a comfortable bed was prepared for me in a little room under the roof and I was told not to worry about anything, but to have a good sleep while they thought over what was best to be done about me. As he showed me into my room, Léon opened the curtain a bit and pointed out a section of German soldiers patrolling the road alongside the railway line in front of us.'

By the time Bill woke, Léon had had information from his railwaymen friends that the remains of P for Peter had been found very close to the Luxembourg frontier, three of his crew had been picked up and an intensive search was being made for the rest. Léon insisted that Bill must stay where he was and was confident that he would be able to make arrangements for moving him out of the area.

'I spent a pleasant if somewhat anxious day. The teenaged daughters, Lucille and Gilberte, were sweet and did their best to entertain me. Their mother was very kind, but obviously anxious − with good reason.'

Next day Léon heard that the hunt was coming closer. Danger and cheating the Boches of their prey under their very eyes apparently delighted and stimulated him. 'He told me with enthusiasm that he had arranged to take me in the cab of his engine, as his stoker, to the neighbouring town of Libramont, where a friend of his, Jacques Reveland, would put me up until they could help me further on my way.'

They set off soon after dark. Léon lent Bill blue overalls and a railwayman's cap similar to the ones he himself wore. 'After the fondest of au revoirs and good wishes, we nipped across the road to the edge of the railway line. A train was already approaching and, as the engine came opposite us, it slowed and almost stopped. The driver and his mate jumped off on the far side; Léon and I climbed aboard. He opened the throttle, or whatever one does, and we puffed slowly into the station. There the train was inspected by a couple of German soldiers. They looked into the cab. Léon greeted them. They didn't give us a second glance and went on down the train.

'Not long afterwards we were on our way again and soon pulled into Libramont station. Léon deliberately overshot a bit, so the engine was beyond the platform and in the sidings area illuminated by shaded standard lights. He had already told me that as soon as we stopped I was to hop out on the left side, cross the sets of lines and under or between the cargo trucks, under the fence and into a road that ran at right angles to the rails. Rather nerve-racking, but I was soon approached by a man who spoke to me in English and told me to follow him at a reasonable distance. He was Jacques Reveland and he took me to his house.

'Jacques was a splendid chap, thin, quick and with a great sense of humour. He and his Polish wife rented part of a rather large house in a row of adjoining houses. They had the ground floor, consisting of kitchen and living room, and on the second floor two bedrooms and bathroom.'

The other two rooms on the second floor were the offices of a department of the German administration concerned with rationing, whose staff used the same front door and staircase as the Revelands.

'When I arrived the office was closed, but Jacques thought it a great joke that next day his Boche neighbours would have me practically under their noses. His wife didn't think it quite so funny. These charming and courageous people entertained me for three days. Jacques was out most of the day about his business and Madame was often out too, making long trips on her bicycle to get food, quite often a long way into the country.'

On the second evening Jacques brought 'a smart, middle-aged Belgian' home with him, who informed Bill that he belonged to a Resistance organization formed to help evaders and escapers. The organization was going through a very difficult time just then, but something would be worked out to get him safely on his way. Commenting on this long after, Bill wrote, 'After all these years I am still amazed, and overcome with admiration for these people.' Before leaving, the visitor took some photographs of him for a false identity card.

Also, news had come from Léon; he believed that two of Bill's crew had been caught, but Reggie King was still free and being helped by other Resistance friends. He had tried to send a message to Bill, so was obviously aware that the Germans had not laid hands on him.

Cool though Jacques was about the presence, during daytime, of the enemy under the same roof as himself and an R.A.F. evader, it would be foolhardy to keep Bill there for long. A plan had been made for a doctor member of the Resistance to pick him up that night and take him further on his way by car.

After dark Jacques and Bill cycled out of the town. Their route took them through a pine forest where, after they had gone a mile or so, they dismounted. 'You must hide in the trees,' Jacques said. 'I will take your bicycle back. The doctor will come this way within half an hour. He will stop and open the bonnet of his car, as if something has gone wrong with the engine. Come out of hiding and get into the front passenger seat.' He rode away with one hand on the handlebars of the spare machine and Bill was on his own again, under the falling snow.

An occasional car went by but none stopped. Thirty minutes passed ... and more. Uncertainty and anxiety, for those who had harboured him as well as for himself, began to worry Bill. 'I gave up hope and started walking back into town. I hadn't the slightest idea of Jacques' address and had lost my bearings.'

He thought he could find his way by going back to the railway station and retracing the route along which he had followed Jacques on his first evening; but what if a German patrol stopped him and addressed him in French?

He set off, but had not gone far before Jacques and another cyclist met him. 'They had received a message that the doctor couldn't make it and were as worried as I was. Jacques's companion turned out to be another Léon, also an engine driver, and he took me to his house, where he lived with a large and very kind daughter.'

There Bill stayed for a couple of days, during which he was given an identity card with a false name that he found difficult to articulate. 'Jacques came to visit and alternately roared with laughter and practically cried with despair at my efforts to pronounce my new name.'

They had also made him a travel permit that allowed him to visit a sick brother. He was to travel by train — this time as a fare-paying passenger — to Brussels, where a member of the Resistance would meet him. Usually, railway tickets were bought by a helper and given to the evader, but, 'They briefed me well as to buying my ticket and how to recognize my contact in Brussels.' He was then to follow her until she dropped her handbag, the signal that he could now catch up with her and introduce himself.

'All went well,' he reports blithely, 'no snags at all. Within a few hours I was walking along a Brussels street with a gay and charming girl called Lulu.' No doubt she would have been flattered by both adjectives. It is deplorable to reflect that if the first were repeated today, she might take offence; the language has been deprived of a delightful word, with its connotation of a merry disposition and lively manner.

This was his first acquaintance with the Comet Line, in whose care he would remain until he reached the Spanish frontier.

'We walked to her flat where I met her older (sic) father.' One could hardly be surprised by a father being older than his daughter; did he mean elderly, perhaps older than he had expected? 'He was as kind as all the other wonderful people I had already met, and made me feel at home, telling me of the years he had spent in England between the wars. The following day Ann Brusselmans came to see me and brought me a smart grey suit that fitted very well. She explained that I had arrived at a rather difficult moment (I discovered years later that this was a masterpiece of understatement).'

Evaders and their helpers evidently moved about Brussels as nonchalantly as those who spent some time in Paris. Bill stayed a few days with Lulu and her father and 'went about Brussels quite a lot, helping her to fetch and carry'. He adds, 'It was rather entertaining to be standing in a crowded tram car, jammed in a group of German soldiers.' He found out later that Reggie King was also in Brussels at that time, doing the same sort of thing; 'But he had the misfortune to be picked up by a patrol and put in the bag.'

In any of the countries, Holland, Belgium and France, whose people helped Allied aircrew to evade capture, it was wise not to harbour anyone for long. After a few days Bill was moved to a flat in the outskirts, belonging to Madame Versmullen, where he found a young American airman, David O'Boyle, who had baled out of a Flying Fortress. 'We shared a rather bumpy double bed and made great friends.'

At this point, reminiscing several years afterwards, Bill Eddy said, 'He now runs a service station in Florida. Not so long ago an Argentine friend touring in the U.S.A. stopped for gas there. Dave evidently saw mention of Argentina on the car and asked if he knew Bill Eddy!'

After a short stay with Madame Versmullen, he returned to Lulu and her father. On the following day she accompanied him to Charleroi, where she handed him over to Simone Gazet — 'large, calm and altogether delightful' — in a café, before returning to Brussels.

Simone took him to a friend's house on the town's outskirts, where they had 'an excellent lunch served on a perfectly laid polished dining table. It seemed like a dream'. Their hostess was 'gay and charming, in spite of the fact that her husband was in a concentration camp, where he died not long afterwards.'

From Charleroi, Bill and Simone took a train to a small place near the French frontier. They crossed into France on foot, 'a long and anxious trek'. After a night in an inn run by friends of Simone's, they travelled on by train to Paris. There they were sheltered by an elderly English lady, Miss Abbot, who, before the war, had earned her living as a teacher of her native language. The next person to harbour Bill was a Russian lady employed at the USSR Embassy.

While there he kept a pre-arranged appointment with his guide to Spain, Michèle. 'She looked about fifteen. She was tiny and very pretty, wore a plain grey coat and skirt, short white socks and a school bag over her shoulder. She may have been tiny but she was a great heroine and was honoured accordingly after the war.' During these few days he spent several hours at the Gare de Lyon, the terminus for trains to the south, observing what checks were made on passengers.

Together, Bill and Michèle made the long rail journey to a small station immediately preceding Bordeaux, their destination, to which they continued on foot. The next stage was a short one, by rail, to Bayonne. On hired bicycles they rode from there to 'a friendly pub just short of St Jean de Luz'.

By this time he had developed an avuncular or paternal attitude to her and she had begun to address him as 'Daddy'. 'I was thirty-five years old, an ancient in her eyes, and must admit I wasn't so pleased about it.'

Next evening they cycled to St Jean de Luz. 'Crossing the river was for me the worst moment since leaving P for Peter. So near the Spanish frontier, but a bridge, with a sentry at the end, to be crossed.'

They went separately, Bill first. He waited until several home-going workers were crossing, then strode boldly across among them. The sentry was talking and did not even look at him. When Michèle caught up with him they climbed a hill on the coast to what appeared to be the ruins of an old fort.

'We watched the twilight over the sea, smoked and talked for an hour or so.' When darkness fell they were joined by two Basque smugglers with whom he was to cross the frontier.

Michèle left him, to return to occupied France and ever-increasing danger. Soon after, having been arrested and escaped, she herself took the route to Spain and on to England, where she was given a commission in the Auxiliary Territorial Service (later the Women's Royal Army Corps). 'She visited us often and became great friends with Blackie. And needless to say we hear from each other at Christmas and such occasions.'

Their railway journey had been undisturbed by any of the potentially disastrous episodes that had brought many other evaders to the brink of discovery. No German soldier had interrogated him when examining his documents. No French traveller had tried to engage him in conversation. But, years after the war, he did mention to his old friend, Ronnie Sheward, who was flying ground attack operations in Typhoons, that when some of these aircraft attacked the train, he 'had a nasty touch of the jitters' and hoped that Flight Lieutenant Sheward wasn't among those present.

For Bill there was a night-long tramp across the hills to a village outside San Sebastian which 'was great fun. A bit of excitement crossing the river opposite, but that was all.'

The 'great fun' was being able to chat in Spanish, in contrast with his lack of French.

They passed the rest of the night sleeping in a Basque farmhouse, redolent with the 'delicious smell of cow and sheep stabled on the ground floor'. In the morning an excellent breakfast was followed by a rest on the upstairs porch, while someone called Pedro — guide, or member of the farm household? — took a note from Bill to the British Consul in San Sebastian. The news of his safe arrival in a neutral country was sent to his wife; it was 25 April, exactly two months from the day he took off to bomb Augsburg.

The Consul sent him money, English cigarettes and the address of a friendly Spanish family in San Sebastian. He also explained that it would be unwise to visit the Consulate or his home, or make any further contact with him, lest the Guardia Civil arrest him, which would mean a long and intimate acquaintance with the squalor of an internment camp.

Bill decided to visit San Sebastian, a matter of a short walk and a tram ride, and call on the people whose address he had been given. They were an elderly couple who 'shared a small flat with two ancient dogs, one a large Alsatian and the other a small and cantankerous Pomeranian'. They were not pleased to see him, but manifestly his natural charm and friendliness prevailed: 'We made friends in the end.'

Later that day a Spanish driver from the British Embassy came to see him at the farm. They arranged to meet near the entrance to one of the tunnels through which the road round 'the magnificent San Sebastian bay' runs. The driver described the car and said it would be flying a (union flag) pennant.

They made the rendez-vous without mishap and reached the Embassy in Madrid that evening, where 'people were very kind'.

A few days later a member of the staff who was driving to Seville gave Bill a lift. On arrival he found that he knew the step-father of the British Consul there, Mr Montgomery, who happened to be from the Argentine.

He had arrived opportunely to finish his odyssey from the Vosges to Andalusia with elegance and gaiety. It was the first day of the famous Feria, the grandest and most colourful of fiestas. The Montgomerys invited him to join their party. 'Two days of soaking up sun and evenings of dancing and dining.'

After this brief spell of hedonism, Montgomery drove him to 'a small port a bit further south'. Before they reached the Guardia Civil checkpoint near the coast, they stopped and Bill transferred from the front of the car to the back, where he was concealed under a rug and several pieces of luggage. On the threshold of leaving Spain, this was a critical moment. 'Montgomery joked in Spanish with the Guardias and opened the boot for them. They had a look in there, a glance in the back and on we went again. I soon got back into the front seat.'

At midday they arrived at the coast, where they lunched with a Swedish shipping agent and his wife. Another guest, the captain of a British cargo ship that was in port, agreed to give Bill passage to Gibraltar. Before returning to the docks after lunch he told Bill and Montgomery to follow in half an hour. Although there was a police guard at the foot of the gangway, he assured Bill that there would be no problem about getting him aboard. On arrival at the quayside they found 'there was no sign of the guard. In fact the gangway was deserted and so was the deck it led up to. We just walked on board and into the captain's cabin. He had arranged for some of his crew to invite the Guardias Civiles below for some good English beer!'

Next morning he was put ashore at Gibraltar in a rowing boat. An Army sentry met him on the wharf and took him to a guard post. 'I there suggested to the sergeant on duty that he send for the Duty Officer, which he did by telephone. He invited me to sit down. I noticed he was reading the *Buenos Aires Herald* and remarked on the fact.

'He said, "Yes, I'm from the Argentine, and I see that J. M. Eddy, the Argentine railwayman's son, William Eddy, has gone missing."

'I said, "He's not missing any more."

'"How do you know?" was the reply.

'"Because I'm Bill Eddy."

'The officer arrived in a car and whisked me away for interrogation. I never had the chance to ask the sergeant's name and have never met him again.'

He spent two or three days in the R.A.F. mess, 'enlivened by a short trip in a Coastal Command Catalina with a crew I made friends with, and some lovely swims and sunbathing'.

He was flown home in a Dakota and arrived in England on 'a lovely spring morning'.

After interrogation at the Air Ministry, he telephoned Wing Commander Nelson, who informed Blackie and a friend, 'Barney'.

Blackie joined Bill in London that evening and he had a message from Barney to say that 'he and Frances were on leave the following day and that the four of us would meet in South America House and have a super party'. But the party, he adds, was postponed. For aircrew, in those days, any appointment made for a few hours ahead was fraught with uncertainty. His friend Barney was shot down that night.

Captured, Barney found himself in a prisoner of war camp, where one of the first people he met was Reggie King, who told him that he was not looking forward, after the war, to having to tell Blackie that Bill's crew had left him alone, 'without a chute or a hope in hell'. He was able to reassure Bill's navigator that his pilot had not only survived unhurt but also returned home in a little over two months.

When the Air Ministry Intelligence Branch had finished with him, Bill and his wife went on leave. His inherent qualities of unselfishness and leadership are demonstrated in the way they spent this time. 'Blackie and I visited the families of all my crew and gave them the latest news. Most had been reported POWs already, but I think it was Miller who was still unaccounted for. I was able to assure his wife that he had jumped out all right and that, with his experience, I was sure he would have no bother. He was kept in a safe house while his burnt hands were looked after, but was later picked up. They all returned to the U.K. in quite good health and excellent spirits after the war. As mentioned in the official report, my crew were loath to leave me alone in the aircraft when I told them to jump, but I insisted and out they all went, Jack Woodward still grumbling that he couldn't find his civvy shoes.'

Bill was awarded the DSO not only for evading capture and accomplishing his journey so quickly, but also for his sense of duty in staying with his aircraft while his crew baled out and his skill in making a crash landing. On his return to operations he transferred to a Pathfinder squadron to fly Mosquitoes and earn a DFC.

When the war had been won he returned to Argentina and bought an estancia. He also bought a light aircraft which, says Ronnie Sheward, 'came in handy to see where the sheep had got to'.

Those who had helped him home were always in his thoughts. In a letter to Ronnie Sheward, he wrote: 'What worries me is my inability to express my admiration, gratitude and affection for those wonderful patriots that light-heartedly helped me and so many others.'

He showed these sentiments in a practical way. Ten years after Lulu left him at Charleroi, he visited her. 'I also had the great pleasure of meeting Anne and her wonderful husband Dr Brusselmans again. I was also able to go to Bertoix and visit Emile and his mother, Léon and his wife and daughters and, back in Brussels, Michèle and her husband Pierre, and their children.'

If the best definition of a gentleman is, 'one of kindly feelings, high principles, a sense of responsibility, a man of honour', Bill Eddy amply exemplified it. A verse of Edward Fitzgerald's befits his memory.

'Lo! Some we loved, the loveliest and best
That Time and Fate of all their Vintage prest,
Have drunk their Cup a Round or two before,
And one by one crept silently to Rest.'

CHAPTER TEN

SERGEANT ALAN MATTHEWS

'I LANDED IN THE middle of the River Charente,' says Alan Matthews, who baled out over France at night. 'I couldn't swim.'

His life vest supported him and he improvised a back stroke that took him towards some trees, which he thought must be on the bank. When he scrambled ashore he found that he was on a small island, so he returned to the water. 'That was the worst part of it; it was cold.' Apparently this concerned him more than the proximity of the enemy. Tall and hefty, twenty-one years old, with a determined look about him, he was tough enough physically and mentally to take care of himself. But a little help in drying his clothes and some information about the enemy hereabouts wouldn't come amiss. He swam back in the direction from which he had come and this time he did find the river bank.

He had begun his Royal Air Force career by training to be a pilot, but failed in navigation. With the inscrutable version − or perversion − of logic peculiar to the armed forces, he was sent on a navigator's course, which he passed. Volunteers were wanted for a squadron based at Tarrant Rushton. Alan lived in Southampton, so knew where this station was: in the beautiful Dorset countryside between Blandford and Wimborne, not far from his home. He was accordingly posted to No 644 (Halifax) Squadron as a bomb aimer, which meant that he also had to qualify as an air gunner.

The squadron was ostensibly training to tow gliders. Indeed, the first six gliders to land in Normandy when the Allies invaded in June, 1944, came from Tarrant Rushton. No 644 was actually one of the few squadrons carrying out Special Duties for the Special Operations Executive. The others were based elsewhere. Between them all they flew Lysanders, landing and picking up secret agents and taking escapers and evaders to England, Hudsons for carrying passengers and supplies, and Halifaxes to drop arms, ammunition, explosives and agents by parachute.

644's training involved many hours of navigation and map-reading at low level. 'Bomber crews often couldn't find their targets,' Alan comments. 'We had to be able to find a *field*.' They had to find it first time, what was more. Members of the Maquis, the Resistance forces, would be waiting for them to gather the parachuted containers without loss of time. To linger, looking for the place where they were to drop their load, could alert the Germans and bring them racing to the spot.

The pilot whose crew he joined, Flight Lieutenant R.F.W. Cleaver, had already won the DSO. They took off at 2226 hrs on 5 April, 1944, on Alan's eighth operation with the crew, to drop arms and ammunition to the Resistance in the south of the province called Charente Maritime. They had to fly down at 2,000 ft to ensure an accurate drop, which meant that they were well within range of light − 20mm − flak, whose ceiling was 6,500 ft, as well as medium 37mm and heavy 88mm.

When they reached the Dropping Zone the flashlight signal from the ground was not given, so they turned for home.

Flight Lieutenant Cleaver's de-briefing report says: 'We were unable to complete the operation, and on the return flight got off course and were hit by light flak over an aerodrome.' Their track had taken them into the gun-defended area around Cognac airfield, across which they flew. 'The starboard inner engine was set on fire and the starboard outer engine stopped.' Asymmetrical flying with a vengeance! 'We were unable to extinguish the fire and about 0200 hrs (6 Apr) I gave the order to bale out, starting at about 1500 ft, and I crash-landed.' The starboard wing was burning by then.

The aircraft was down to about 1,000 ft when Sergeant Alan Matthews jumped for his life.

The point at which he emerged from the river for the second time was near the village of Vibrac, not far from Chateauneuf, in an area where the Resistance had been active for nearly four years. His modest way of recounting events makes being adrift, sopping wet, in enemy territory sound trivial: 'At about 2.30 in the morning I knocked on a door and found myself in touch with the local Maquis within minutes.' It was not as simple as that. There were at least a dozen German troops billeted in every village, any of whom might have caught him. With a blazing aircraft to guide them, they must already be out hunting for survivors. He did not know how close at hand the nearest of them might be, nor could he count on a friendly reception from every French household.

Knocking on the door of the first house he came to resulted in more than the provision of concealment and food. It was to gain him admission to a way of life such as which, and the company of people like whom, he had never expected to encounter when he volunteered to fly with the R.A.F.

On 13 October, 1940, a warning notice had appeared all over Occupied

France. 'Anyone who is sheltering British subjects is compelled to inform the nearest German Army Garrison Headquarters before 20 October at the latest. Anyone who continues to shelter British subjects after this date without reporting the fact will be shot.' And they were.

When the Allies invaded Algeria and Morocco in November, 1942, the Germans moved into the former Unoccupied Zone. The district into which Alan Matthews dropped was part of the Zone that the Germans had always occupied. The enemy presence was therefore strongly established, but so was the Resistance, the Maquis. This name originated from the expression *'gagner le maquis... take to the woods'*, used by its members who went into hiding in the wild countryside when arrest was imminent and from which they waged clandestine war against the Nazis.

By the time that Alan arrived unexpectedly on the scene, the danger to loyal Frenchmen and women of discovery and betrayal had grown even more widespread. In June, 1942, the Germans formed *la Milice*, literally the Militia, a black-uniformed paramilitary police force. An active member of the Maquis said of this, 'It was the most painful and the most revolting episode of this period, at the very least for our conscience as French people and patriots. Sad, because we could not understand how Frenchmen could become mercenaries and fight their compatriots for money. Revolting, because in addition to treason against their country, these renegades very often behaved in the most odious manner, stealing, assassinating and martyring.'

But he exonerated the police and gendarmerie. There was no reason, he said, to classify them as a whole as adversaries of the Maquis, least of all in Charente. 'On the contrary, many Charentais policemen and gendarmes joined the Maquis. Others turned a blind eye or actively helped.'

The first Charentais victim for an act of defiance was a youth of nineteen, Pierre Roche. On the night of 1/2 September, 1940, he cut the telephone cable between La Rochelle and Royan. The civil court sentenced him to two years in prison. A German court martial sentenced him to death for sabotage and he was shot on 7 September.

Resistance groups were being formed all over France. In Charente the setting-up of the group in whose territory Alan found himself was precipitated by a catastrophe.

In June and July, 1943, two parachute drops had been made on to an unfrequented meadow, hidden by trees, in the Taponnat region. The arms thus delivered were secreted for future issue to the maquisards, on whom the Allies relied for an insurrection when the Normandy invasion took place. At the end of August the Resistance group responsible for receiving these weapons and ammunition was warned, by a BBC coded message, 'Zoupinette will go for a bicycle ride this evening,' that a third drop was due. The reception team had reached a crossroads a kilometre from the Dropping Zone when they heard an aircraft approaching at low altitude. After a moment's hesitation they flashed the correct signal with their torches. It was, of course, the wrong decision. Hard though it was to turn away a delivery, it would have been the right thing to do. The Halifax released its cargo, which was, as usual, scattered. Within the bounds of a carefully chosen field, it was not difficult to gather the spread load. Here, it was a different matter. Some fell among the trees in a village, where, says an eye witness, 'the containers and parachutes gave a beautiful multicoloured impression [there was moonlight] to the villagers, who, rudely woken, came out to see what was going on.' In a properly reconnoitred Dropping Zone, there were no prying eyes to breach secrecy. Here the populace witnessed all that was afoot, and tongues wagged.

A new day dawned and not all the parachutes and containers had been recovered. What was more, 'Some "good" Frenchmen told the local Milice, who at once informed the Gestapo.'

Nearly all the Resistance members were arrested, denounced by one of their own. They were tortured, deported to imprisonment in Germany, or shot. The arrests continued for several weeks, during which the Gestapo penetrated the network right up to the national head of the organization, General Jouffrault, who was himself imprisoned in Germany and died there.

Shortly before the *parachutage* that went so disastrously wrong, the second in command of the Resistance movement, Colonel Penchenat, had come from Paris to attend a meeting of the local group at their usual place, the Café Blanc in Taponnat. At this he appointed André Chabanne, a former schoolteacher and wartime infantry officer, who had escaped from a prisoner of war camp in Germany, to take charge of the Secret Army in Charente if he himself were arrested, which did happen soon after.

Chabanne was a resolute and resourceful man, twenty-nine years of age. He had made his first escape from a prison cage in France. In Germany he made three more, on the second of which he reached the Dutch frontier before being caught and sent to a disciplinary camp in the Rhineland. From there he finally got away by bribing guards. In his new capacity as chief of the Charentais Maquis he took the name of 'Jacques Blanchi'.

During the summer of 1943 several comrades had helped him to build a hiding place, dug into the slope of a hill, in the Forest of Cherves, near Fougère. Here he was joined by seven men, one of whom, Guy Pascaud, was, like himself, a teacher. They had been in hiding while they carried out various acts of sabotage, one of which was to derail a train on the Angoulême-Paris line.

Chabanne now set about establishing his own group, the Fougère Maquis. He had two principal lieutenants; Guy Pascaud, who adopted the name of

'You', and Madame Hélène Nebout, a schoolmistress, who had joined a Resistance group near Limoges in 1942. She, who took the Maquis name of 'Luc', was introduced to him by yet another schoolmaster, named Gagnaire.

When winter came, not only was this small group armed with merely a revolver and a few rifles, but also were finding their hideaway very uncomfortable in the cold, wet weather. They adopted a new sanctuary in the château de Chatelars, a ramshackle uninhabited building, which was a good vantage point from which to survey the surrounding terrain.

On 5 February, 1944, thirty of them, well armed by then, were installed there when the Regional Military Commissioner, Lieutenant Colonel Claude Bonnier, alias 'Hypothênuse', visited them. Before the war he had been a mining engineer. Now he had been sent from London to reorganize the Maquis in this area after the betrayal at Taponnat. He was welcomed with the Maquis song, composed by Jean Luissel, one of Chabanne's original companions in the forest. Says someone who was present, 'He was surprised and moved to the point of tears in his eyes. Impeccable, all in blue pullovers, these young men were a proud sight.'

It was on this occasion that Chabanne's group was named le Maquis Bir Hacheim. The name, spelt in this way by the French, when correctly transliterated from Arabic script into Roman, reads 'Bir Hakim' and means 'Well of the Sage (or Doctor)'. It was chosen in honour of the only notable action to that date fought in this war by the French Army, when in May, 1942, Rommel attacked the Gazala Line in Libya. The southernmost end of this defence line at a desert spot named Bir Hakim, was held by General Koenig's 1st Free French Brigade. The battle there had a special significance for the French. It was the first time they had fought the Germans since capitulating to Hitler in 1940. They showed exemplary gallantry in helping the British and Commonwealth forces to repulse the enemy.

Hélène Nebout designed a badge for the members of her maquis to wear on their pullovers or jackets: a shield on which was a V (for Victory) with the cross of Lorraine between its arms, surmounted by the words 'Bir Hacheim'. The embroidery was done by girls in the local villages.

This meeting at the château was the last time that the Bir Hacheim or any other Maquis was to see Claude Bonnier. Four days later he was arrested in Bordeaux and immediately committed suicide by poison, to avoid torture that might have extracted secrets from him.

On the evening of that visit, the Bir Hacheim was fortuitously engaged in a fire fight at Saint-Mary. Eleven of them were on their way by motor van to replenish their food stocks and to bring back with them two members of the Resistance from Saint-Cloud, when they were stopped by a German patrol. The maquisards' instant reaction was to open fire with their machine pistols and kill the lot. The sound of shooting alerted an enemy detachment that happened to be near at hand and rushed to the scene. In the renewed fighting one Frenchman was killed. Three others kept the Germans at bay while the rest hurried back to the château de Châtelars. More than a hundred German troops engaged the four maquisards who were covering their comrades' withdrawal. The enemy retreated with heavy losses. When one of the Bir Hacheim, Albert Gin, was wounded by grenade fragments the four withdrew into a wood. During the night the whole of the rest of the maquis joined their comrades, to help the wounded to cross the River Bonnieurs and make the long trek back to the château.

If this first battle of the Bir Hacheim cost the enemy dear, it also alerted them to the fact that an organized and armed maquis existed in the Chasseneuil neighbourhood. It would be unwise to stay at the château until a systematic search was made. They moved to another, le château du Gazon, whose owners, the Mesdames de Villemandy, harboured them. The three leaders, Chabanne, Pascaud and Madame Nebout, decided to disperse their men in three groups. One set up a camp in the forest of Horte. Another, preferring mobility, moved frequently from one wooded area to another. The third stayed with André Chabanne, Guy Pascaud and Hélène Nebout in the forest of les Jaulières, in the commune of Cherves-Chatelars, where their number was gradually increased. During this time Guy Pascaud was caught and deported.

This was the environment in which Alan Matthews was to figure for six months. Life there proved no less active or dangerous than operational flying.

The occupants of the house at which he tried his luck, Monsier Razé and his daughter, Madame Marinette Vignaud, welcomed him unreservedly. Monsieur Razé gave him some clothes to replace his wet uniform and, because the Germans were making a house-to-house search, took him to hide in a wood. He also arranged for the English teacher at the local school to go and explain to him that he would presently be taken to a safer place.

With amusement, Alan recounts how he was tested to prove his nationality, by being asked to repeat the tongue-twister 'She sells seashells upon the sea shore'. For good measure he added, 'And the shells she sells are seashells, I'm sure'.

It was Monsieur Roger Charles who turned up and drove him home to Douvesse hidden in his van, which had been converted to run on gas generated by charcoal. A German patrol stopped them on the way, but did not find the passenger. Later, Roger Charles took Alan to the nearest Maquis unit, whose headquarters was at Armel Farm, in Douvesse, a small village between Bouteville and St Même-les-Parrières. It belonged to Fernand

Tatou, owner of the château d'Anqueville, and was situated on the edge of a wood, accessible only by several minor roads, which were easily kept under surveillance and defended. With the maquisards, Alan spent the rest of the night breaking into the wreckage of the Halifax and unloading as much of the arms and ammunition as they could in the few hours that remained before dawn.

The Bir Hacheim maquis had by now grown to such a size that it comprised several groups, each of which was identified by a local name. The one to which Alan Matthews belonged was known as either 'le maquis d'Armel' or 'le maquis de Bouteville', and commanded by a retired officer of the colonial infantry, Captain René Valantin, whose Adjutant was another former regular officer, Lieutenant Alex Barreau. A third important figure was an American Army captain, sent to France by the S.O.E., whose true identity was concealed by the single name 'Joe'.

Asked about his activities during his six months with the Maquis, Alan says, modestly, that he took part in 'several nice little ambushes'. He was able to participate in these properly dressed in R.A.F. battledress; three weeks after his unplanned immersion in the River Charente, Madame Vignaud had delivered his uniform, dried and ironed, to the farm.

After the Allied landings in Normandy on 6 June, 1944, the Maquis' activities increased considerably. The Germans were being driven back and trying to withdraw northwards. The maquisards were doing everything possible to stop them.

One action, which became known as 'the Douvesse fight', will have to suffice as an example of the kind of fighting in which Sergeant Matthews was embroiled. It was set in motion by a kidnapping, a practical joke, perpetrated by Léon Giraudon, the baker at St Même. When setting out on the morning of 29 August to deliver bread to the Armel farm, he overtook two German soldiers armed with machine pistols, but did not notice that they wore the skull and crossbones badge of the SS. They called 'Good morning'.

'I wondered what these *cons* were doing there,' he said afterwards, 'so I stopped and asked them where they were going.'

In their mangled travesty of the language, they replied that they were on their way to walk in the grounds of the château. He offered them a lift and they climbed aboard among the loaves.

He drove straight to Armel and stopped in the farmyard, amid several of the Bir Hacheim men. When these opened the doors at the back of the van and pointed their guns at its occupants, the Germans, according to an eye witness, 'were at first dumbfounded, then turned green with fear'. The maquisards had added two useful weapons to their armoury.

This was not the only time that the baker used this ruse to deliver unsuspecting Germans into the hands of the maquis. He managed to keep his participation in the Resistance so secret that many people suspected him of collaborating with the enemy. Alan, who stayed in the baker's house for a week before going to live at Armel, says, 'I had to walk down the street with him to convince the doubters that he was on our side.'

In their enjoyment of the trick, the maquis men overlooked the fact that there was a strong German garrison in the Cognac neighbourhood. The German Commandant soon realized that two of his men were missing and sent patrols to search the area where they had intended going. At eleven o'clock the small château was invaded by some 300 SS troops in lorries, who lined up everyone in the place, two married women, a teenage girl and three youths, against a wall with their hands up. The Germans searched everywhere and questioned everyone, without avail. They were about to leave empty-handed when an officer, searching the surroundings through field glasses, saw that two tree trunks had been put across the road to Bouteville, barring their route back to barracks. In a fury, he left a few men to guard the château and led the rest off in their lorries towards the barricade.

The maquisards had made a grave mistake in detailing only four men to wait behind the road block and four others to hide in the bushes on either side. They let the leading enemy vehicle, a car, get within fifty metres of them, then opened fire with machine guns. They killed all five of the officers in the car and destroyed the lorry immediately behind it. The rest of the Germans leaped to the ground and tried to encircle the barricade. But the terrain was bare and flat and offered no protection. One by one the eight men at the barricade were picking them off.

Maquis reinforcements arrived through a small wood behind the barricade and the enemy realized that, despite their numbers, they could not get through the undergrowth, from which the intensity of fire was increasing. The defenders, making a grievous error attributable to their youth and inexperience, did not take advantage of the respite to withdraw.

Getting a grip on themselves, the SS, with the weight of fire from their great number of automatic weapons, made another, and this time successful, move to encircle the defenders. These fell back, but it was too late. Three of them died and two wounded were captured. Another wounded man who had hidden in a field was found and killed by forty-eight bayonet thrusts, under the eyes of a brave farm worker who had gone to his aid.

Among the forty Germans eliminated from the battle by wounds was one, hit in the neck and bleeding copiously, who was taken back to the château. Seeing the six occupants and farmhands still lined up along a wall with their hands up, he raised himself on his stretcher, snatched a machine pistol from one of his comrades and, mad with rage, was about to shoot at them but could not lift the weapon on aim. The effort brought blood spurting from an artery and he fell back dead.

The SS troops turned their attention to their two wounded prisoners. They tied them by one wrist to the back of a lorry and drove off, dragging them at fifty kilometres an hour. This torture endured over a distance of fifteen kilometres, their clothes ripped off, their skin and flesh excoriated and burned by friction. When the lorry stopped, the Germans were so infuriated to find the two Frenchmen still alive, although reduced to quivering lumps of raw flesh, they set about finishing them off with such cruelty that their screams were heard by workers in the fields a kilometre away. The Germans stabbed what was left of the two captives' arms and legs with their bayonets. With pincers they cut all their fingers off. They gouged out the eyes of one of them and emasculated the other. Finally they bayoneted both in the throat. This is corroborated by an extant photograph.

This was not a unique example of the savagery of the SS. Those who fell into their hands after a gun fight were always treated with similar cruelty.

Nemesis awaited the two whom the baker had captured. On the day following the battle, the maquisards made them dig their own grave. When it was done, they turned towards one another, shook hands, then raised their right arms in the Nazi salute and cried, 'Heil Hitler!' One then lay down in the trench and was despatched with a bullet through the head. His friend stretched out beside him, head to foot, and was given the same quick death. Barbaric though their habits were, they died bravely and with dignity.

Joe, the American, had made contact with the pilot and navigator of an R.A.F. Mosquito, who were in hiding, and four American aircrew. Throughout Alan's time in France, Joe had been promising him that he would ensure his return to England but he could not say when this would be possible.

The time came at last. Guided by a French Canadian girl, who stayed a couple of hundred yards ahead of him, he cycled to Angoulême, where he spent a week before being informed that he was leaving that night.

On the airfield, from which the enemy had barely departed, he and Joe's six other British and American airmen waited. A Hudson landed, its crew throwing out packs of medical supplies as soon as its wheels touched down. It turned and taxied back, then turned again, into wind. The seven passengers climbed aboard. Four hours later Sergeant Alan Matthews was in London, three stone lighter than when he baled out six months previously.

He resumed his operational tour and was promoted to warrant officer. After the war he chose a more tranquil way of life as a decorator.

Since 1981 he has returned to the Charente every year to visit his Maquis comrades and their families. But it was not until early in 1992 that the authorities realized that they had omitted to award him the Resistance Medal. He and his family were invited to spend a week in his old battleground, during which he would be presented with his decoration.

There was a significant corollary to the shooting down of Flight Lieutenant Cleaver's Halifax that reflects the most admirable aspect of the traditional relationship between the British and the French. Despite the many wide differences in most facets of their two characters, the frequency of friction between them, the readiness with which each expresses exasperation with the other, there is a hard core of mutual respect. The wars they fought against each other over the centuries are diminished to the dimension of mere squabbles; *family* rows – taking into account the Norman Conquest of England – when compared with the tremendous comradeship engendered by fighting side-by-side, in modern times, in the two World Wars. Rancour at what Wellington did to Napoleon is overshadowed by what Foch and Haig, Montgomery and de Gaulle did to the Kaiser and Hitler.

Alan Matthews was not the only survivor after the aircraft was hit. The pilot made a successful crash landing. All the other members of the crew baled out and three survived. Two of them paired up and made their way home, with help from the Resistance, via Spain. The pilot did the same on his own. One fell into German hands.

Tragically, the rear gunner was unable to leave the aircraft until it was too low for his parachute to take full effect. He broke his neck when he hit the ground. The Germans took him first to hospital in Angoulême, then moved him to Cognac, where he died and was buried.

To the inhabitants of the area in which the hitherto anonymous airman met his death he personified all the aircrew who had sacrificed their lives in helping to liberate France from the Nazis. Public feeling was so intense, so gratefully affectionate, that, soon after the war, the Châteauneuf-sur-Charente Municipal Council decided to erect a memorial to him at the very place in Fontaury where he had landed beside the Berbezieux-Châteauneuf road. Here, every year since the memorial was set up, a remembrance service has been held.

In 1977 a native of Châteauneuf returned to his birthplace after many years' absence. His name was Jean Fargeas and he had been a Liaison Officer with the British Expeditionary Force. After the war he became a keen Associate Member of the Royal British Legion. On coming back to live in his own *coin*, he became the Legion's Representative for Charente. He and Jim Clark, the Chairman of the Bordeaux and South-West France Branch of this admirable ex-servicemen's organization, determined that the identity of the R.A.F. man whose memory was formally revered each year must be established.

They began by discovering why his name was not known: his clothing and identity discs had been left at Angoulême Hospital when he was transferred to Cognac.

When an American graves registration unit came to the area after the armistice, it reasoned that, because the U.S.A.A.F. had bombed the Angoulême area at the time of his death, he was probably American; so they had his body re-interred in the United States cemetery at Champigneul. There was nobody in Cognac to tell them that he was British. After nearly two years of assiduous investigation and correspondence with the Ministry of Defence and the R.A.F. Escaping Society, Jean Fargeas and Jim Clark discovered that his name was Flight Sergeant Donald John Hoddinott. They arranged for his remains to be transferred to the British cemetery in Choloy.

Although Choloy is far away in north-eastern France, distance did not affect the reverence and gratitude in which the memory of how and where Flight Sergeant Donald John Hoddinott of the Royal Air Force was killed in action is still held in the Charente. His name was duly carved on the memorial and a special service was held there in November, 1979, at which a member of the crew and several senior military and civilian personages, including the British Consul General from Bordeaux, were present. Alan Matthews attended the memorial ceremony in 1981. Since then he and his wife have returned every year and been warmly greeted by his Maquis comrades and their families.

There is an object lesson in this for all European politicians, pre-eminently the British and French. *Les politicards*, with their petty antagonisms and reciprocal maladjustments, have lost sight of human issues that are far more important than the pompous principles over which they wrangle like mangy hyenas over a lion's carcass. The real people of Britain and France have an *entente* that is as *cordiale* as it ever was, even though it is demonstrated only in a peculiarly esoteric manner at certain times and in certain places; such as at Fontaury once a year.

Reflection on what de Beaumarchais wrote a couple of hundred years ago would be salutary for international statesmen of both nationalities: '*Parce que vous êtes un grand seigneur, vous vous croyez un grand génie! Vous vous êtes donné la peine de naître, et rien de plus.*' (Because you are a great lord, you believe yourself to be a great genius. You took the trouble to be born, but no more.)

For 'lord' read 'politician'.

CHAPTER ELEVEN

FLIGHT LIEUTENANT R.F.W. CLEAVER DSO

THE REPORT THAT Flight Lieutenant Richard Frank Wharton Cleaver, DSO, DFC, the captain of the crew in which Alan Matthews was bomb aimer, made on his return to England conceals conduct of outstanding bravery, sense of duty and determination beneath its stark and unemotional formality of expression.

'I was pilot of a Halifax Mk 5 aircraft which took off from Tarrant Rushton about 2200 hrs on 5 Apr 44 on a special operation over France. We were unable to complete the operation, and on the return flight got off our course and were hit by light flak over an aerodrome [Cognac]. The starboard inner engine was set on fire and the starboard outer engine stopped. We were unable to extinguish the fire and about 0200 hrs (6 Apr) I gave the order to bale out. The other members of the crew baled out, starting at about 1500 feet and I crash-landed.

'I came down in a field near Chateauneuf-sur-Charente. The aircraft was still on fire and I left my parachute, harness and Mae West in the aircraft in the hope that they would be destroyed.'

What he omits to say is that, once he was down to 1500 feet and irrevocably losing height while he waited for his crew to leave the Halifax, he was committed to a hasty landing, in the dark, on unknown terrain that might have been fraught with all manner of fatal obstacles; hillocks, ditches, trees. Moreover, not only was his aeroplane on fire, but also he had a load of ammunition and explosives on board that might well have detonated before he could scramble clear of the wreckage.

'I began walking right away S.S.E., keeping off the roads and taking my direction from the moon. By daylight I had covered only about four miles, and hid in a patch of woods about two miles N.E. of Maine-Loup. Here I examined my escape kit and rested until 1600 hrs.' When he continued on his way, he met an unexpected frustration. 'I went to a small farmhouse nearby, but the owner was stone deaf and I got no help from him.' Despite the awfulness of his predicament, with enemy troops carrying out a widespread search for him and other survivors, reading his laconic statement

142

nearly half a century later brings a flicker of amusement: the young Englishman patiently reiterating his request for help at increasing volume, the – presumably elderly – French farmer cupping a hand to his ear and shaking his head in bafflement. And time running out, with German vehicles perhaps approaching.

'I continued walking east till dark, my idea being to make for the Line of Demarcation [between the occupied and unoccupied Zones]. About 2200 hrs I reached a small wood about five miles N.W. of Blanzac.

'The following morning (7 Apr) as soon as it got light I walked for about two miles and asked for help at a farmhouse. After I had persuaded the people that I was a British pilot they took me in. They were very sympathetic, as a son of the house of about my age had been in Germany as a labour conscript. They gave me food and a bed and some civilian clothes (a very old black jacket, tweed trousers, and a shirt), for which I gave the son 100 francs from my escape purse.

'At 1600 hrs that day I left the farm and, walking alone, went round Blanzac and continued south till I reached the outskirts of Montmoreau about 2000 hrs. I walked round the west side of the town and then crossed the River Jude and the adjoining railway near [he gives the map reference]. I rested in a wood near here till 0200 hrs on 8 Apr and then continued by compass in the moonlight across country to about two miles east of Aubterre. It began to rain about dawn and I got into the outbuildings of a farm. When it got light I found there were a good many people about and that the outbuilding gave me very little cover. I left about 1000hrs and walked by compass to Parcoul, which I reached about 2000 hrs. The village was full of Germans, but I walked through quickly and was not stopped.' Here, again, there is an offhand coolness of narrative style that surely belies intense qualms of uncertainty and apprehension. 'I got into woods N.E. of the town and asked for assistance from a peasant, but only got a drink of wine, the people being obviously afraid of the Germans. At dark I rested in the wood.

'At 0200 hrs on 9 Apr I began walking again.' It was his twenty-fourth birthday. 'About 0500hrs I reached the River Isle at St Antoine de l'Isle. I crossed the river here by a bridge which was unguarded. From about noon until early afternoon I sheltered in some farm buildings and then continued walking towards the Line of Demarcation. About 1700 hrs I reached Villefrance de Louchant which, although I did not know it at the time, is actually on the south side of the Line of Demarcation. The town was not occupied by the Germans. Three miles south of the town I asked a man where I was and he told me I was over the line. I had not seen any sign of any patrols. I went on till about 2100 hrs, by which time I was a few miles from Moncaret. Here I got food at a farmhouse but was refused shelter.

'I slept out in the woods till about 0500 hrs (10 Apr), when I went through

Moncaret, continuing to Velines where I intended to get a train for Bergerac. There was no train until midday, and I spent the time walking about Velines, where all the shops were closed, as it was Easter Monday. About midday I got a ticket for Bergerac without difficulty and went on by train.

'At Bergerac I found there was no train leaving that evening because of the holiday. I went about five miles N.E. of the town and got food at a farmhouse, where I was also allowed to shave. The people advised me to avoid the next station as the station master there was a collaborationist. I slept the night in the woods and about 0500 hrs (11 Apr) started out for Mouleydier where I got a ticket for Ales le Buisson, the terminus of the line. At Ales I got a ticket for Agen. In asking for the ticket I mispronounced the name and the man in the booking office gave me a piece of paper and a pencil to write it down, apparently not suspecting who I was.

'From Agen I went out into the country to the east of the town and after about five miles I met a farmer who gave me bread and milk and information about crossing the River Garonne. In the evening I crossed the river by the road bridge at [he gives the map reference] N.W. of Layrac. I slept the night in woods two miles west of Layrac and at dawn I caught a train for Auch. I knew that Auch was about 50 miles from the Pyrenees and I thought this would be a suitable place from which to start walking.'

His unruffled acceptance of repeatedly having to sleep out of doors without the benefit of any covering, not even being able to burrow into a haystack, is admirable. Those shivering nights must have provided precious little sleep and his mind, during hours of chilly wakefulness, must have been busy with speculation about what his chances were of evading capture for another day.

'I walked S.E. by road and across country till I was four miles west of Castelnau Barbarens, where I spent the night in the outbuildings of a farm. In the morning (13 Apr) I continued walking S.E. While I was resting by the side of the road between Tachoires and Simorre two gendarmes came along on bicycles. They asked for my identity card, which I did not have, and then searched me, finding my R.A.F. identity card. This pleased them very much, and they told me that they belonged to the Resistance movement and that they were my friends. The junior gendarme fetched a farm lorry, and he and the other gendarme took me on the lorry to a farmhouse at a small village (no name) where six members of a Toulouse Resistance group were living in hiding. From this point my journey was arranged for me.'

He had travelled far in seven days, but crossing Spain was not so quick a journey and it was not until 16 June that he left Gibraltar by air for England.

Due recognition came his way when he was put up for the Distinguished Flying Cross on 3 August, 1944. After describing the circumstances in which he ordered his crew to bale out, the Wing Commander commanding 644 Squadron wrote: 'By this time it was too late for him to do the same, so he decided to make a crash landing. This he did successfully in a field without injury to himself, in spite of having both starboard engines out of action and the aircraft on fire, with the load still on board. For his prompt decision when in great danger, which saved the lives of at least 4 other members of the crew of 6, and for his great skill in landing the aircraft in almost impossible circumstances, it is recommended that F/Lt Cleaver be awarded the D.F.C.'

The Group Captain commanding Tarrant Rushton passed it on: 'Strongly recommended. Throughout the time he has been on this station F/Lt Cleaver's flying has always been a splendid example to the rest of the crews here.'

Air Vice Marshal Hollinghurst, Commanding No 38 Group, added: 'The crux of this deed is that F/Lt Cleaver was carrying a number of containers, many of which were filled with explosives — and he knew it. Time did not permit of the bomb doors being opened and the load jettisoned and F/Lt Cleaver preferred to remain with the aircraft in order to give his crew the best chance of escaping instead of fending for himself. The aircraft blew up shortly after F/Lt Cleaver had crash landed and made his escape. Recommended for the award of the D.F.C.'

Air Marshal Sir Roderic Hill, Commanding Air Defence of Great Britain, endorsed the document 'Recommended for the immediate award of the D.F.C.' and Air Chief Marshal Sir Trafford Leigh-Mallory, Air-Commander- in-Chief, Allied Expeditionary Air Force, signed it 'Approved' on 29 August, 1944.

The Royal Air Force lost a fine man and valuable officer when Frank Cleaver was killed in a flying accident in 1953.

The escape line based in Toulouse was the surviving link in the line established by Pat O'Leary. In March 1943, one of its members, Le Neveu, 'Le Legionnaire', a double agent, betrayed O'Leary to the Germans. This destroyed most of the 'Pat Line', but did not put it totally out of action.

In Toulouse lived an indomitable sexagenarian lady, Madame Françoise Dissart, whose deep detestation of the enemy made her resolve to carry on. She was never for a moment daunted by the fact that the Gestapo Headquarters was a stone's throw from her home where she lived alone with her cat, Mifouf, which lived to the remarkable age of eighteen. Madame Dissart continued to pass escapers and evaders down the line, often escorting them herself, right up to the day when the Allies liberated southern France.

CHAPTER TWELVE

FLYING OFFICER M. W. SMYTH

IF, AS WILLIAM COWPER DECLARED, 'Variety's the very spice of life / That gives it all its flavour', then Squadron Leader Maurice Smyth's experience of flying against the enemy must be deemed uncommonly pungent. His operational career began on 12 August, 1941, with eight months as a sergeant pilot in No 111 Squadron, flying Spitfires, mostly on sweeps over northern France from fighter stations in England. It continued from 21 July, 1942, when he joined a Hurricane squadron, No 73, in North Africa, to carry out the night defence of vital installations, night intruder operations over enemy airfields, and daytime tasks that ranged from destroying enemy vehicles to shooting down hostile aircraft. During this period he was commissioned. On 9 August, 1944, he was posted to 253 (Hyderabad) Squadron, based at Canne, six miles south of Termoli on the Adriatic coast of Italy, to fly Spitfire VCs, a variant whose wingtips had been clipped to improve low-level performance.

Canne was one of a cluster of three small airstrips made of pierced steel planking and all laid on sloping ground. The Wing Commander, Group Captain A. H. ('Ginger') Boyd DSO DFC, had fought in the Battle of Britain and had a career total of eighteen enemy aircraft destroyed. There were two Desert Air Force squadrons at Canne, Nos 6 and 32, an Italian fighter squadron flying (occasionally!) Macchi 202s and a Russian fighter squadron.

The squadron's tasks were to attack every manifestation of the enemy on land and sea: vehicles, buildings, parked aircraft, troops and small surface vessels. It had come to the Mediterranean as part of the air component that covered the North African landings in November, 1942. Advancing from the west across Algeria and Tunisia, it had joined up with Desert Air Force, which had fought its way westwards over Egypt, Libya and Tunisia. It was now with the recently formed Balkan Air Force. This somewhat misleading title did not imply that the majority of its personnel hailed from Balkan countries, nor that its squadrons were based there. There was no association whatsoever with zithers or other plangent stringed instruments, robust dancing that consisted largely of men with arms about each other's shoulders stamping the floor like rutting stallions; nothing to do with wearing astrakhan hats, or a garlic issue to the squadron cooks. It was so named because it had been formed to help the Partisans in the Balkan countries and to harass fourteen German and Italian divisions that were in the process of evacuating Greece, Albania and Jugoslavia. While stationed at Canne the Spitfires usually carried long-range tanks and used an airstrip on the island of Vis, in the Jugoslav Archipelago, for emergency landings and forward refuelling.

On 17 October, 1944, Flying Officer Smyth was detailed to lead a section of four, briefed to fly direct to an enemy airfield at Termovich, near Sarajevo, to see if there were any signs of activity. If necessary, they were to strafe it, then carry out a road sweep from Sarajevo to Mostar. There was also an airfield at Mostar, from where Messerschmitt 109Gs were known to be operating, which had to be reconnoitred.

They were flying over spectacularly beautiful scenery, but aesthetic appreciation was the least of their considerations. The road they were to strafe and the railway line and river beside it were the main supply routes to Sarajevo. These lay at the bottom of a deep valley with mountains rising to five or six thousand feet on both sides. Maurice describes it as 'a difficult place to strafe.'

'We had a good look at Termovich, couldn't find anything, so went down the Mostar Valley. We saw nothing on the way, but, from about 4,000 ft over Mostar, near the airfield, I sighted a small staff car. I told the others to stay up and said I'd go down and fix it. I did a broad sweep back and came up behind this chap at very, very low level, doing about a hundred and eighty miles an hour. He was driving quite happily along the road – it was an open small Mercedes – and didn't hear me coming. Obviously dreaming of his girl-friend. I just didn't have the heart to shoot him in the back with a Spitfire, so I did a steep turn and parted his hair with my wingtip. I looked over my shoulder. I must have given him an awful twitch: the car half-spun and hit the side, nearly turned over, came upright again and the driver got out and made a bolt for it. I did a wide turn to port to give the driver a chance to get away, came in again and strafed the vehicle.

'As I passed above it I heard some nasty noises coming from behind me, the radio went dead and the coolant temperature began to climb rather rapidly.'

He could see the occupant of the car lying some twenty-five yards from the vehicle and blazing away at him with a submachine pistol that must have been a Schmeisser MP40, standard issue at that time. His radio and engine were hit; he does not know whether by 9mm Parabellum bullets from the man whose life he had spared, or 20mm anti-aircraft shells. The Germans had ceased using tracer bullets and had also gone over to smokeless powder.

It was therefore no longer possible to see at once from where one was being shot at when under fire from light flak. As for the possibility of the Schmeisser having found its mark, he says, 'It could have been, because I had slowed down to 160 m.p.h., with the prop in fine pitch, for strafing'. Well, of course, if one *will* loiter at snail's pace within close range of an angry man with a large-calibre automatic weapon...

'It was obvious that the aircraft couldn't last long, so I decided that as we were over Croatia, where the natives were fighting for the Germans, and if you came down among them you could be shot or have your throat cut, or have a very rough time, I would head towards the coast and the island of Vis. I used maximum throttle and when I had crossed the coast I flew along the Korcula Channel, climbing. I was at seven thousand feet when the engine seized and the resulting torque when it stopped suddenly tore the engine through the side of the aircraft. A small trickle of flame appeared down the side, so I immediately cut off the magnetos and cut the fuel off. Before I could do any more there was an enormous "whoosh", a roaring noise and the side of the cockpit started melting, so I jettisoned the hood. After a couple of attempts, during which I got slightly burned on the face and my uniform was scorched, I managed to get out.

'I was then between the islands of Hvar, where there was flak that usually fired at us, but which this time left me alone, and Korcula. I landed in the Korcula Channel, between these islands. There was a very strong wind blowing and when I hit the sea I was dragged along the surface, swallowing large amounts of water. Flying Officer Evans, who watched it, said I looked like a speedboat going along. I attempted to inflate my life jacket, but the bottle was flat so I had to blow it up by mouth, which was difficult. I then looked round for the dinghy, which was attached by a lanyard to my Mae West, but couldn't see it until it hit me on the back of the head. Fortunately it inflated and I was able to climb into it quite easily. The boys above me were still circling and diving over me. I felt quite happy because I knew they were reporting my position, and I waited for an air-sea rescue boat to come out from Vis, which was only about forty miles away.'

So Maurice Smyth was happy and 'the boys', certain that a high speed launch would soon come forging along at 45 knots, were not too distressed on his account. They stayed to what they believed to be their prudent limit of endurance, intending to lob in at Vis and refuel. But when they got there, they were refused permission to land; more than twenty U.S.A.A.F B17 Flying Fortresses and B24 Liberators on their way back from bombing raids, damaged by flak or short of fuel, were cluttering up all available space. The Spitfires just made it to the Italian coast and crash-landed on the beach, writing off all their aeroplanes. This was not the calamity that it might seem. None of the pilots was hurt. The squadron was in the process of re-equipping with the Spitfire Mk VIII, which was also clipped-winged and had an even better performance. Deliveries were not as quick as the Squadron Commander, Squadron Leader J.R.C.H. ('Gravy') Graves would have liked. The accidental loss of three Mk Vs enabled him to obtain instant Mk VIII replacements.

'The strong wind was whipping up a choppy sea. I put the drogue out to stop the dinghy drifting. I could see Korcula on my left and Hvar on my right and wondered if the Germans would come out and get me. But either they hadn't seen me going down or were waiting for a rescue craft to come and then have a go at that. The radio which should have been in the dinghy was missing. The telescopic mast was jammed tight and the sail was also missing. It was very cold sitting there with water swilling about. It was late afternoon when I was shot down and darkness fell before there was any sign of an Air/Sea Rescue high speed launch showing up. I heard an aircraft pass overhead, so tried to fire one of my red flares, but my hands were so cold that when I did so it shot backwards into the dinghy, shooting red balls about, so I hastily went over the side, but luckily it didn't do any damage. I got back aboard.

'By this time a storm was blowing up. I decided that the best bet was to get to Hvar and hope to get in touch with somebody who'd hide me. Then lightning started to flash, which was quite alarming. The dinghy had a spray sheet, which a man in it could fasten around his neck. The wind was blowing from the north-west, so I decided to make a sail of it in the hope of reaching the tip of Hvar and at least getting ashore.'

The reason that he was not picked up by A.S.R. was that all its craft were busy in the northern Adriatic searching for ditched bomber crews. The R.A.F. was trying to arrange for a landing craft to go out and find him, but the heavy weather prevented this.

All that night he had the greatest trouble in steering the dinghy. Dawn was breaking and the sea was calmer when he did reach the island but he didn't know exactly at what point. He paddled the last few hundred yards with his hands, grounded on a beach and found that he was at the foot of a German-built concrete pillbox. After all his efforts and having survived the night without being found by the enemy, his spirits fell. Luck seemed to have played him a nasty trick. When he got out of the dinghy, expecting to see unfriendly riflemen in field grey uniforms coming to frog-march him to their blockhouse, he was so stiff with cold that he couldn't walk. He sprawled on the sand, contemplating the empty captured English cigarette packages littered around the pillbox, 'And I thought what a dirty lot the Germans were'.

Nobody appeared, so he concluded that the pillbox had been

abandoned. Greatly cheered by still being at liberty, although cold, hungry, sleepy and tired, he heaved himself to his feet and began to footslog inland, following a path through the woods. It was a long trudge. For the next day and a half he subsisted on the Horlicks tablets and benzedrine in his escape pack, so was 'a little light-headed when I saw an old woman with a bundle of sticks on her back, like something out of a children's book'. Luckily for him she was no witch; rather, a fairy godmother. 'She beckoned to me and took me to a very small village on the hillside. Her family were kindness itself; they gave me a meal of cheese and hard bread and put me to bed.'

He slept for some thirty-six hours. When he was about to venture out of doors the old lady's family prevented him: a German anti-aircraft battery was sited on the hilltop. After dark, a member of the Partisans arrived, greeted him warmly and led him down to the coast where some others were waiting. They rowed him out to a motorboat, which, when someone started the engine, made such a noise that he expected the enemy to descend on them within the next few minutes. Once again he was freezing cold; his uniform, tattered and torn by now as well as burned, was damp and the wind cut through it as the boat forged towards the mainland. He never knew where it was that they eventually went ashore; probably somewhere near the village of Gradic, he thinks.

Here, a small party of partisans took charge of him. Once again he was faced with a long tramp in his battered, seawater-rotted shoes.

He was shocked to see that the first village they came to had been 'literally demolished'. His anger and disgust grew with each village through which they passed. All had been laid waste, put to the torch, and he could imagine what had been the fate of their inhabitants. 'There wasn't an animal, not a human being. There wasn't a sound. It was most eerie.'

In the desert and in Italy, though the fighting had been hard and relentless, there were no scenes of ruthless Hunnish pillaging and ruination to distress the eye. In the air, combat had been without malice, apart from instances on both sides of the line when fighter pilots had strafed and killed the occupants of aircraft they had shot down, instead of sparing their lives as the unwritten rules of aerial combat decreed. In Jugoslavia it was as though Attila had been reincarnated and turned loose to scorch the earth. The scenes that Maurice Smyth saw during that trek were a reflection of the massacre at Oradour, in France, on 10 June, 1944, when 150 S.S. troops locked the entire population of this large village into the church, set fire to it, then watched and heard them all being burned to death. It was an act to make Saddam Hussein lick his lips and wish he had been there to apply the match to the petrol-soaked tinder instead of merely murdering Kurds with poison gas and cannonfire. All over Africa, rival tribes dispose casually of similar numbers every month with equally unemotional barbarity. In India, the conflicting religions would consider the slaughter of a mere few hundred men, women and children who profess a different religion a waste of time; there, they kill by the thousands. But to a twenty-three-year-old Englishman, in 1944, even though he had seen and contributed to violent death many times in the past three years of warfare, this wanton cruelty was the ultimate horror. Thenceforward he fought the Germans with more than a sense of duty; to it were added loathing and contempt.

Eventually they reached an encampment, 'where they appeared to have a radio'. Maurice was thankful to get there unscathed. Not only had they escaped any enemy attacks, but also there was the small matter of the hand grenades that the partisans who accompanied him wore slung round their waists. These looked as though one might come loose at any moment, every step of the way, and explode. His legs had already been peppered with shell fragments over the desert (wounds that plague him now, five decades later), and he could do without any more bits of metal embedded in him. It was uncomfortable. And one could lose one's air crew medical category that way.

'I was pretty clapped out by this time. They got hold of a donkey and put me onto this wretched animal to make it easier for me. They really were kindness itself.'

This stage of his journey ended at a village where a British sergeant and a private were in radio contact with the island of Vis. 'They immediately brought all their tinned rations out and I had to eat about three tins of steak and kidney pudding, by which time I was bloated.' They also signalled Vis and, soon after, a Lysander arrived and landed in a small wooded clearing and took Maurice to that island. The Commanding Officer there, thinking he must be starving, gave him another good meal, 'then kindly gave up his room in his villa to me for the night. The thing I remember about that was a huge mirror above the bed. I thought "Nice sort of people must have owned this". Jealous, of course!'

The next day some wounded partisans were flown to Italy and Maurice was put on the same flight. He travelled in the cockpit. 'The smell of gangrene from these poor chaps was appalling.'

When he landed at Bari, 'I handed to our Headquarters there a captured German Army code book the partisans have given me. Nobody at H.Q. could have cared less about me; they just left me to find my own way back to the squadron. I hadn't any money, my trousers were in rags and my battledress blouse was rumpled. An American officer arranged for me to be flown to a place near Termoli, from where an Anson took me back to Canne.'

Joseph Addison was an elegant essayist, but his lines, 'What pity is it that we can die but once to serve our country,' assume too much. He had never worn uniform, let alone fired a shot in anger or been shot at. If he had, he would not have written such a hyperbole. The greatest desire of every man who goes to war is that he will emerge from it alive and, if possible, unhurt. What your fighting man has to do, however, is to *behave* as though he were in accord with Addison's sentiment.

Maurice Smyth was back on operations against the enemy after one week's leave.

After the war he served on in the R.A.F., then spent five years as an instructor to the Saudi Arabian Air Force.

CHAPTER THIRTEEN

OBERLEUTNANT FRANZ VON WERRA

HE HAD THE CHEEK OF THE DEVIL. He rivalled Baron Münchhausen with the lies he told about the enemy aircraft he claimed to have shot down. He spoke English fairly well and the first British police sergeant who had charge of him said he was 'quiet, polite, correct, very much master of himself'. His rank was Oberleutnant, equivalent to a first lieutenant or flying officer, but he was sarcastically insolent to a middle-aged squadron leader (a major, in Germany) who interrogated him. He had many unpleasant qualities, but cowardice was not one of them and he was a man of iron determination backed by considerable intelligence and ingenuity. He was short (5 ft 7 ins), slight (10 stone) and handsome, with a ready smile and a good measure of charm. Although his name did not appear in the Almanach de Gotha, the equivalent of Debrett's 'Peerage', he claimed to be a baron and wore an ostentatious ring engraved with a crest surmounted by a coronet. His father had indeed inherited the title of Freiherr, but our *junger Herr*, being merely the fourth son, was not the heir to it. Hard times had hit *Papa* von Werra and he had handed over the two youngest of his eight children, Franz and a sister, to a childless couple, Major and the Baroness von Haber, to foster, which probably heightened the foster son's delusion of grandeur.

His name was Franz von Werra and he was twenty-six years old when he was shot down over Kent on Thursday 5 September, 1940.

He was flamboyant and a keen seeker of publicity. He kept a lion cub that he called Simba, the Swahili word for 'lion', about which much had been written and illustrated in newspaper and magazine articles. He sported a red jerkin, in cheap imitation of the Great War's famous fighter ace, Manfred Ritter von Richthofen, so the Press dubbed him 'The Red Devil'. Richthofen hadn't faked his victory claims, but the name that journalists gave him because he flew in a crimson aeroplane had been as spurious as his pretentious counterpart's. Known as 'The Red Baron', Richthofen was a mere knight.

The Battle of Britain was approaching its climax when Oberleutnant Franz von Werra, of Jagdgeschwader 3, got his comeuppance, retribution for being a braggart and liar. September the 5th was one of a succession of fine, warm days although cloud formed in the late afternoon. On the previous day the R.A.F. had lost fifteen aircraft and the Luftwaffe twenty. On this unlucky day for Werra the R.A.F. was to suffer the loss of twenty while shooting down twenty-three Luftwaffe bombers and fighters.

A Geschwader was not, as the sound of its name suggests, the equivalent of an R.A.F. squadron. It was the largest tactical unit of the German Air Force and comprised three Gruppen. Each Gruppe numbered three or four Staffeln and it was a Staffel that approximated to a British squadron. The prefix '*Jagd*' meant 'fighter'. The Geschwader Kommodore and each Gruppe Kommandeur operated as leader of a Stabschwarm (staff flight) of four, flown by himself, his Adjutant, Technical Officer and another.

It was around 1000 hrs when the first raids came in to attack the fighter stations at Croydon, Biggin Hill, Eastchurch, North Weald and Lympne. Fourteen Fighter Command squadrons went up to intercept them and most of the enemy force failed to reach their targets.

Werra was flying his Messerschmitt 109 in IIJG 3, No 2 Gruppe of Jagdgeschwader 3, of which he was the Adjutant. Some accounts of the relevant events say that there were three aeroplanes in the Gruppe Kommandeur's flight. This is incredible. Luftwaffe fighters always flew in pairs and fours. These accounts also attribute to 'the Tail End Charlie' the warning that Spitfires were attacking. There was no 'Tail End Charlie' in a German fighter formation at that period. These flew in 'finger fours', spread laterally, not in the R.A.F.'s threes with one (known by the less mealy-mouthed colloquialism of 'Arse-End Charlie') weaving astern, a system devised in 1916 by the Royal Flying Corps.

Whoever gave the warning, it didn't do much good for Werra. A Spitfire, flown by a flight commander in No 41 Squadron, Flight Lieutenant J. T. Webster DFC, who then had a confirmed score of at least fourteen victories, settled on Werra's tail and sent him down with short bursts that put paid to his engine. Webster was killed in action when a second wave of raiders appeared over the Thames estuary, Biggin Hill and another airfield, Detling, soon after lunch the same day.

Werra's varied accounts of his performance that morning had one common factor: they were all untrue. In one he alleged that he had collided with another Me109. He even falsified the description of his capture, in accordance with his compulsive histrionics. In reality, he made a belly landing in a field near a searchlight battery, from where an air defence Lewis gunner had fired at him. He clambered out of the cockpit unscathed, but according to what he said and wrote later, the aeroplane came down in flames and he was hurled clear on impact.

The troops on the site were jubilant in the belief that one of their machine-gunners had brought him down. The unit's cook abandoned his stove and dashed to the crashed fighter, followed by some of his comrades carrying rifles. Escorting their captive to the battery site, they were the first Britons to witness a display of his habitual impertinence; he strolled with one hand in his pocket, and when they went through an orchard he picked an apple and munched it as he ambled along.

According to him, however, his arrest was melodramatic. To admit that a Freiherr and member of Hitler's – and the entire German nation's – favourite armed force had been apprehended by a non-combatant in shirtsleeves and not even armed with so much as a kitchen knife, would be humiliating. In his fictitious narrative it was the Home Guard who had surrounded him, and, all with guns of sundry types, advanced in waves, the standard military procedure, taking it in turns to move forward while the rest covered them. Only ignorant or stupid listeners and readers could accept that one helpless man would be the object of such precautions.

But that was a harmless fabrication. The victory symbols he had had painted on the tail fin of his Messerschmitt were a heinous deception. So was his story of his achievements that day. There were thirteen emblems on the aircraft: eight narrow oblongs to indicate bombers he had allegedly shot down and five smaller ones with arrowheads pointing down, for fighters. This shameless and shameful display put him, falsely, among the leading aces of the time. The great Werner Mölders, who was at that time Germany's leading ace, had scored thirty-two by then in this war (of which nineteen were various French machines of poor performance, easy victims). He had also scored fourteen in the Spanish Civil War (also more or less sitting ducks), to which Hitler had sent a large air contingent. Galland had twenty-four to his name, Schöpfel fourteen and Joppien thirteen. The next highest was Manhard, with nine. It is disgraceful that Werra remains to this day credited with a total of twenty-one kills in the annals of the German Air Force; thirteen over England, of which most were bogus, plus eight he actually did pull off on the Russian Front.

Less than a week before he was taken prisoner he had given an interview that was broadcast by the main German radio station. In this he reported having been embroiled in a furious battle with a large formation of Hurricanes and Spitfires. He said he was attacking a Hurricane when he noticed a Spitfire behind him, which, of course, he outmanoeuvred and shot down. His bizarre way of doing this, according to him, was to dive into cloud, followed by his adversary, then do a loop that put him on the Spitfire's tail. Visibility in cloud being nil, this was a blatant figment of the imagination. Now separated from his flight, he claimed that he went down and flew low towards the coast. In one version he was hedge-hopping. In another he was at 500 metres. He lied that he saw an aerodrome 300 metres ahead, where six Hurricanes had just landed and six more were about to touch down. He described how he formed up behind the rearmost one, was mistaken for a returning British aeroplane, and shot down three of them. If he had tacked onto them from 500 metres altitude he would have had to dive so steeply that he would have drawn attention to himself. He then, according to him, flew round the airfield and, having saved his cannon shells until now, strafed and destroyed three parked aircraft and a petrol tanker. Making a second run, he said, he destroyed another fighter, then carried out three more ground attacks during which he set one more fighter alight. All this time, he pointed out, the light anti-aircraft guns around the aerodrome were shooting at him and he was returning their fire. He concluded this totally untrue story by telling the interviewer that he returned to base two hours overdue.

No such occurrence was recorded at any British airfield on the claimed date or any other. It was unbelievable that the R.A.F. watchers on the ground and the Hurricane pilots would not have recognized a Me109, with its German markings and different shape from a Hurricane. It was unbelievable that he could have made so many low passes over the field without being riddled with holes made by cannon shells. The only damage to his aeroplane was three machine-gun bullet holes. It was unbelievable above all that a 109, whose maximum endurance was an hour and a half, could remain airborne for some three hours. It is astounding that Werra's Commanding Officer did not reprimand him for telling such obvious falsehoods. Nevertheless Hitler was apparently credulous, for he awarded Werra the Knight's Cross on the strength of this tale of fantasy.

Werra was taken from the searchlight site to the Kent Constabulary Headquarters at Maidstone, where he was kept for several hours. He enjoyed chatting, but divulged nothing beyond the bare personal details demanded by the Geneva Convention. The sergeant in charge of him, who dealt with hundreds of German airmen during the war, said that Werra impressed him as 'confident, alert and highly intelligent'. He added that he was glad that this prisoner would not be his responsibility for long and was not surprised when he heard, many months later, of his escape. That evening Werra was transferred to Maidstone Barracks.

Next morning he was driven to the London District Cage in Kensington Palace Gardens, where he expected a harsh and deeply searching interrogation. But the German-speaking captain who interviewed him evinced no interest in the Luftwaffe. His questions were confined to asking how Werra had been treated and whether he needed medical attention. He offered him a cigarette, before turning the conversation to politics. As the discussion progressed, Werra felt that he was getting the better of their debate. When the interviewer dismissed him, Werra asked when he would be given back the personal possessions that had been taken from him immediately after he was shot down, and when he would be taken to a prisoner of war camp.

The second question was highly significant to the captain. It revealed the prisoner's unquenchable intention to escape. The whole conversation had been skilfully devised to give an insight into Werra's intelligence, morale and the strengths and weaknesses in his character.

Next, Werra had another motor journey, to a mansion in grounds surrounded by barbed wire − Trent Park, in Cockfosters, a northern suburb of London. There, he was given a medical examination before being issued with clothing and toilet articles. He was put in a bedroom on his own. He had neither seen nor heard any indication that there were other prisoners here. His spirits slumped. Obviously, this was not a permanent prison camp. When would he get the chance to plan his escape? What further interrogation awaited him here?

The following evening he was escorted to an interview with a squadron leader who wore pilots' wings and Great War medal ribbons. At once, having accepted a cigarette, he went onto the offensive − literally − by making a brief, derisory and sneering speech, then ridiculing the squadron leader and trying to taunt him into a display of anger.

He reaped a crushing retaliation. In impeccable German the squadron leader quoted articles written about Werra's invented exploits and demolished them as pure nonsense. He showed him the transcript of his recent radio interview and logically tore his ludicrous claims to shreds, pointing out discrepancies and contradictions in his statements. He ended by telling him that he was a lying humbug and the laughing stock of Fighter Command for the fabricated yarn about destroying nine Hurricanes in one attack on an unidentifiable airfield, on a three-hour sortie.

Werra spent several days at Cockfosters where he was tricked into an indiscreet conversation with a comrade, which was picked up by a concealed microphone, which he was astute enough to find, but too late. He was then returned to the London District Cage, where an Austrian British agent purporting to be a Luftwaffe fighter pilot failed to trick him into any indiscretion. After four days here he was transferred to No 1 POW Camp, at Grizedale Hall, in the Lake District.

This stately mansion stood three miles south of the Lancashire village of Hawkshead. Two miles to the west lay Coniston Water and Lake Windermere was three miles to the east. Ambleside, which used then to be in Westmorland and had a population of some 2,500, was fourteen miles north. Ulverston, in Lancashire, a coal-mining and iron-founding town whose population at that time numbered a little over 9,000, lay sixteen miles to the south.

At the southern end of each lake was a river. These converged, leaving only one route, to the north, that was not barred by water. And even that was crossed by a road between the lakes that was patrolled by the Army and police. The bridges over the rivers were also guarded. If an escape from Grizedale Hall were reported, police would send out launches to patrol the lakes.

In all prisoner of war camps, whatever the country, the senior imprisoned officer or NCO was responsible to the Camp Commandant for the discipline of the prisoners. Members of the British forces always formed an escape committee to consider whether an escape plan had a good prospect of success and to turn it down if it did not. It also organized the provision and production of clothing, false identity documents, maps, compasses, food and other escape aids.

German war prisoners, typically, established a supreme body, under the Senior Officer, which exuded menace: *der Altestensrat*, the Council of Elders. This was not only responsible for maintaining discipline but also examined all escape plans, censored all mail and held courts martial. At these last, if the death sentence were passed, the *Altestensrat* carried it out in secret so that it seemed that the condemned man had died from a natural cause, suicide or an accident. The heel of the jackboot that threatened to trample on and crush anyone who did not display ardent Nazism or was considered to have been captured as a result of cowardice was ever-present.

In Werra's time the members of this supreme body were Major Fanelsa, Hauptmann (captain or flight lieutenant) Pohle, both of the Luftwaffe, and a naval officer, Kapitänleutnant Lott, former submarine captain. Lott seems, in retrospect, to have had dubious qualifications for passing or rejecting other men's escape plans; he had tried to escape and been caught while still in the camp precincts.

Ten days after his arrival, Werra applied to the council for approval of his escape plan. Major Fanelsa began by warning him that, after Lott's attempt to get away, security had been improved and the ruthless bombing of Britain since then had probably so angered the population that any German airman who fell into civilian hands ran the risk of being severely mauled or even killed.

Werra was never a willing listener. A supreme egotist, talking about himself was his greatest conversational interest. A born confidence trickster, he was also a natural salesman. He propounded his plan with the persuasive charm that had deluded his Geschwader Kommandeur and comrades into believing that his performance in action had put him among the Luftwaffe's leading aces.

The council agreed that his plan was the best they had ever heard. They felt he was capable of executing it successfully, not only because of its intrinsic excellence, but also because he had made as much of a study of the forbidding surrounding terrain as was possible, so knew that it was rugged and inhospitable, and, further, had been getting fit by running round the exercise area. In addition, a fellow prisoner had made him a compass and another had drawn him a map of the region and the eastern part of Northern Ireland. His aim was to reach the west coast of England or Scotland and get across to Ireland, or to stow away on a neutral ship and go to whichever neutral country happened to be its destination.

All this in ten days, when none of the other prisoners, all of whom had been there for weeks or months, had been able to present an acceptable plan, except Lott, who, in the R.A.F. jargon of the time, had ignominiously 'had his lot'.

The 'elders' were able to amplify what little he himself had been able to appreciate about the hazards. The hills and valleys were steep and the fields where sheep grazed were divided by dry stone walls. He would have to clamber over scores of them. The Lake District had the highest average annual rainfall in England, so he must expect to be wet and cold. There were rivers to cross and bogland to struggle over. The British expected parachute troops to be dropped in this district, so there were infantry battalions in Ulverston and Windermere. Living rough for several days and trudging up and down rocky hills and dales, perhaps having to swim a river, would make him look like a tramp by the time he arrived at a port, which would excite general suspicion. If he got as far as the coast, he would not be able to steal a boat in which to cross the Irish Sea, because, by Government decree, all small craft had been immobilized in case of an invasion.

Werra told them that his jackboots would stand up to the hard walking, and he was offered a pair of leather trousers and a leather jerkin, both the property of U-boat crew. He was also given a faint and blurred copy of a map of north-western England.

As soon as he was granted permission to put his plan into effect, he was impatient to be off. On Monday 7 October, 1940, only two days afterwards, merely four weeks and four days since he was shot down, he made his break.

At 1400 hours, as was done several times a week, usually on alternate days, twenty-four prisoners in three ranks, were taken for a route march. They were escorted by an officer, a sergeant on horseback, four armed troops in the van and four more at the rear. The sergeant constantly rode up and down and around the column, so there was no chance of a prisoner breaking away while on the march. The only opportunity arose during the ten-minute rest.

There were two innovations this time. The party had always left camp at 1030 hours, but at the Senior German Officer's request the time had been changed, on the grounds that morning exercise interfered with the educational timetable. The real reason was that escaping in the afternoon would give Werra three and half hours less time before darkness fell than he would have to endure if he decamped in the morning. The second innovation concerned the route. None of the prisoners knew beforehand whether they would be ordered to turn right at the gate and go northwards, or left and go to the south. There was no regular pattern of alternation; sometimes the same route would be followed two or three times in succession. As the squad was about to pass through the gate, the officer commanding the escort, positioned towards the rear, where he could keep an eye on the Germans as they left camp, or the sergeant who led the way, would give the command to wheel right or left. But the voice that gave the order 'Left wheel' was not the British officer's, it was Hauptmann Pohle's, who was in the front file.

On the northern route there was no cover within reach at the point where the halt was always made. On the southern one, there was good cover at the habitual resting place five hundred yards past Satterthwaite. Where the squad was fallen out on the left of the road a dry stone wall bordered it, with a field beyond. Fifty yards past the halting place the road sloped downhill and curved to the left and then to the right. On the opposite side of the road stood a wood on the flank of a steep hill.

During previous marches Werra had found the road almost deserted. This time, as the column approached the point at which the march would be halted, he was dismayed to see a horse-drawn cart coming towards it.

As usual, the prisoners stayed alongside the wall and all the guards crossed to the far side of the road, from where they could best keep watch for any attempt to get away.

It was an established habit for some of the prisoners, before leaving camp and again on returning, to 'make much of', in equestrian jargon, the sergeant's horse. On the march that Werra had made immediately before this one, he had got one of his comrades, whom the sergeant knew was a keen rider, to cross the road for a moment and do this. It was a test of the sergeant's attitude, and he had permitted this attention briefly. This morning, however, as soon as the same man crossed the road to gentle the horse and distract the sergeant's attention, he was ordered back.

As arranged, Werra was hidden from sight by the eight biggest men in the party. Two others, leaning against the wall, laid their overcoats on top of it to protect him from its jagged stones and to prevent any loose ones from falling and making a noise. Werra climbed on to the wall and stretched full-length along the coats.

When the cart, which belonged to the local greengrocer, came near, it was seen to be loaded with vegetables and fruit. The officer gave permission to stop the cart. The sergeant bought some apples and gave one to his horse. Some of the troops also bought.

The prisoner standing nearest to Werra gave him a nudge and he rolled off the wall into the field.

He ran, crouching and hidden by the wall, making for the bottom of the slope. There he would cross the road and take to the wood.

He saw two women, several hundred yards away, running up the road, waving and calling out. The prisoners and their guards saw them too. Pohle, as quick on the uptake as Werra, immediately started waving back and the other prisoners followed suit. They were ordered to desist. Thinking this incident no more than a frivolous exhibition by a couple of shameless hussies to whom a German prisoner was a man like any other, not an enemy, the officer marched the column away.

The sergeant rode round counting heads. The twenty-three remaining Germans did what they had practised in advance; the outside man on the left of a file moved forward to the one ahead and the man on the right of the file in front dropped back. They repeated this several times. On a previous march, Werra had moved from a file near the rear to one near the front, and back again, without any of the escort being aware.

Now he jumped back over the wall and, as he crossed the road, gave the two women a grin and a wave.

While pressing on through the undergrowth and among the pines he heard his comrades singing the song which let him know that the guards had not noticed his escape. Thrusting his way through bracken and tangled creepers, he climbed to the crest of the hill 400 feet above the road. Then he scrambled down the reverse slope and on over the next rise and the decline beyond it. And so on until he reached a stretch of woodland bordering a moor. It was 1640 hrs and he waited there for darkness to fall over the silent, deserted landscape. Before the light faded, it began to rain.

He had wondered how long it would take the escort to tumble to the fact that they were one prisoner short. The column had covered half a mile and was nearing the northern edge of Satterthwaite when the officer called a halt and counted heads. As soon as he had confirmed that he had lost a man, he sent the sergeant galloping back the way they had just come and took the rest on at a quick march. There was a telephone box ahead, from which he called the camp. A few minutes later vehicles from there appeared, going south, and a lorryload of reinforcing troops drove up to join the escort. When they all arrived back at Grizedale Hall a roll call at once revealed the identity of the escaper.

Meanwhile the sergeant had encountered the two women who had tried to attract the guards' attention and they told him why they had shouted and waved and which way Werra had gone.

By 1730 hours the hue and cry had been raised far and wide. The Lancashire, Yorkshire, Cumberland and Westmorland police were all in the hunt. The Home Guard and Special Constables took over various duties from the Army, so that the soldiers could begin to beat through the immediate countryside, helped by bloodhounds.

Within the next twelve hours the BBC and newspapers gave the news of the escape. Public anxiety and tension were acute. The whole population had been nerving itself to repulse an invasion for the past three and a half months, so Fifth Columnists were widely suspected of sheltering Werra. 'Fifth Column', like 'The Third World' nowadays, was a term glibly used by press, radio and public, ignorant of its origin. Most people were also unsure of its precise meaning. It was coined by General Franco towards the end of the Spanish Civil War. Four columns of his troops were advancing on Madrid, one from each point of the compass. 'A fifth column awaits us in the capital,' he declared. So the expression was taken to mean spies, collaborators, saboteurs and armed partisans.

Werra was leading a damp, chilly and hungry existence. In his pockets he carried a few chocolate bars. Most of the space was taken up by toilet articles with which he would do his best to make himself look presentable when he had to mix with people. He had a little English money. He had no waterproof or overcoat, which he thought would have encumbered his movements.

It rained almost incessantly. On his fourth night at liberty, 10 October, he was sheltering in one of the small stone huts that are scattered about the fells to store sheep fodder. The Home Guard were searching these. At about 2300 hours that night two shepherds in Home Guard uniform, one carrying an acetylene cycle lamp and a shotgun, the other armed with an automatic pistol, found that the door of this hut had been forced open. The lamp beam fell on Werra. There was no effective resistance he could offer when they challenged him by name. One of them tied a cord round his right wrist and wound the other end about his own left hand.

They were going down a slippery hillside in pitch darkness when Werra jerked the cord free, knocked down the man who had been holding the end, turned and pelted back uphill to hide in a wood. He spent the night there watching the dim lights of cars and lorries on the road far below as they searched for him.

The following afternoon he was spotted by a sheep farmer on one of those hills that, in this part of England, have quaint names. Some, such as Bowkerstead Knott, Green Hows and Cicely's Brow, are romantic and euphonious. This one sounded discouragingly as though named after an ill-favoured streetwalker: Bleak Haw. The farmer gave the alarm, troops, policemen and bloodhounds spread line abreast moved up the hill.

On a patch of boggy ground, into which, lying on his back, Oberleutnant von Werra had partly sunk and was difficult to see, they stumbled upon him.

The Commandant sentenced him to twenty-one days' solitary confinement. He had expected the maximum thirty.

Several prisoners had been transferred to Swanwick Camp, a mansion called 'The Hayes', set in large grounds, five miles north-east of Belper, Derbyshire. The Nottinghamshire border lay three miles to the east. On 3 November Werra was released two days early from his punishment cell and taken there by train, handcuffed to a corporal and escorted by a captain.

Among those who greeted him, among several other friends from Grizedale Hall, was Major Fanelsa, who was again the Senior German Officer. Here he made a new friend, Leutnant Wagner, a thirty-two-year-old fighter pilot in the Reserve.

Still intent on escaping, within a few days Werra had persuaded Wagner, Major Cramer, and Leutnant Wilhelm, Malischewski and Manhard, the last a heavyweight boxer, to join him in excavating a tunnel. They agreed to burrow, from an empty room in the part of the building closest to the surrounding barbed wire fences, under the two fences and sentries' path between, to some waste ground where bushes and trees grew. The tunnel would have to be nearly fifteen yards long and pass close to one of the armed watch towers surrounding the perimeter.

They found a disused well, covered by a heavy stone slab, down which they would dispose of the earth. They did not tell Major Fanelsa of their intention. A lookout at an upper window would give warning if anyone approached the section from which the digging might be audible. This work was done by Werra and Malischewski. Wagner and Manhard lugged the excavated earth away and handed it to Wilhelm and Cramer for disposal down the well.

They began work on 17 November, 1940. The next day Major Fanelsa heard of it, sent for Werra, gave him a blasting, and was flabbergasted to hear than an officer of his own rank was involved.

Malischewski soon found the nervous strain too much, retired from the team and the hefty Manhard took over his share of the tunnelling. It was a dangerous undertaking, not only on account of the obvious risk of an earth fall, but also because of the lack of air and the threat of electrocution, made more acute by water seepage, from the frayed old wire with which they had rigged up a light. They received several shocks and were lucky that none proved severe. As the tunnel's length increased, the time a man could work in it decreased rapidly from fatigue, heat and lack of oxygen. By the time they were half-way through they barely filled six buckets with earth each day.

The moment came when the roof did cave in and buried Manhard. Werra barely managed to drag him free by the ankles. But the fall allowed air in and eased their task.

Precisely one month after they began the project, the tunnel was completed.

The five who had done all the physical work were going to leave first. Any others who were willing to try to escape could follow them. The five gathered the clothing they would need and the *Altestensrat*'s minions provided forged identity cards. Werra was going to pose as a Polish pilot. For this he would need identity discs.

At this point, one has to consider how accurate in detail the accepted accounts of Werra's escapades are. It has been stated that, by tricking one of the guards into showing him his identity disc, which was round in shape and dark brown in colour, Werra was able to register exactly what was on it and have a copy made. But members of all three armed Services wore *two* identity discs: a round, brown one and an octagonal, dark green one. The latter was stamped 'Do not remove' and was left on the body when interred in a temporary grave. The red one was removed as proof of the wearer's death. Werra's, and other people's, narratives have to be called into question over their accuracy in this matter. If a soldier had indeed shown Werra what he and others claim, then he would perforce have been wearing both discs. The necessity to forge two discs has never before been mentioned.

Werra's choice of imposture was based on the fact that his accent could not pass for British, but there were many Poles in the R.A.F., and few Britons could distinguish between the way a German and a Pole spoke their language. None of the others was in better case − Manhard understood no English − and they had different plans. Werra was going to wear flying overalls over his uniform, a tartan scarf and flying boots. He had four shillings (20p), some chocolate and cigarettes in his pocket. To authenticate his impersonation, he carried that day's *Times* tucked inside his outer garment.

He was to be the first to leave, which meant that he must hack through the thin layer of soil that remained above the exit. Lock-up was at 2000 hrs and he intended to break free an hour later. He wore a beret made from blanketing, and pyjamas dyed black with shoe polish, over his flying overalls.

There was faint moonlight and there were mist patches. Derby, twenty-five miles south and Sheffield, the same distance north, were being bombed. The camp's perimeter lights were off.

Werra thrust his head and shoulders above ground to scan the scene and listen. Voices rang out from the camp, where a carefully rehearsed choir was singing to mask any sound of his final labours when digging through the surface. He moved on all fours towards some bushes. A farm lay ahead. He crawled on, over a footpath. A gate slammed, he heard voices. Lying prone, he saw two men and two women approaching. The loud voices of his comrades died away. The two couples, drawn apparently by curiosity about the singing, turned back and disappeared.

When he reached the barn where all five were to meet, he found Cramer and Manhard there. They soon left and presently the other pair turned up and departed again. Cramer was caught soon after midnight.

Werra intended to steal an aeroplane and fly home. His destination was any R.A.F. station where a single-engine type was flown. He did not want his dash for home to end in ignominy with a ground loop when taxiing or taking off in a twin-engine job for the first time. To make sure that he got to an airfield, he planned, with his habitual audacity, to trick the R.A.F. into providing the transport.

He walked through the night and at about 0500 hrs came upon a railway line. Somewhere along it he would find a station or signalbox. He followed the track. The first sign of life was a locomotive in a siding, and he accosted its driver. 'I am Captain van Lott, Dutch Air Force, with the R.A.F. My aeroplane is hit by flak, I made crash landing, I must go to nearest R.A.F. airfield. Please help.'

The engine driver told his young fireman to take 'the Dutch pilot' to the signalman at Codnor Park station nearby. When they got there, they found it had no telephone, so Werra had to wait until the booking clerk, Mr Eaton, arrived just before 0600 hrs and he had to tell the tale again, making great play of the newspaper as he talked. It is astonishing that none of the people with whom he dealt seems to have wondered why a bomber pilot would take a daily paper with him on a raid or why, when he crashed, he should salvage it and carry it while he tramped miles in search of help. Why didn't he take one of the flasks of coffee aboard, or some sandwiches?

He belonged to Coastal Command, he said. He had intelligently selected this Command because it was little publicized, in contrast with Bomber and Fighter, so would render him less liable to suspicion and questioning. He told Mr Easton that he was stationed at Aberdeen, and had been flying a Wellington. He chose Aberdeen because its long distance away would make it as difficult as possible to verify his statement. He also said he had bombed a target in Denmark. If that were true, he would not, of course, have been so far south, or indeed inland at all, on his way home, but nobody raised this point.

Mr. Eaton surmised that his targets were ships and U-boats. Werra agreed, but alleged that his was a special squadron and he had just attacked a land target at Esbjerg. As a professional Service pilot, he should have known better. It would have been totally beyond the competence of a Coastal crew to carry out such a task: maritime operations demanded different equipment and skills from overland ones. Both categories had various types of speciality. Maritime crews were trained either to drop depth charges on submarines, or to drop bombs on surface vessels, or to launch torpedoes at the latter. But few civilians would know that.

What Mr Eaton did ask was where he had crashed and where his crew were. 'Captain van Lott' assured him that nobody was hurt and the crew were guarding their Wellington. There was a farm nearby, but it had no telephone; he had come down about two miles away, so he said.

To Werra's consternation, Mr. Easton telephoned the police. The German knew too little about England to be aware that an Englishman's – or woman's – first reaction in an emergency was to ask the nearest Bobby to come along, unless an ambulance or fire engine were urgently needed. He sat in the booking office, drinking tea, showing off his newspaper, while Mr. Eaton sold tickets for the early train.

While waiting for the police to arrive he learned that the nearest R.A.F. camp was Hucknall, a flying training school. He elaborated his statement by claiming that his aeroplane was fitted with a new, secret bombsight and other new instruments, which he had been sent to Esbjerg to try out. It was imperative for him to get back to base and report on these. On hearing this, Mr. Easton telephoned Hucknall and eventually spoke to the Duty Officer, then gave the telephone to Werra to speak for himself. Werra had heard Mr. Easton mention the Adjutant, so assumed that this was the identity of the Duty Officer, to whom he spun his bogus yarn yet again and the assertion that an aircraft would be sent to Hucknall to fetch him. The Duty Officer conceded; a vehicle would be at the railway station in twenty minutes.

Then a uniformed police sergeant and two plainclothes men arrived. Werra could not know that they were aware of Cramer's escape and capture and were doubly suspicious of him. They and the station staff all thought it was odd that nobody had heard an aircraft crash, nor had it been reported. But after a great deal of interrogation, the policemen departed and an R.A.F. car drove up. Werra presumed that this was proof that the Duty Officer had believed him. On the contrary, it was because he suspected him of being an impostor and had lent the driver his revolver.

The most obvious reasons were that Werra had given his rank as 'captain', whereas if he had been transferred to the R.A.F. for the duration of hostilities, he would have had the equivalent rank of flight lieutenant, and that he said his unit was 'The Mixed Special Bomber Squadron'. Whether the 'mixed' applied to its duties, types of aircraft or to the nationalities of its personnel, its only official identity would have been a number.

On arrival at the aerodrome, Werra told the driver to take him straight to the Control Tower, to find out when the aircraft coming for him was due. But the driver had been ordered to deliver him to the Duty Officer.

During the car journey Werra had asked the Adjutant's name and been told that he was on leave and Squadron Leader Boniface was standing in for him. The Duty Officer was using the Adjutant's office. He noticed at once that Werra was not wearing regulation R.A.F. flying boots or overalls. He tried to get him to take off his overalls, so that he could see what uniform this would disclose, but Werra demurred. The Duty Officer made him repeat what he had said on the telephone about his previous night's sortie and asked several arcane questions that the police had omitted. Next, he asked for his 'twelve-fifty', (Form 1250, the R.A.F. identity card). Werra had never heard of a 1250, but his lightning-fast brain deduced that it must be an identity document, so he retorted impertinently that, as the Duty Officer (who wore a pilot's brevet) knew, one was not allowed to take such items on operations. That saved him for the moment.

At that instant the call to Dyce, the airfield near Aberdeen, came through. Knowing that his sham was about to be exposed, Werra indicated that he urgently wanted to go to the W.C. and, while the Duty Officer held onto the telephone, he nipped out of the room, right out of Station HQ, and walked fast towards the hangars, where he saw Hurricanes on the tarmac apron in front of them.

He darted into one where a mechanic was at work on a Hurricane. He was disconcerted to see that the man wore civilian clothes and a coat-like coverall. He introduced himself under his assumed identity and said that '*Mister*' Boniface had sent him there to be shown the cockpit drill and take a Hurricane up.

This area of the airfield was used by Rolls-Royce, manufacturers of the Hurricane's Merlin engine. After some more talking the mechanic concluded that Captain van Lott was a ferry pilot, accepted what he said and directed him to a foreman who was also sucked in. But before he could authorize Werra to fly away there was paperwork to do. This accomplished, Werra triumphantly climbed into a Hurricane's cockpit on the hard standing.

Here again a professional doubt enters one's mind. A ferry pilot would have brought his own parachute along. Where was van Lott's? Without a parachute, what was he going to sit on, anyway? It appears that he claimed that it would be brought in an aircraft that was about to arrive. That still doesn't answer the question of what this short man sat on.

All he needed now was for someone to start the engine and, although sitting too low to see properly when he taxied, took off and landed, he was on the brink of probable success. He pressed the starter button, but the engine was too cold to fire on internal batteries. It turned the propeller a couple of times, then died. An irritated mechanic shouted to him that he needed external power. Werra begged him to do something.

The mechanic went off, came back with an accumulator trolley and was connecting it when Squadron Leader Boniface pointed a revolver at Werra and told him to get out.

Some versions of this event say that the weapon was an automatic pistol.

It cannot have been; R.A.F. officers were issued with the Smith and Wesson .38 six-chamber revolver. Moreover, anybody who has served with Squadron Leader Boniface knows that he would never have ignored Service regulations or done anything so flamboyant as to carry a non-regulation sidearm. There is, moreover, a certain vulgarity about a heavy automatic; vide the U.S.A.A.F crews' Colt Forty-five in a holster with thongs that are tied around the thigh.

Squadron Leader Boniface ('old Bonnie' as he was known when a popular Station Administrative Officer at R.A.F. Middle Wallop in the late 1940s and early 1950s), a Great War pilot, sportingly described Werra as having a pleasant personality and being worthy of admiration for his enterprise and boldness.

It was 21 December, 1940. All five escapers had been caught and were leniently sentenced to 14 days' solitary confinement.

On the day after Werra's two weeks in cells expired, all prisoners in the camp who were medically fit to travel were taken by train to Greenock. There they boarded ship for Canada.

News of intending transfer across the Atlantic was a severe blow to everybody's morale. In Britain, separated from mainland Europe only by the English Channel and North Sea, one could foster the hope of somehow reaching France or the Low Countries. A runaway from a prison camp in Canada would have to cross into the United States, which remained neutral until the Japanese attack on Pearl Harbor on 7 December, 1941, forced America to enter the war as Britain's ally. Crossing the frontier meant avoiding the police and customs officers and the military posts on both sides of it. To be caught in Canada meant return to prison camp. In the U.S.A. it threatened internment.

The ship sailed in convoy on 10 January, 1941. Prisoners, both officers and other ranks, from other camps in Britain were also aboard.

Werra's main occupation was, as always, planning his escape and return to Germany. The first opportunity would come when the ship docked; he might be able to jump overboard and swim ashore. He trained for a long immersion in icy water by daily lying in a bath full of sea water for as long as he could endure it. To learn their destination and as much as possible about Canada, he stood in for a German ranker who was working in the galley. By gossiping with the ship's cooks and scullions he learned that she was to make port at Halifax on 21 January. The POWs would be taken by train to prison camps away in the west.

During the days that he washed dishes, emptied refuse and peeled potatoes, he roamed beyond the kitchen. This gave him the notion that it might be possible to seize control of the ship. There were naval officers and ratings among the Germans who could crew her. A plan was worked out, but before it could be enacted the ship was in sight of land.

Comprehensively though he was endowed with rascality, Werra commands respect for his resolution, the thoroughness of his preparation and the promptness with which he converted intention into action. The swiftness with which he had broken free after arriving at both previous prison camps had taken his British gaolers by surprise. The Canadian guards would probably not be expecting an immediate attempt to escape either.

On the train the prisoners were herded into pullman carriages — thirty-five to each, with twelve armed guards who were on watch three at a time, one at each end of the gangway and one in the middle. There was snow on the ground, but the coaches were well heated. Also, each prisoner was given a blanket and the windows were double-glazed. Werra had a window seat with Manhard on his left. Wagner faced him from the opposite window seat and Wilhelm sat beside Wagner next to the gangway. The seats and luggage racks were designed to form bunks so that passengers could sleep stretched full length.

It was 1930 hrs, and snowing, when the train pulled out of Halifax. Presently some of the German O.Rs served their officers a hot meal. In the drowsy warmth, prisoners and guards began to relax and converse. From the talk emerged the information that the Germans were bound for a new POW camp on the northern shore of Lake Superior, over a thousand miles away and set in a wild part of Ontario. From his enquiries about the geography of Canada, Werra knew this meant that the route lay via Montreal and Ottawa. Between these the railway ran close enough to the American frontier to make an escape across it feasible. The section of track closest to the U.S. border came earlier, but he did not think it would be wise to try to take advantage of this. There were two reasons. The terrain on the American side was forested and sparsely inhabited, so he would almost certainly lose his way and freeze or starve to death. Also, there were many other intending escapers aboard who would probably try to get away from the train on this stretch, and the security patrols would be duly prepared.

He would, therefore, leap from the train somewhere between Montreal and Ottawa. First he had to devise a way of raising the inner and outer window panes without the guards' awareness. How could he open them at all, since ice and frost held them fast? Each time the train halted for several minutes, however, the heat inside the carriage caused a slight thaw. If he could ease the inner window up even half an inch, after a long stop, it would allow enough warm air to circulate between the double glazing to free both the inner and outer panes. After one long halt he pushed the inner glazing up a trifle and a slow thaw began. To accelerate it and prevent a fall in temperature that the guards would notice, he asked everyone else to put the heat regulators at maximum. It was so hot that people took of their jackets, but he would have to don his overcoat. How could he do so without making the guards suspicious?

More than twenty-four hours later the train arrived at Montreal. The time to act was almost upon him. Fate came to his aid. Since leaving Halifax the prisoners had enjoyed richer food than they had eaten for many months and there had been a surfeit of fresh fruit. This had caused widespread discomfort with the bowels. Normally, only one man at a time was allowed to go to the lavatory, escorted by one of the three guards on duty. In the sudden emergency two at a time had to be allowed out, each with a guard, leaving only one guard in the carriage. Many of the prisoners felt so ill that they were shivering beneath an overcoat and blanket.

Werra was wearing his overcoat now, without looking conspicuous. When the train stopped at a station somewhere beyond Montreal and was moving slowly out, Wagner rose from his seat, holding a blanket, and began to fold it, concealing the escaper. Werra dragged both inner and outer windows up and, because it was not possible to jump through the opening, he bravely dived out head-first, arms outstretched as though plunging into a swimming pool. His accomplices closed the windows and the guards did not notice his disappearance until the next afternoon.

He landed in deep snow. Navigating by the Pole Star, he headed south. He had to wrap his scarf around his head to prevent heat loss through his scalp and to protect his ears from frostbite. Across open ground and through pinewood, he plodded through the snow. First light banished the darkness and at last he reached his immediate objective, a narrow road. Any road would do, to make progress less strenuous and to take him towards the river. An hour more of walking brought him to a signposted highway and after a while he hitched a lift in a lorry.

He told the driver that he was Dutch, a merchant sailor whose ship had been bombed more than once and who had seen many others sunk by German submarines. He had given up the sea and was on his way to visit relations in Ottawa, where he would find work. The lorry driver took him as far as he could and Werra continued on foot. By sunset the St Lawrence River was in sight. Now he had to reach the far side without being caught on some guarded bridge.

He ventured closer to the river and found that it was frozen. He would walk over! From the far side the lights of a town beckoned and he followed the Canadian bank of the river until he was almost opposite it.

But he had not gone far across the ice when he found that it did not lie solid all the way to the American shore. An ice-breaker had been at work and cleared a channel. He turned back.

More trudging, with weariness, hunger and the biting cold weakening him, until he came across some unoccupied wooden huts on the outskirts of a small Canadian town, where he found what he was looking for — a boat, lying inverted. First he had to scrape away the snow that thickly enveloped it, then heave it over the right way up. But the frozen snow around its gunwales bound it tightly to the ground. He must lever it up. A search yielded two fencing planks. Using one as a fulcrum and the other as a lever, straining with all the force that his light weight could bear on the task, he rolled it on to its keel.

Neither oars nor rowlocks were in the hull. He would have to use the planks as paddles. But how could he move the boat to the water? There were no poles that he could have used as rollers. He put his hands on the transom and began to shove. Very gradually the boat slid forward. His feet kept slipping on the impacted snow that caked the soles of his boots. Each shove shifted the heavy craft only a few inches. By the time he had pushed it to the water's edge he was tottering with exhaustion. He threw one of the planks aboard, ran the boat into the water until it was nearly afloat, climbed in and shoved off with the other plank which fell from his grasp and was carried away by the current. He picked up the remaining plank and tried to paddle, but it was too bulky and heavy. Nor could he steer with it. But the current slowly carried the boat across to the opposite bank.

He clambered out and made his way towards a road where he could see a parked car with its bonnet open and a man leaning over the engine. There was a young woman in it. He asked where he was.

'Ogdensburg,' she told him.

Was it in America?

Yes, and who was he?

'I am a German Air Force Officer... escaped prisoner of war... from Canada.'

The man drove him into the town, but did not reveal that he was a Canadian. He had Werra arrested by the first policeman they came across who took him to the Police Station, where he was charged with vagrancy.

When the police saw his uniform and letters written to him while he was a prisoner in England, they gave him into the custody of the Immigration Inspector. Later that night he was allowed to telephone the American Consul in New York.

Then the local newspaper reporters descended on him and he regaled them with a boastfully exaggerated account of the feats that he had performed to get here. Although the distance he had covered from the railway line to the St Lawrence was some thirty miles, he gave it as a hundred, and all his other assertions distorted the truth on the same scale. Then the radio stations broadcast his story, the New York press arrived and within forty-eight hours his name was known all over the United States. He was acclaimed as a hero, but the journalists found him cocky, conceited and arrogant.

Legal proceedings for illegal entry were started against him, but, on payment of a large sum, he was released into the charge of the Consul General who came to take him to New York. The processes of the law dragged on for three months, during which Werra was being treated as a celebrity. By late April it seemed likely that he would be deported to Canada. So, with the connivance of the German Embassy and disguised as a Mexican labourer returning to his homeland at the end of his daily work across the border, he mingled with a crowd of genuine Mexicans and sneaked into Mexico where its frontier marches with Texas.

Thence, he went by train to Mexico City, where an official car met him at the station and took him to the Embassy. There, he was given a passport under a false name and civilian occupation. With this he went by air to Peru and on via Bolivia, Brazil and Argentina to Spain, staging through the Cape Verde Islands. His penultimate air passage was to Rome. The final one took him to Berlin, where he landed on 18 April, 1941.

Hitler decorated him with the Knight's Cross, awarded for his alleged destruction of nine R.A.F. aircraft a few days before he was shot down; or, in his version, collided with another Me109. He was lauded by the press, radio and cinema news reels.

He was promoted to Hauptmann and sent on visits to R.A.F. prisoner of war camps, to compare them with the Luftwaffe camps in Britain, and advise on security. To his credit, Werra also recommended several improvements in the living conditions of the British prisoners. Of most value to Germany was his experience of British methods of interrogation, which were far superior to the Germans'.

He had been engaged for some months before being taken prisoner and he and his fiancée were married soon after his homecoming. When Germany declared war on its former ally, the U.S.S.R., in June 1941, he was posted to the Eastern Front, where he shot down eight Russian aircraft.

Three months later his unit was transferred to Holland. On 25 October, 1941, he took off as leader of a Schwarm on a defensive patrol over the North Sea. Twenty minutes later his engine cut, his Me109 dived into the sea and he was killed.

Conveniently, the Court of Inquiry, as these, both military and civil, have a habit of doing when a pilot cannot be present to defend himself, gave its verdict as 'pilot error'.

Franz von Werra was a rogue, but a charmer with as many good characteristics as bad. It was ironical that this man, who could talk himself out of any predicament, had to depart this life with an unfair entry on his Service record and one that would so much have offended his vanity had he lived to contest it.